PROFITS AND POWER

Navigating the Politics and Geopolitics of Oil

UTP insights

UTP Insights is an innovative collection of brief books offering accessible introductions to the ideas that shape our world. Each volume in the series focuses on a contemporary issue, offering a fresh perspective anchored in scholarship. Spanning a broad range of disciplines in the social sciences and humanities, the books in the UTP Insights series contribute to public discourse and debate and provide a valuable resource for instructors and students.

For a list of the books published in this series, see page 323.

PROFITS AND POWER

Navigating the Politics and Geopolitics of Oil

David A. Detomasi

UNIVERSITY OF TORONTO PRESS
Toronto Buffalo London

ISBN 978-1-4875-0016-0 (cloth)   ISBN 978-1-4875-1033-6 (EPUB)
ISBN 978-1-4875-2010-6 (paper)   ISBN 978-1-4875-1032-9 (PDF)

Library and Archives Canada Cataloguing in Publication

Title: Profits and power : navigating the politics and geopolitics of oil /
    David A. Detomasi.
Names: Detomasi, David A., author.
Series: UTP insights.
Description: Series statement: UTP insights | Includes bibliographical references.
Identifiers: Canadiana (print) 20220159491 | Canadiana (ebook) 20220159564 |
    ISBN 9781487500160 (cloth) | ISBN 9781487520106 (paper) |
    ISBN 9781487510336 (EPUB) | ISBN 9781487510329 (PDF)
Subjects: LCSH: Petroleum industry and trade – History. | LCSH: Petroleum
    industry and trade – Political aspects. | LCSH: Petroleum industry and
    trade – Economic aspects. | LCSH: World politics – 21st century.
Classification: LCC HD9560.5 .D58 2022 | DDC 338.2/7282 – dc23

We wish to acknowledge the land on which the University of Toronto Press
operates. This land is the traditional territory of the Wendat, the Anishnaabeg, the
Haudenosaunee, the Métis, and the Mississaugas of the Credit First Nation.

University of Toronto Press acknowledges the financial support of the Government
of Canada, the Canada Council for the Arts, and the Ontario Arts Council, an
agency of the Government of Ontario, for its publishing activities.

Canada Council **Conseil des Arts**
for the Arts **du Canada**

ONTARIO ARTS COUNCIL
CONSEIL DES ARTS DE L'ONTARIO

an Ontario government agency
un organisme du gouvernement de l'Ontario

Funded by the   Financé par le
Government gouvernement
of Canada   du Canada

Contents

Acknowledgments

It is a myth that books are a product of a solitary individual working alone at a desk. They require the effort, and forbearance, of a lot of people for a long period of time. This book is no exception: you could say it was decades in the making. My interest in oil started long ago, growing up as I did in Alberta, Canada, in the 1970s and 1980s. The province's economy waxed and waned with the fortunes of the industry. More memorable were the people: enthusiastic, optimistic, energetic, and independent were the key adjectives describing their attitudes about where they were and what they were doing. So that is a great place to begin: I had the good fortune to start life where, when, and with whom I did, which planted oil and politics firmly in my worldview.

In the decades since I have benefited from a very large number of people who contributed in ways large and small to this finished product. There are too many to be listed and thanked properly, but here is at least my best attempt. In my university years, both undergraduate and graduate, I had professors and mentors who showed me how politics and economics were inherently interrelated. Studying the discipline of political economy in graduate school gave me chances to explore these links myself. There I was also introduced to the community of scholars who also have spent much of their working life exploring the intricacies of oil and the political problems it generates. Their work has influenced mine greatly and became the foundation for what is explored in the following pages. I have tried to give them their due via fair treatment in the footnotes.

However, when studying oil, academia only gets you so far. The oil business is if anything a practical, results-orientated one. Over my career I have been fortunate to interact with a large number of business executives who did not write books or articles but who knew all there was to know about meeting bottom lines. Unlike the storied negative stereotypes that sometimes attach themselves to oil company executives, to a person I found them thoughtful, insightful, fair, community-minded, and very much aware of how what they did in managing oil companies mattered far beyond what the confines of a balance sheet might show. In addition to oil executives, I have benefited from the work and contributions of public economists, forecasters, and business analysts who generated the context for understanding the oil business. Of particular note are the insights provided by Stephen Poloz, who has been a friend and mentor for more than twenty years now. I have tried to convey in these pages the competitive realities with which business executives must deal, I hope I have got it close to right.

I also have to thank the Smith School of Business at Queen's University. They gave an opportunity to an international relations PhD graduate when few other business schools would have. The School has been generous in their ongoing support, encouraging me to write and teach about the things I felt mattered and wanted to do. I have done my best to repay that initial leap of faith and can now count thousands of school alumni who at some point were students who suffered through at least some of the content contained in this book. It is not an easy gig working as a professor at Smith: the school draws scarily bright and competent students who keep pushing me to stay at the forefront of whatever it was I am doing. As a reward I get to watch what they do after graduation. I hope some of them find the time to read what this manuscript contains.

A few of these students were particularly instrumental in allowing me to complete this book, either by performing outstanding research assistance or aiding me in classroom duties that freed up time for writing. David Godsell and Mathew Boland did both while they completed their doctorates as Smith, and both have gone on to forge very successful academic careers of their own. More recently Raynold Alorse and Tiffany Chua continue to do the same and were always happy to speak about book ideas, providing invaluable alternate insight into whatever issue I was then grappling with. Without their help I would not have been able to even think about writing this book. Tim Kitchen and Shameer Ahmad at Barclay's Bank were also immensely helpful, and Maddie Hubbard at Queen's proved particularly adept at helping me with graphs and charts.

Finally, family was critical. They all proved far more patient than anyone ever has a right to expect. My parents, Don and Kaye, and brother, Don, continued to reside in Calgary and during the writing phase were gentle with their prodding about "when will the book come out?" I discussed many of the ideas in this book with my father and deeply regret that he was unable to see the final product. My brother also offered thoughts based on an oil-outsider, sometimes lawyerly point of view, which also added necessary adjustments to the final manuscript. My brother's wife and father-in-law also offered pointed questions and illuminating insights about the book when I discussed it with them, often things I had not thought about. My in-laws, who reside primarily in the Brantford-Hamilton corridor, put up with my preoccupation about a book on oil on family occasions even though that topic does not burn as deeply in the Ontario psyche as it does in the Alberta one.

Finally, my immediate family in Kingston deserve the most thanks. Sarah, Jack, Emma, and Curtis all had to endure my preoccupation with the manuscript. Much of the manuscript was written jammed between the dance recitals, hockey games, and school events that are a necessary part of an active teenager's world. Sarah also tolerated my absences in the office, despite her own challenging schedule. Without their support and love, this book would never have been conceived, let alone finished. It is to them that I dedicate whatever truth this book reveals. The errors I of course reserve to myself.

PROFITS AND POWER

Navigating the Politics and Geopolitics of Oil

chapter one

Introduction

"I cannot believe you are allowed to teach this. Don't you know how close the world is to environmental catastrophe? People like you are the reason my generation has no hope."

The genesis of this book started here, with an accusation. When your day job is teaching undergraduates, you do get some impassioned students and probing questions. But it is rare to be confronted with blanket and undisguised hostility, particularly before the final grades have been tabulated. Something I had said or done had clearly struck a nerve and generated a reaction beyond what my teaching experience might have predicted. My goals in undergraduate teaching could be described as ambitiously modest. I try to capture as much of the students' attention as I can in the little time I have with them, but I know there are limits, given the endless amount of more entertaining electronic distractions lying at their fingertips and my admittedly not-always-captivating stage presence. I am not helped by the arcane course subject matter, which is rarely as interesting to them as it may be to me, and my telling of it sometimes induces sleepiness as much as it does anything else. Thankfully students are usually charitable: if they do not like, are bored by, or disagree with what I am saying they usually are restrained in how they express it.

Yet not that day. Our mutual expectations of comfortable classroom process had been thrown out the window by those three sentences. My transgression came well disguised, as I did not see the intellectual landmine I had managed to lay. In the course syllabus

I had included a week of material dedicated to studying the global oil industry, how it worked, and why it mattered. Learning of that seemingly innocuous and, to me, obvious choice was enough for at least one student to call for hellfire and damnation to rain upon my head. It forced me to do a bit of scrambling.

To my credit or discredit, this is what I came up with. I had a few points to proffer in my defense, beginning with the more-or-less obvious. Some of the more oil-critical students in the class were foreign, having taken advantage of the extensive international exchange relationships my home university had built. All had presumably gotten to Canada on an airplane. Their Canadian compatriots came literally from all over the (very big) country. They too presumably had had to rely on some combination of planes, trains, and automobiles to get to the off-the-beaten-path Kingston. I was pretty sure all of them wanted to keep warm in the sometimes-frigid Kingston winter: many of the aging houses they rented still relied on oil-fueled furnaces. Once settled into the day-do-day life of an undergrad, a big part of their daily exercise quotient comes in the furious typing of lecture notes, which I sometimes pause my sessions to let them do. Their fingers dance and blur on their bestickered laptops, machines encased in hard plastic shells that are derived from petroleum. I assumed these students liked inexpensive and plentiful food, enjoyed driving on asphalt-paved roads, and perhaps even appreciated the industrial chemicals used to manufacture medicines and fertilizers and the dozens of other petroleum-derived products that help keep us safe, warm, productive, and more-or-less happy. Even after pointing out that all of that depended on oil, I did not change many minds. Oil was still an unsavory thing to study and not something discussed in polite company. Me proposing that it was worthy of such discussing was enough to make some want to banish me to the recesses of Luddite knuckle-dragging hell.

In subsequent discussions with other students I discovered that an anti-oil stance was not an isolated opinion: many of the students' colleagues agreed, at least partially, with what had been said. They did not like oil, wanted as little to do with it as possible, and studying it made them feel dirty, like they had become forced accomplices to the perpetuation of some kind of global crime. To them the topic was not just an academic discussion of the workings of a particular commodity. Instead it constituted a morality litmus test, one that those endorsing oil, or even saying anything mildly positive about it, failed utterly. Such miscreants were clearly and woefully misguided and probably were well beyond salvation. They likely also believed the earth was flat, Elvis was alive and working at a Memphis Burger King, and burning witches at the stake had merely gotten a bad rap.

As the initial shock wore off, my more academic, inquiring (and sometimes insecure) side kicked in. What exactly was it about oil that elicited such a virulent response? Why was it directed toward a middle-aged, slightly overweight professor who students evidently believed had sold out to the corporate man (but who had in reality given up dreams of grandeur and global domination decades ago)? More importantly, what did these students actually think was going on in the world of oil? Did they know where gasoline came from, how internal combustion engines worked, why the lights went on when they flipped a switch (which is more a natural gas story), why a furnace burned a fuel that kept out the ravages of a Canadian winter? The more I probed, the more it seemed the answer was no, most did not know these things. It was even worse: what they thought they knew about oil was wrong, and not just by a little bit. To me, that seemed more worrisome and pressing: if recent global experience is any guide, it is not what you don't know, but what you do know that ain't so, that causes real problems.

Clearly there was and is an informational hole to be filled, and I thought I was as good a candidate as any to fill it. I grew up in a small town in southern Alberta located close to Calgary, one of the world's primary petroleum cities, one that is often mentioned in the same breath as Houston, Riyadh, and Dubai. Oil was in the air, literally, as it was common then to see derricks flaring natural gas as a by-product of the oil they extracted, which of course they can no longer do. Parents of friends I went to school with worked in the industry, and many high school classmates themselves ended up working on derricks and oil camps in the summer and eventually took office jobs in oil companies. Oil logos and placards decorated the downtown high rises and provided a foundation for the bustling energy and entrepreneurialism that remain Calgary's hallmarks today. So, writing about oil is not much of a stretch.

Growing up, it was also clear that energy politics permeated people's thinking about Alberta's place in the Canadian confederation. The province seemed infused with a political tension and a feeling of being perpetually under siege, as Alberta's rich oil and gas bounty always seemed vulnerable to the grabbing hand of the federal government. I can remember the gist of the titanic federal-provincial governance bouts between Alberta premier Peter Loughheed and the Canadian prime minister Pierre Elliot Trudeau, where control of oil and gas and its associated revenue was always a key battlefield. Those contests became the stuff of Canadian political legend, and their outcomes generated bitter feelings and lingering resentment. It was not uncommon then to see bumper stickers on Alberta's backroads arguing that the province should "Let the Eastern Bastards Freeze in the Dark," and Alberta's residual anger and mistrust of the feds smolders today and is often directed at Trudeau's son, Justin. When it comes to oil, the country apparently still has issues.

Interest in oil continued as I began my academic career. After completing graduate school, I began working at the School of Business (now known as the Smith School of Business) at Queen's University. There I have had for two decades the privilege of working with some of the nation's brightest young minds, as well as having the additional good fortune of teaching many highly capable international students as well. Their experiences with oil and energy are as varied as they are, and their opinions about it run the spectrum from enthusiastic proponents of Canadian energy to the entrenched opponents quoted earlier who wish it would just go away. A good many simply do not know much about it at all, and what they did know usually led them to conclude that oil was bad. At best it was a necessary evil, and at worst the oil industry and the companies working in it were emblems of a corrupt industrial system that kept the world hooked on crass consumption fueled by the opioid of burning carbon. These were sentiments of business school students: anti-oil feelings likely ran hotter in other parts of the university.

During the last fifteen years I have also witnessed successive Canadian governments, both provincial and federal, struggle with the question of what the country should do with its vast oil and gas reserves. To be more accurate, successive federal governments did know what they wanted to do: but they wanted to do polar opposite things. The federal Conservative Party, led by Stephen Harper, governed Canada between 2006 and 2015. As prime minister Harper was unapologetically supportive of Canadian oil and gas development, at one point even branding the country as an energy superpower. He had no interest in signing on to global carbon emission reduction agreements unless the world's largest polluters did so as well, which at the time they gave no indication of doing. By the end of his tenure Canada was the fifth-largest producer of oil in the world, powered primarily by additional production in the Canadian oil sands.

The Liberal government, headed by Justin Trudeau, that succeeded him had very different ideas. Trudeau's government put combating climate change at the top of its domestic agenda and pledged that the country would reduce its overall carbon emissions. That pledge is hard to square with increased oil extraction, particularly from the Alberta oil sands, which ranks among the most carbon-intensive sources of extracted oil in the world. Canada's provincial governments, who control the right to regulate and extract resources in their territory, vary both in ideological stripe and in the preferences of their constituents. They consequently rarely express any kind of consensus in their support for or opposition to oil and gas development. Many have proven unwilling to let additional oil pipelines traverse their territory and consequently have made the country's landlocked oil resources increasingly hard to get to international markets. Faced with political uncertainty and ongoing low oil prices, foreign investors have over the past half-decade fled the Canadian energy sector in droves, taking their capital and jobs with them, though recent price increases due to supply constraint and the geopolitical shock of the war in Ukraine may reverse that trend. Taken together, these forces have not made it easy to be in that sector, still less to trumpet its virtues.

This book makes no pretense at solving these long-standing problems in the Canadian body politic: it just acknowledges they are there. Nor is it targeted at Canada specifically: the debate about the future of oil is one countries the world over are having. It instead was born out of a conviction that more accurate knowledge of how that system worked, and the politics underneath it, might lower the volume on an increasingly fractious debate. Understanding may even inspire better and more reasoned policy debates and create more workable outcomes to the very real challenges oil use poses. It might even do an end run in those debates around the seemingly instinctual desires to extol or condemn oil, or pigeonhole the debates' participants as either greedy, uncaring, borderline psychopathic oil barons or naïve, self-righteous, hypocritical, tree-hugging activists. Understanding is perhaps more critical now than ever, given the rapidity with which our energy systems appear to be changing. It might even prevent further classroom fusillades being lobbed my way.

As far as possible, the book is neither "for" nor "against" oil. To repeat, as far as possible. Biases, preexisting beliefs, and formative experiences condition my outlook as much as they do anyone else's. Despite that, the book tries to follow the data and research and make fair use of it. Most of that evidence indicates that current oil dependency is something with which we must deal for a while yet. Moreover, if lowering that dependency and reducing oil use is a sound goal enjoying popular support, we should acknowledge that achieving it will create problems and challenges, as well as benefits. The book hopefully avoids the pushing of any agenda or any blatant attempt to change minds one way or the other. If it does, it will be because the reader has decided to do that on their own. But there are choices to be made, locally, nationally, and internationally. None are consequence free or will easily or quickly end our current oil-dependent reality. So yes, Virginia (not her real name), we are going to study it.

Why Oil?

It is worth knowing something about the economics, politics, and geopolitics of oil. Oil matters in ways other commodities do not and continues to exert sway over the world's governments in powerful ways. Oil, and the money its sale generates, lubricates, funds, or otherwise infiltrates most of the geopolitical conflicts that populate today's headlines. The brutal civil conflict in Syria generated massive domestic suffering to the Syrian people and damage to the Syrian state. Contested control over oil supply routes helped motivate that conflict, and pilfered oil revenue generated a lot of the funds used fight it. China continues its investments in building economic infrastructure at home and abroad, investments that total in the trillions of dollars. It has intensified trade and monetary links with its neighbors and economic partners that raise worries about the geopolitical ambition their economic efforts portend.[1] Driving that strategy is China's need to secure critical supplies of natural resources, in particular oil, of which it must import a lot. The unsettled politics besetting the Middle East remain as complex and volatile as ever: Iran and Saudi Arabia both possess large reserves of oil and huge potential production capacity. They also continue to wage a proxy war in Yemen that has, at this writing, cost tens of thousands of lives and threatens millions more with starvation.[2] Russia's habitual sabre-rattling on the borders of Ukraine morphed into a full-fledged invasion in February 2022, further roiling energy markets and exposing Western Europe's continued reliance on Russia energy exports. Many more links could be drawn between oil and geopolitical conflict.

The mix of oil, politics, and geopolitics also affects the most advanced of economies, many of whom continue to import a lot of it. In the United States, recent waves of populism and nationalism have spread across the electorate, absorbing adherents who support protectionist economic policies that they think will protect them against the threat foreign competition poses. That mix of populism and economic nationalism propelled Donald J. Trump to the presidency in 2016, and once there he pursued a nationalist economic agenda that included strong support for domestic energy production and the rollback of environmental regulations designed to limit the environmental damage such production generated. His inaugural address trumpeted nationalist economic rhetoric and, within a week of taking office, he had issued an executive memoranda authorizing construction of the Keystone XL oil pipeline that had been blocked under the previous administration of Barack Obama.[3] Increased oil production seemed to be a pivotal thing that would "Make America Great Again" and was central to the political agenda that got him elected. It mattered to his successor too. Upon winning the 2020 election, President Joe Biden canceled the pipeline as rapidly as Trump had authorized it, and Biden's domestic agenda appears to prioritize the transitioning off of oil as much as Trump's agenda had been built on promoting it.

To be sure, all these disparate events have multiple causes, consequences, and attendant issues. Yet, in all of them, the politics of oil somehow always seems to matter. Oil is admittedly not everything, but it always seems to be something. Perhaps that is due to the sheer size of the industry, which today consumes hundreds of billions of dollars of investment capital each year and is by many measures the world's biggest business.[4] The need to procure oil affects – infects, underpins, drives, fuels, motivates, limits, poisons, choose your adjective – the political decisions governments make. Importing governments care about security of supply and keep a wary eye on the price they have to pay for a barrel. Oil affects the domestic politics of producers as well: controlling the revenue oil sales generate can become the basis for wielding political power. No one can afford to ignore the economics and politics of oil, and that seems to be true no matter what the institutional structure of the government might be, what policy goals it might have, or whether that government is a democracy, a dictatorship, or something in-between.

The more one looks, the more oil appears to have seeped into all the nooks and crannies of the global economy. Its price and availability can constrain or accelerate the economic growth countries achieve. Its perceived availability colors the geopolitical debates that governments have at national security tables. The industry features some of the worlds' largest and (at times) most profitable companies, who collectively employ millions of people, spend billions of dollars annually in investment capital, and operate in some of the world's most remote geographic areas. Billions of consumers rely on daily delivery of oil products to move around, keep warm, and otherwise live their lives. These consumers intuitively understand that oil and politics are inherently mixed. Though they are not always sure how, they are often nevertheless convinced that that interaction between oil, politics, and money rarely seems to benefit them.[5] Many of the most challenging issues governments face today – including national security, ensuring energy abundance, coping with climate change – depend significantly on how the oil market evolves and the choices its key actors make.

To understand those choices, we need to first examine how the industry works. That is no simple thing because the system is big, has a lot of moving parts, and sometimes generates baffling and inconsistent outcomes. For example, take the idea of "peak oil," which dominated public debate a decade ago.[6] It posited that the world was rapidly running out of oil and that existing reserves could not meet the exploding demand rapidly industrializing emerging economies would need. If production fell, as it seemed like it would, all manner of dire geopolitical consequences would follow. The theory made intuitive popular sense: after all, oil was supposedly a finite resource, and the earth's crust presumably only held so much. At some point more would have been extracted than what remained, at which point output would go down and countries would engage in a mad scramble to control what was left. That prediction proved wrong. By 2014 global production had caught up and began exceeding world demand. Market observers realized this, and in the fall of 2014 prices suddenly fell by half and fears of peak oil evaporated. Companies, having been given sufficient monetary incentive, had proven inventive and capable in either finding new oil or extracting more oil from old fields.[7] Supply overshot demand: price plunged.

Confident predictions about the oil industry's future often crash on the rocks of an unpredictable unfolding reality. To take a second example, so stringently did companies roll back investment after the 2014 price fall that by 2018 analysts were once again warning of another potential supply shortage, one caused not by peak oil but instead by the massive cuts in exploration expenditure companies had enacted to cope with the price fall.[8] Without consistent investment, supply growth would not keep pace with continued rising demand, lending to a new scenario of rapidly rising prices.

Then the COVID-19 pandemic happened. It caused global oil use to plummet, supply bunkers to overflow, and prices to drop almost literally through the floor, erasing fears (or perhaps hopes for producers) that supply shortages would put upward pressure on price. To summarize, in the space of ten years the oil market gyrated between periods of investment euphoria[9] to the depths of economic distress and despair, while actual physical output went from fears of shortage to excessive oversupply.

Understanding things now is no easier. Today's oil industry is also subject to "disruptive elements" that are changing the rules of the production game seemingly daily. Some are improved technologies that now allow more oil to be produced in different places and at lower cost than ever before. Others include the rise of non-carbon-based energy competitors that comprise an increasing portion of the energy pie. Societal attitudes toward the use of carbon as an energy source are evolving rapidly and usually not in the favor of using more of it. There appears to be a growing consensus, particularly among younger people (one of whom was quoted earlier), that using less oil is not just a good idea but is instead an immediately necessary one to prevent environmental collapse. Governments remain their unpredictable and idiosyncratic selves with regard to oil, sometimes acting as a referee, friend, owner, or policeman of oil companies, and often doing all these things at the same time.

To complicate matters even further, a consuming public may hold disdain for private oil companies that can rise to loathing when oil prices are high and profits enormous. Residents of oil-producing regions may in theory support oil production and the revenue it provides but would usually prefer it not be done in their backyard. Going from the local to the global, the industry now features rapidly growing emerging markets that require stable sources of energy: those countries are every bit as attentive to energy procurement as developed economies have been for decades.[10] On the monetary side, the act of producing oil does not simply enrich company executives (though it still certainly keeps doing that): it has also become the fiscal backbone for many of the countries that produce it. Their hospitals, roads, extensive social support programs, security expenditures, and geopolitical heft all depend on the continued flow of oil revenue. Environmentally, the costs of the carbon-based economy appear evident, yet efforts to limit carbon emissions inevitably run up against the entrenched interests of those whose livelihoods, or indeed even political survival, depend on the burning of ever more oil.

After witnessing all this, it might seem reasonable to wonder what good it does to examine the past or think about the future. Given all this complexity, if even the best-informed opinions are within a few short years as likely to be proven wrong as right, why look ahead at all? Why not simply take each market gyration as it comes, keep your chin up, and muddle through? The answer is as simple to state as it is difficult to show. Despite the complexity, buried deep within this day-to-day seeming chaos is a discernible order. The oil industry exhibits rhythms and patterns that create familiar and predictable pressures on producers and consumers alike. When studying oil, it is sometimes easy to feel that we have all been here before because, in many ways, we likely have.[11] Understanding those patterns will help us navigate the choices that collectively must be made today.

The act of finding oil, producing it, selling it, and consuming it produces a discrete set of economic, political, and geopolitical challenges with which both consuming and producing governments must grapple. Those challenges change in hue and shape over time, but they have yet to be cured or eliminated. They can only be managed by diligent and coordinated effort. Compounding the old problems are the more modern ones, primarily having to do with energy transition and lessening the environmental impact our carbon-dependent economies have. That will not be easy: efforts to transition toward alternate and renewable energy sources may, at least over the short term, even intensify rather than alleviate those challenges.

This book is designed to identify what those challenges were, what they are now, how they have been managed, and how they might evolve. It is written for everyone who has an interest in oil and the impact it has on our lives. It (hopefully) provides a clear explanation of how the oil industry works, what political and geopolitical problems it generates, and what the future might look like. It gives the reader a framework for thinking about how the politics, geopolitics, and oil will intersect, and tries to do so in a readable and concise package. That is no simple feat: the politics of oil remains a complex multi-headed beast, and events in the oil business have a way of outrunning and confusing even the fastest pen. Yet without such a foundation, it will remain difficult to separate industry signal from noise[12] and consequently easy to fall into a trap of giving oil either too much or not enough importance in determining what goes on in the world.

Why Study Oil: The Economics

We start by outlining the reasons why examining the oil system is worth it. First, studying oil tells us more than just the travails of a single commodity. It also explains a lot about how the world works generally. The book chooses three interwoven themes to help structure the convoluted story of oil – industry structure, politics and geopolitics, and the effect oil production has on how states are choosing to run their economies. All three are in a great deal of flux at the moment. The next chapter outlines the industry as it exists now, explaining how and why oil is explored for, found, extracted, refined, and delivered in certain ways and not others. Understanding that structure – knowing how the oil business works, and who the key players are in it – is foundational to interpreting much of anything else.

A key economic barometer in the oil business – indeed any business – is the price the product commands. We therefore spend time examining price dynamics because they help us understand the decisions industry players are making at any given time. There is a lot of price evidence to survey, provided by analysts and business journalists who track every small rise and fall and then issue torrents of commentary about what those movements might portend. It would be nice if oil prices acted the way classical market theory argues they should. In a well-functioning market, price distills and interprets all that is known about the market for a particular good or service, thereby rendering an accurate estimation of its value, and investors and consumers use that indicator in deciding where to deploy their investment and consumption dollars. In the oil market, the price mechanism rarely works this clearly or this well. It can in fact be downright hard to explain why the price of a barrel is what it is. Many variables affect price – levels of supply and demand, bouts of extreme weather, momentary geopolitical shock, the uncertainty around the COVID-19 pandemic, to name a few. That variability confounds even the most sophisticated analysts.

It can be difficult to interpret what a given price may saying, why it is what it is, or how long it will prevail. Moreover, that complexity is compounded by a lack of transparency: a lot of key information about the oil market remains shrouded in mystery. The production desires of governments, the reserves many large fields contain, and ongoing investment plans are often hard to uncover and may even shelter under the banner of official state secrets. Analysts can make educated guesses about them, but they remain estimations. The outcome of these collective predictions and estimations often compounds, rather than reduces, price volatility, and can amplify market sentiment in either bearish or bullish ways.[13] The importance of oil prices is even broader than that: oil price is used as a bellwether indicator to explain, interpret, and predict the health of the global economy as well, helping to build a collective "story" that explains why current economic events are happening as they are.[14]

Oil companies make production decisions based on what they expect their product will garner on world markets, which is in turn based on expected demand levels, as well as what they think other producers will dump on the market. Oil executives face further burdens of choice in deciding how much exploration capital to spend and where to spend it. Meanwhile, politicians in economies that either produce or consume large quantities of oil must make budgetary and economic decisions based, at least in part, on what they think will happen in the oil market and what their expected revenue intake will be. Without a sound understanding of how the market works, it is difficult to derive meaningful insight from day-to-day price fluctuations or resist the siren call of "collective market wisdom" that in hindsight often proves to be anything but wise. So, we necessarily spend some time looking at the industry itself.

Why Study Oil: Politics and Geopolitics

A second reason to study oil is because that study will lend insight into the political and geopolitical decisions states make. The strategic considerations surrounding the procurement of oil are considerable and are almost as old as the industry itself: stories about geopolitical intrigue are woven throughout the industry's history.[15] Students of international relations and national security pay attention to oil because it affects the central puzzles they care about: identifying the causes of conflict between nation-states and deciphering the foundations of a sustainable peace.[16] A political world composed of competing sovereign nation-states operating in an anarchic environment is a dangerous and a largely self-help one. No authority exists that can set and enforce rules, adjudicate disputes, or generally protect the weak from the strong.[17] Consequently, a national government's first priority will always be to safeguard the security of its citizens, and the measures it will take to do that – often measured in blood as well as money – are theoretically unlimited. The study of how states pursue their own protection and survival delineates the field of grand strategy, defined by Barry Posen as "a state's theory about how best it can cause security for itself."[18]

Grand strategy involves both ends and means. The end is the pursuit of the national interest – the things governments' judge vital to national security and well-being. They include such things as physical security, economic growth, and the defense and extension of key values abroad.[19] Enhancing these is perhaps the key reason why nation-states exist in the first place. Interests are permanent, transcend changes in government leadership or regime governing type, and their pursuit usually enjoys widespread domestic support. Countries employ what tools they have at their disposal to pursue that interest, ranging from quiet diplomacy to the outright use of military force. Building military alliances, crafting economic and trade agreements, launching information and education campaigns, and today even developing social media strategies are all part and parcel of what states do to enhance their position and power in the world.[20] Of course, because other states are doing similar things, conflict often ensues. Grand strategy studies how, where, and why such conflict could take place and outlines the conflicting political interests that give rise to it.[21]

These insights remain pertinent today, even as the international system continues to evolve. Strong powers continue to define the rules of the game for the overall system, yet challenge to established rules appears inevitable, as some powers weaken and others strengthen. Rivalry between different sets of rules, and who gets to set them, typifies the ongoing struggle for influence and power.[22] This dynamic of power ebbing, flowing, and transitioning means that states are concerned with relative, not absolute, gains in international affairs.[23] They evaluate economic and political transactions with an eye to ensuring their gains exceed those of their rivals. Only by outpacing, or at least matching, the power gains of others can states ensure they maintain their relative strength, the route that gives them the best chance at survival.

Oil is central to all these calculations. Countries need oil to power their economies and fuel their military forces. The consequences of oil shortage could be military defeat and possibly even foreign subjugation.[24] Most highly industrialized economies do not have enough domestic oil supply to meet what they need and consequently must rely on imports. So too do many developing and emerging economies. The need for imports may grow rapidly if their economy is booming or if their military forces are engaged in conflict. Securing necessary supplies, and if possible denying those supplies to adversaries, has therefore become part and parcel of what military planners habitually think about. Importers craft political relationships with oil suppliers to ensure reliable flow and may craft alliances and build military capabilities that protect that flow. Competing powers strive to exert diplomatic influence over key oil suppliers and/or physical control over supply routes. Securing access to stable and reasonably priced energy has become a well-established geopolitical interest:[25] taken to its extreme, this interest creates a disturbing potential scenario where oil-consuming nations fight to access remaining supply.[26]

Geopolitics and political interest also influence the calculations of exporters. Exporters depend on oil revenue to fund their military forces, as well as to pay for the social programs they have promised their domestic citizenry. They want to maintain their established export market share and also want to reap as high a price as they can get. Exporters, much like importers, foster political relationships designed to further national interests. They manage available supply if they can, work to ensure that a reliable buyer is available for the oil they produce, and keep a sharp eye out for any sign that their market share is dwindling. They deploy oil revenue into financial markets to further extend their geopolitical influence through the power of invested money. The sheer amount of wealth created by oil exports – often coming in windfall boom-bust cycles rather than by a measured and predictable increases in revenue inflow – can also create the incentive to spend or steal as much of that revenue as possible when times are good. Such incentives and tactics compose the traditional stuff of the geopolitics of oil. Importing countries will continue to care about security of supply and will employ state power to ensure it. Exporting countries view selling oil as equally vital and will do what is necessary to protect their supply outlets as well.

New geopolitical issues now compound these established ones. Today there are more players in the oil and energy game. All of them require a steady supply of energy to keep their economies growing. Moreover, oil often fuels the messy substate conflicts that today afflict the international system, conflicts that result from a weak domestic institutional structure that cannot withstand the pressures poverty, disease, and contesting political forces might place upon it.[27] Combating and containing substate conflicts composes much of what the world's current armed forces are called upon to do:[28] countries so afflicted may earn the dismal label of "failed states" and can then become breeding grounds for instability in the global system.[29] When surveying that bleak landscape, it becomes clear that oil, and the struggle to control it or profit from the revenue its sales generate, can contribute to prolonging and intensifying civil conflict and societal breakdown endemic in many of the world's more difficult geopolitical hotspots.

A final emerging national security and strategic challenge is in halting, or at least mitigating, the potentially catastrophic problems a steadily warming climate might create. Judging from its potential capacity to inflict human misery, extreme climate change ranks second only to all-out nuclear war on the "list of things we would like to avoid." The scientific evidence citing the burning of fossil fuels as a major contributor to a warming atmosphere is, shall we say, strong. Yet, given the magnitude of the world's current reliance on those fuels, halting or significantly slowing that use will be a decades-long task that poses geopolitical challenges. Countries that rely on oil sales to fund their economies today are going to have to develop alternative industries quickly, and rapid global declines in oil use will cause their economic and geopolitical fortunes to dwindle. Meanwhile, countries that burn a lot of carbon-based energy are in a race to develop technologies that reduce that use or mitigate the damage a carbon-dioxide infused atmosphere might create. Those most successful at doing so will enjoy an economic as well as a geopolitical windfall: freeing themselves from carbon dependency while also creating long-term economic advantages in the renewable energy systems of tomorrow.

Geopolitical tension therefore permeates the oil business. The act of securing oil supplies affects all the things students of geopolitical competition care about. These problems continue to wax and wane as the oil industry moves through its production and price cycle and are now complicated by a host of twenty-first-century challenges. Oil remains a key facet to them all.

Why Study Oil: The Future of the Global Economy

A final reason to study oil is that its workings will tell us much about how the global economy will likely evolve and what type of capitalism the future will see. At first blush, this may seem too grand a claim. After all, the business of international economic relations, especially when compared to the weightier matters of geopolitics and grand strategy, seems like pedestrian stuff. Discussions of the global economy are peppered with references to trade, capital account balances, currency exchanges, commodity flows, and economic growth levels, all of which have a tendency to make eyes glaze over. Indeed, economic matters are sometimes confined to the basement of "low politics": treatises on grand strategy are often either entirely silent upon, or give only cursory treatment to, economic matters.[30] This may seem reasonable: though economic disputes and conflicts happen and are painful and disruptive enough to the contending parties, they rarely threaten overall national security or demand an immediate state-based response.

That characterization misses a key link between geopolitics and economics. Military conflicts may be geologically akin to earthquakes and volcanoes, whose eruptions and tremors shake the international system. Episodic and violent, they certainly capture the collective attention of national governments and focus their political will. But they are (hopefully!) temporary: conflicts end, peace treaties are eventually struck, and new institutional governing arrangements are made. By contrast, acts of economic exchange – the movements of goods, services, money, ideas, and people across borders – generates a relentless and grinding economic competition that is more geologically akin to the shifting of tectonic plates, whose subtle but constant movement increases geopolitical pressure. Over time, as countries feel their economic position strengthen or weaken, it generates a corresponding sense of self-confidence or fear. The pressure accumulates, and if not managed, the accumulated stress can rupture the "fault lines"[31] striating the global economy.[32]

Those tectonic plates are certainly grinding in the oil industry. Its size alone guarantees that what goes on in it will affect the economic fortunes of a sizable chunk of the world's economy. Moreover, the global oil business lies at the very epicenter of the contests currently raging about how the global economy should work. Oil operates in stark contrast to the accepted wisdom of globalization, defined loosely as the progressive and intentional lowering of barriers to economic exchange across national borders. Globalization has been a central international economic story since at least the end of the Cold War, and its intellectual heritage draws on the writings of Adam Smith, David Ricardo, and many modern economists who have outlined the benefit to consumers the doctrines of comparative advantage and free trade can have.[33] However, much of what they recommend does not always come naturally to national governments, who are prone to protectionism and economic nationalism, particularly when their economic fortunes turn sour. National governments may even erect trade and investment barriers when confronted with hard economic times, measures tending to make things economically worse, not better.

Over the last three decades, efforts to integrate the economy have helped ignite global growth and raised the income levels of hundreds of millions of people, particularly in the developing world. Those efforts have included the construction of a network of trade and investment agreements that coordinate and manage trade and investment flow:[34] these are the rule sets that govern an interlinked global economy. Globalization also encouraged governments to remove themselves from the "Commanding Heights" of their domestic economies, thereby entrusting that the market would effectively self-police its players through international agreements and rules. Governments have deregulated and privatized their state-owned enterprises and endorsed measures to remove barriers to international trade and investment.[35] Confidence in economic liberalization and globalization once seemed universal: the adoption of capitalism by former communist states gave rise to the "End of History"[36] arguments that populated popular discourse. Economic cooperation would supposedly banish to oblivion the dark side of geopolitical competition that had written much of the world's history.

Often unnoticed was that, during this same period, events in the oil market often marched in the other direction. While much of the global economy went merrily about its liberalizing and privatizing ways, overall state control in oil increased. In the specific case of oil, advanced economies liberalized their oil markets – a process that occurred over a period of years and decades[37] – developing market economies, the ones holding the largest known oil reserves, increased state control over theirs.[38] State control over oil had begun to grow in the Middle East since at least the 1970s,[39] and remains firmly entrenched today. Today state-owned oil companies dominate much of the world's oil production. Those companies do differ significantly in their managerial prowess, sophistication, and the amount of control their government owners exert. But, even when such companies claim a private-sector patina and argue that they care only about market metrics and shareholder return, the presence of their home government always looms. That government may claim to be but a passive owner, but few believe that this entirely holds, still less that it holds all the time. State ownership implies at least the potential for state influence, if not outright directive, and governments clearly have a financial interest in what their companies do, particularly if a crisis or disruption hits the oil market.

The debate contest between markets and state control present in the oil industry will be a significant battleground in the ongoing contest determining the direction the global economy will take. Some observers are now clearly questioning whether the globalization juice is worth the loss-of-sovereignty squeeze. A liberalized global economy has pitfalls, which have revealed themselves via the financial crisis, increasing income inequality, and perceived heightened economic instability in once previously secure jobs that have afflicted even the most developed nations. More recently, globalization's disaggregated production chains have also suffered from external risks that could be disrupted by unforeseen events, like a global pandemic. Liberalized international markets clearly hold dangers as well as opportunities.

The decades-long embrace of economic liberalism may have caused some to forget that there are indeed other ways of doing things. Given recent global economic tumult, some are wondering if it makes sense for governments to exert a more focused hand in managing their economies. A competing economic logic has reemerged that challenges liberalism's dominance, that of state capitalism, a doctrine in which national governments take just such a guiding and directive role. State capitalism uses government instruments to help domestic companies achieve not just success but perhaps even dominance in international competition. Its clearest example is China, whose dominant Communist government has proven to be anything but shy in using the domestic levers of government to aid the rise of its companies, shelter its currency, and protect its export-led economy.

But China is hardly alone: state capitalism is gaining popular legitimacy and the number of its adherents is increasing.[40] The discipline of geo-economics, where countries compete in the economic realm as much as they do in the geopolitical one, is making an academic and practical comeback.[41] Economic nationalism is even making strides in more developed countries, who had been among globalization's greatest beneficiaries. Its sentiment echoes in the populist political movements noted earlier that have generated such startling political results, including the election of Donald Trump and Great Britain's decision to leave the European Union.

State-directed economic nationalism has its own intellectual legacy that is also deeply cemented in economic history: its most stringent form is mercantilism. Mercantilism argues that the purpose of economic activity is to build state power, arguing "that economic activities are and should be subordinate to the goal of state building and the interests of the state."[42] Physical control of tangible assets matters, as does the accumulation of financial reserves via trade surpluses. It is the government's duty to try to foster the acquisition of those assets and reserves wherever it could and to deploy them to increase state economic power. Doing so freed countries from the vulnerabilities that foreign ownership created and protected key productive assets from the exploitation by adversaries. A quote from Friedrich List, one of the doctrine's intellectual forbearers, demonstrates the philosophy permeating mercantilism and the very high stakes for which that game was played: "The object of the economy of this body is not only wealth as in individual and cosmopolitical economy, but power and wealth, because national wealth is increased and secured by national power, as national power is increased and secured by national wealth ... Its leading principles are therefore not only economic, but political too. The individuals may be very wealthy; but if the nation possesses no power to protect them, it and they may lose in one day the wealth they gathered during ages, and their rights, freedom, and independence too."[43]

It is a bit of a jolt to be reminded that economic activity can be phrased in such nakedly power-based terms. Yet there is nothing new about it: before globalization swept popular imagination and policy advice, evidence of states using their resources to directly acquire the economic goods fueling their political power were as common as not, and such references are the bread and butter of the history of what countries were trying to do.[44]

The oil market will be a key test case determining what direction the world's economy is going to go. It is an arena where alternate economic ideologies continue to wage a contest for adherents. Private-sector enthusiasts advocate for the wisdom of markets and price signals in determining how much and where oil is produced. Markets, if left alone to work their magic, will allocate capital toward the most productive investments, will reward those companies able to extract oil cheaply and will thereby ensure delivery of adequate supply at the lowest price. State-control enthusiasts retort that markets are unpredictable, erratic, create inequality, leave small countries vulnerable to foreign dominance, and cannot ultimately be trusted. Embracing markets to develop oil resources will rob producers of their sole source of geopolitical leverage. The oil industry is a microcosm of the enduring and endemic struggles within the international economy, which increasingly looks like a house divided against itself. The choices countries make signal their confidence that an interdependent economic system will help them over the long run.[45]

Outline of the Book

The book proceeds as follows. The following chapter provides a primer on how the oil industry works. After a century and a half of cumulative experience, the industry has developed its own way to rock, so to speak. It has specific ways of doing things and responds to pressure in particular and regularized ways: this chapter outlines what these are. Chapter three then summarizes the history of oil, outlining a series of discrete political and economic challenges that have repeatedly occurred and linger today. The rest of the empirical sections of the book are divided into distinct eras delineated by trends in price. Chapter four looks at the period 2002–14 chronicling the economic challenges emerging in a period of generally rising and sustained high prices. That period, interrupted only briefly by the financial crisis, witnessed changes within the industry that generated political and geopolitical worries: chapter five chronicles what these were. Chapter six examines the economics, politics, and geopolitics of a price drop followed by a sustained period of low prices, which characterized the years between 2014 and 2020.

The final chapter deals with momentous years of 2020–22 and beyond. That was a period in which a global pandemic ripped through the world's population and forced changes upon the oil market, along with pretty much everything else. Yet, despite the pandemic's headlines, it is clear that the patterns witnessed throughout the history of oil remain with us. New challenges – demands to use less oil, heightened concern over the environment, an increasingly demanding financial community wanting oil companies to do more in the realm of environmental, social, and governance (ESG) performance – arose and now need to be incorporated into how the oil system works. That chapter summarizes the ongoing practical and academic problems that will have to be solved if those demands are going to be met. The chapter then offers projections on how those problems will play out and what the future of oil might hold.

The book adopts an interdisciplinary flavor, drawing on scholarship in economics, politics, and international relations. Each of these disciplines have contributed independently to the scholarly treatment of the problems the book examines: much of the more significant literature on a particular issue is contained in the references. The politics of oil also continue to receive scrutiny from security specialists, who acknowledge that the separation between grand strategy, political economy, and domestic politics is highly artificial and largely unhelpful in an increasingly globalized world.[46] The issues remain intertwined: security and geopolitical influence depend on fostering a competitive national economy, a point sum-marized well by the Princeton Project on National Security: "The importance of integrating economic policy into national security policy should be self-evident ... (however) despite this strong case for policy integration, U.S. policymakers have had a difficult time achieving it, at both the conceptual and operational levels ... in the situation we confront in the world today, there is potential for considerable mutual reinforcement between economic policy and national security/foreign policy aims."[47]

An earlier section of this chapter criticized the inaccuracy of pre-vious predictions about the oil market. Yet that will not stop people from making new ones: the human propensity to try to predict the future seems powerful and ingrained, no matter how wrong those predictions eventually prove to be.[48] While this book will make a few of its own, it will hopefully help readers do a better job of that themselves. At the very least, the book ought to allow readers to make sounder judgments about whatever headline they might read or oil rumor they might hear. Understanding how any system works helps unmask underlying, often inaccurate assumptions that often generates the word on the street: it forces analysts to be more explicit about the conditions upon which that judgment is based.[49]

Today, the challenge is both maintenance – managing estab-lished and known problems so that they do not become worse – as well as transition, moving away from oil toward alternative fuel sources and doing so without igniting the various political hotspots such a transition might engender. This book provides a reasonably coherent picture of what those challenges are and how they can be addressed. We start by looking at the fundamentals of the industry, laying the foundation for the political and geopoliti-cal discussions to follow.

chapter two

A Primer on the Oil Industry

It is difficult to navigate the politics and geopolitics of oil without first understanding how the industry works and why it is the way it is. This chapter builds that understanding, telling the reader what they need to know about how oil is procured, sold, and consumed. By chapters' end readers will know such useful things as how much oil the world uses, whether we need to worry about running out, what current production and consumption patterns and trends look like now, and in what direction those things are trending. It is structured to provide enough detail to demonstrate the industry's size, its centrality to the overall global economy, and the obstacles that will hinder a simple or rapid transition away from its use, all hopefully without overwhelming or over-boring the reader.

It proceeds as follows. First, it outlines supply and demand statistics and breaks those statistics down by geography. Second, it looks at the problem of maintaining overall supply and the reality (or not) of "peak oil." Third, it looks at the various species of oil companies that do the world's exploring and producing, noting that they are varied beasts that operate with different production logics and have different corporate priorities. Finally, it examines contemporary developments in the industry, focusing on the implications US shale production could have for the oil market. This chapter covers the statistics of the oil-producing world up until the beginning of 2020 – that is, all the pre-COVID-19 time. The pandemic's impact on the oil market will be the subject of the last chapter.

A Primer on the Oil Industry

Most of the world's oil lies in a semi-viscous liquid state trapped beneath the earth's surface in "fields" of various size. Some fields lie so close to the surface that a portion of their oil seeps upward and coats the topsoil and landscape. Consequently, humans have been aware of oil's existence for hundreds if not thousands of years and have regularly employed it for various purposes. Indigenous North American peoples sealed canoes with oil residue, and accounts of nomads in the deserts of the Middle East referencing "lakes of fire" – ignited pools of surface oil set aflame by lightning – date back centuries.[1]

Oil fields vary tremendously in size, recoverable volume, and comparative ease of drilling access. They may lie anywhere from a few hundred to many thousands of feet below the surface of the ground or even the ocean floor: such sourced oil holds the label "conventional" oil extraction, and they are the typical image people have of what drilling for oil looks like. Other "non-conventional" sources of oil include that trapped in a semi-viscous rock-and-sand mixture commonly known as oil sands, vast deposits of which lay buried underneath the frozen tundra of Northern Alberta and along the Orinoco river delta in Venezuela. Additional sources of non-conventional oil include that trapped within shale rock, oil that is released once that rock is "cracked" via the application of fracking technology.

The engineering effort and accompanying expense required to access these different sources varies considerably. Some fields hold the ideal combination of being comparatively cheap to access while holding a deep reservoir that can pump out high volumes of oil over an extended time. Their production virtues easily pay for the necessary associated engineering infrastructure: oil extracted from these fields may cost but a few dollars a barrel to produce. Remaining sources of oil require more infrastructure to extract and refine, and their extraction costs rise accordingly. The oil sloshing through the world's pipeline infrastructure and transport ships holds different production-cost profiles: a barrel of oil costs less than $10 to produce in Saudi Arabia; it costs around $30 to produce in Mexico, $41 in Canada, and around $50 in the United Kingdom.[2] Those individual costs can vary as companies work to lower them by improving operational efficiency, which in turn raises the profits they would receive at any given price. The range in production price, field profile, and engineering complexity associated with various sources remains substantial.

Finding oil fields, estimating how much oil they might contain, and thinking through how best to effectively extract that oil is both a practitioner's art and a highly complex and expensive science. Early exploration efforts relied upon an experienced geologist's eye to spot the elevated tectonic domes and rock formations that signaled a potential field. Today, technology augments and amplifies that eye with seismic sensors, supercomputers, three-dimensional sonography, and an array of highly sophisticated and expensive exploration technologies that may cumulatively cost tens of millions of dollars to develop and deploy. Some fields are generous: possessing the ideal combination of easy accessibility, plentiful recoverable reserves, and ease of extraction: these are known in the trade as "elephants." But there are only so many such fields: most have already been "mapped and tapped," and major oil companies, either state-owned or private, already likely hold the required leases to control their production.

The oil remaining in the earth's crust is harder to find, more difficult to access, and more expensive to extract than the oil that has already been found. In some cases that oil may be buried underneath thousands of feet of rock and/or seawater, or even Arctic ice. It may require expensive, energy-intensive and complicated refining, as the bitumen trapped in the Alberta oil sands does. The fields may be located in unstable or poorly governed countries where the above-ground political risk is high. Oil companies not surprisingly must work assiduously to monitor and reduce risks and costs, to increase the chances of successful exploration, and to lower the associated investment, exploration, and political risk. Despite all this, oil exploration remains an imprecise and expensive business, one that has often been prone to high drilling failure rates, requires long-term engineering investment, and where success has often required a significant dose of luck.

Despite these daunting challenges, there remain plenty of individuals willing to take on those risks if they think they will make money. Whether they will or not is determined by the difference between what it costs to produce the oil and the price that oil fetches on the global market. "Available" oil supply is therefore largely a function of price: companies need the economic incentive a high price provides before they will bother doing all the things necessary to develop expensive fields. If prices are low and are expected to remain there, the oil more expensive fields contain will lay undeveloped and will technically remain "unavailable," even if the reserves themselves are known.

To take a quick example, no one knows this better than investors and oil companies looking to develop the Canadian oil sands. Knowledge of the immense reserves lying underneath the tundra in Northern Alberta has existed for decades. But the expense required to extract them is formidable: the oil must be separated from a frozen slurry of dirt, rock, and oil that has earned the trade name "bitumen," which requires a lot of refining to gain a usable product. That has historically limited the pool of investment capital dedicated to developing it. The price simply did not justify it. It remained cheaper to explore in other geographies, and accept the exploration costs and risk, rather than develop the oil sands reserves even if they carried zero exploration risk.

Finding new oil requires a lot of exploration expense and time: sometimes it may take a decade or more for a new oil field to be located and for the required drilling infrastructure to be built before that field begins producing significant volumes. Expected prices therefore have to remain high enough for long enough to make that development worthwhile. The expense of finding new oil, or refining particular grades of oil, acts as an investment deterrent. Why explore in an expensive field when there are sources of cheaper oil available elsewhere and the forecasted prices do not justify it? Yet without continued annual investment, there will be no new sources to replace the output of the fields currently being drained. Under that scenario, eventual supply shortages are a certainty, and without new fields companies would miss out on the profitable opportunities offered by subsequent rising prices. Maintaining the right amount of field exploration is therefore a delicate and constant balancing act.

Individual oil companies will have more or less exploration success depending on their luck and engineering prowess. Yet, taken in its entirety, the industry has repeatedly proven capable of finding and retrieving whatever amount of additional oil the market might be demanding.[3] There are literally thousands of oil companies looking for oil. They collectively spend hundreds of billions of annual exploration dollars, employ thousands of ambitious and talented engineers to do that looking, and have (at least until recently) been backed by a vibrant financial community happy to provide the investment dollars needed to scour the globe. When totaled over all the decades it has been going on, these cumulative exploration and development efforts have created a gigantic industry whose accumulated value – measured in 2016 at US$1.7 trillion – is greater than that of all other raw material and metal industries combined.[4]

Over the period 2014–20, oil prices dropped significantly, and those prices were not helped by the onset of the COVID-19 pandemic and consequent slowdown in travel and transport. Yet even that did not entirely stop ongoing investment. Capital devoted to exploration efforts in upstream oil and gas exploration has ranged between $500 billion and $750 billion annually for the previous decade and a half.[5] In 2014 global upstream spending measured nearly US$800 billion. It dropped significantly due to the price fall of that year: in 2015 it measured almost $600 billion. It measured $400–$500 billion annually in the years 2016–19, and is projected to measure around $330 billion each for 2020 and 2021.[6] Today that cumulative capital investment measures in the trillions of dollars, supports a system capable of producing and delivering around 100 million barrels of oil every day,[7] and could supply significantly more if necessary.

That is just the effort that goes into exploration and drilling. In addition to the task of finding and producing oil, there is also a massive supporting infrastructure in place dedicated to refining that oil into usable products and then transporting those products to thirsty customers. A lot of this is done by pipeline, of which there are over 1.4 million kilometers scattered around the globe.[8] There are also millions of additional miles of railway track shuffling oil to and fro, along with other industrial staples and finished goods. Hundreds of thousands of gas stations stand at the corners of the intersections of the world's highways and local streets, and there are currently 7,350 oil tankers traversing the earth's oceans, picking up and delivering oil from refineries and storage depots.[9] Significant storage capacity has also been built, housing oil to be released in emergencies or to meet spikes in demand. The US alone holds between 500 million and 550 million barrels of crude oil spare capacity inventory,[10] and the corresponding world total measures around 4 billion barrels of stored oil.[11]

This accumulated infrastructure base supporting the oil economy – the refineries, millions of miles of rail track, thousands of oil tankers, gas stations, and everything else – is impressive not only for its size. Ironically, it is often barely noticed. Pipelines are usually buried underground, out of sight and out of mind. The oil carried on trains draws no more attention than does the myriad of other products those trains might be carrying. Unless one lives near, in, or works at a refinery, they too rarely occupy attention, and oceangoing merchant marine vessels remain one of the least visible industries around.[12] Consequently, few customers have a clear idea of what it takes to get oil out of the ground, refine it, and transport it to a local gas station where it eventually gets deposited into their gasoline tank. That the gas station remains consistently well supplied, heating tanks in millions of homes do not run dry, and airline executives never complain about the availability of fuel (though they may grumble at the cost), and that all this works reliably and predictably, is something of an industrial and engineering miracle.

Where does all that oil end up? To begin (and there is no way around this), most of it is turned into some kind of fuel that is then burned in an internal combustion engine, which supplies the power to some kind of transport vessel designed to move people and goods around quickly and efficiently. Oil is the feedstock for the liquids powering most of the world's cars, planes, and ships. Personal transport vehicles are the obvious place to start. Cars are particularly noteworthy, and the statistics on car use are daunting. Between the years 2000 and 2017, 500,000 "personal light duty vehicles" (cars and small trucks) joined the global fleet, increasing that total to a whopping 1.1 billion such vehicles on global roads. Over 95 per cent of those vehicles rely on carbon-based fuels.

To be sure, there are emerging alternate options. Some of these options are driven by regulation: as the concluding chapter shows, bans on internal combustion engines for cars are growing worldwide. The most environmentally friendly alternative for an internal combustion engine is to not have one at all. Countries with higher urban densities and generally smaller geographies make public transport networks more efficient and economically viable, sometimes obviating the need to own a car. Alternatively, one could also replace the gasoline-powered engine with one powered by some other, presumably cleaner fuel. For cars, the obvious alternative to a gasoline engine is an electric one. Sales of electricity-powered vehicles are indeed growing rapidly, even more so as those vehicles gain in range, performance, and affordability. The financial markets are certainly enthusiastic about electric car makers: in the spring of 2021 the market capitalization of Tesla (the electric car company founded by Elon Musk) exceeded the market capitalization of Ford, General Motors, Chrysler, ExxonMobil, and Chevron combined. More electric vehicles are certainly on the way: as many political jurisdictions in Europe have either banned, or are considering banning, internal combustion engines in vehicles,[13] and some governors of US states have asked president Biden to do the same thing.[14]

Yet it will be a long time before electric vehicles fully displace vehicles powered by gasoline. Sales of electric vehicles measured virtually nothing in 2012. In 2018 electric cars accounted for 1 per cent of annual car sales,[15] and by 2019 annual sales of electric vehicles measured well over 2 million.[16] Tesla captured 14 per cent of the electric car market in 2019, when it sold 337,000 cars.[17] Yet, in 2019 alone over 71 million cars were built, over 20 million light commercial vehicles, and over 4 million heavy-duty commercial trucks.[18] In 2019 General Motors sold 2.8 million vehicles.[19] Ford sold 2.4 million cars, and its overall bestseller was by far was its gas-guzzling F-series of pickup trucks.[20] Even at their impressive growth rates, it will take some time for electric vehicles to make a real dent in the number of carbon-based vehicles on the road. Moreover, even if they do, electric vehicles are not going to be the environmental panacea sometimes portrayed. Something must generate the electricity those vehicles use, and often that is a natural gas–fired (sometimes, though increasingly rarely, a coal-fired) electricity plant. Moreover, the specialized metals and batteries used in electric vehicles carry significant environmental concerns of their own,[21] the labor conditions under which those materials are mined are often abysmal, and the disposal of those batteries when worn out is a landfill nightmare.

The dominance of oil in air and commercial ship transport, as well as in transport trucks, is even more complete than it is in personal vehicles. Practically speaking, carbon-based jet fuel powers all of the world's airplanes, and its dominance is almost as complete in shipping and oceangoing transport vessels.[22] Granted, a few hardy souls remain stalwart fans of wind-powered sailing ships, and advanced militaries do have nuclear-powered submarines and aircraft carriers. But beyond these specialized cases, oil- and diesel-fired engines rule the world of oceangoing vessels. Transport trucks are also heavily dependent on gas and diesel: many of these are privately owned by small firms who would not be able to afford a major electric-engine retrofit. Moving beyond transport, oil also provides the feedstock to a host of other products and services. These include industrial chemicals, plastics, and fertilizers that find their way into the supply chains of associated industries, ranging from medical care products to agriculture. Oil also is the feedstock of dozens of everyday products, such as candle wax, insect repellent, kayaks, shaving cream, fishing lures, golf balls, deodorant, pajamas, umbrellas, and heart valves.[23] Taken together, the centrality of oil to the global economy is difficult to deny.

Cutting back on oil consumption significantly and transitioning to some other fuel is therefore going to take substantial political and consumer will and will likely take decades. Doing entirely without it at this point seems the stuff of utopian dreams. This assertion might seem surprising, if not jarring, given the amount of popular attention paid to the idea that we can rapidly shed our reliance on oil. The statistics and realities presented here demonstrate how difficult, and likely time consuming, that transition is likely to be. Oil's presence in the globe's overall energy mix is a structural outcome caused by 150 years of accumulated industrial investment and momentum, which is difficult to change rapidly and resists easy fixes.

Oil Demand Now and in the Future

People pay attention to how much oil the world needs and who supplies that oil. Fortunately, several reputable agencies exist that track such figures, and they have over decades built particular credence with oil market observers for their consistent veracity and reliability. Internationally, a key repository of oil market information is the International Energy Agency (IEA), founded in 1974 under the auspices of the Organization for Economic Cooperation and Development (OECD). The IEA's history interestingly enough emerged out of a combination of both fear and embarrassment, as a series of successive oil crises, embargoes, and price shocks (chronicled later) revealed not only the dependence industrialized economies had on imported oil but also their stunning ignorance about how big that dependency was. They did not possess a systematic shared repository of information about what global production capacity was, what available reserves were, and who was doing the bulk of the producing. Since its inception, the IEA's task has been to gather and track that data and fill these glaring knowledge gaps. It publishes its findings via its influential Monthly Oil Report and annual World Energy Outlook, documents that catalogue supply, demand, and inventory levels of different types of energy stocks.[24]

The IEA is not alone in tracking that information. There are also national agencies that are highly reputable sources of data. One of these is the US Energy Information Administration (EIA), which reports on global and domestic production levels across the energy spectrum. Private-sector oil companies, such as ExxonMobil, BP, and Shell also provide additional reliable annual energy outlooks, as do many investment banks and consulting organizations, not to mention the data and analysis arm of the Organization for Petroleum Exporting Countries (OPEC). Taken together, these multiple sources act as a mutual check on each other's accuracy and reliability: if one produced a forecast diverging significantly from the consensus views of others, it would then require a lot of explaining. Each data report and forecast in effect competes with others, forcing them to clearly lay out their assumptions and planning foundations, helping generate mutual confidence in their overall veracity.

The data presented in the following paragraphs draws collectively from these reputable sources. It is not surprisingly selective and offers the proverbial highlight reel: we pick and choose key statistics that give an accurate picture of what is going on without drowning the reader in an avalanche of available facts, figures, and data.[25] Those desiring a more complete data dump should consult the quoted sources independently.

Figure 1 takes a summary look at oil-demand projections from various sources, each of which develops various scenarios in which oil use varies depending on how aggressively governments enact policies to reduce carbon consumption and emission. The figures range from projections where government policy remains unchanged toward scenarios where governments enact aggressive and ambitious carbon emission reduction targets.

These forecasts indicate consumption is predicted to rise and will likely continue doing so for several more decades. Yet predicting just how much future consumption there will be is tricky and becomes progressively more so the farther out one looks. Projections vary between the noted forecasters and necessarily fluctuate depending on the assumptions built into the forecasting models. The key variables affecting future oil demand are what policies governments enact (and consistently execute), what improvements are made in non-carbon energy sources, and how consumer preferences evolve, all of which are difficult to forecast. Some forecasters therefore offer multiple forecasts that are predicated under different scenarios of what changes occur and what governments decide to do or not do.

Figure 1. Summary of Oil-Demand Projections, Various Forecasts (Millions of Barrels/Day)

Summary of Global Oil Demand Forecasts

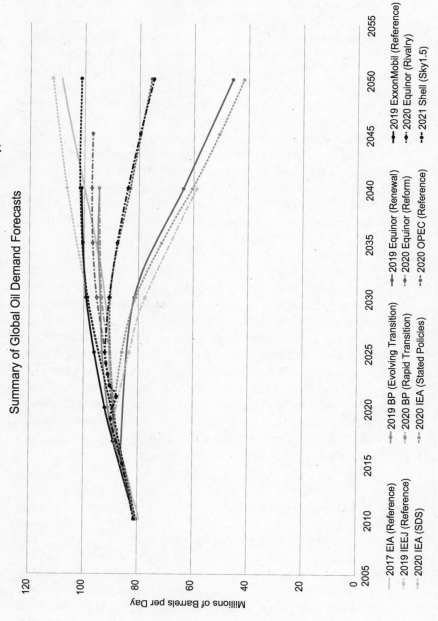

— 2017 EIA (Reference)
····· 2019 IEEJ (Reference)
-·-· 2020 IEA (SDS)

— 2019 BP (Evolving Transition)
····· 2020 BP (Rapid Transition)
----- 2020 IEA (Stated Policies)

—•— 2019 Equinor (Renewal)
··•·· 2020 Equinor (Reform)
--•-- 2020 OPEC (Reference)

—•— 2019 ExxonMobil (Reference)
··•·· 2020 Equinor (Rivalry)
--•-- 2021 Shell (Sky1.5)

** Data sourced from the International Energy Agency, the United States Energy Information Administration, Energy Forecasts from Equinor, BP, Shell, ExxonMobil, and the Institute for Energy Economics, Japan

Most scenarios reveal some consistent facts. First, the world consumes a lot of oil, and that consumption has grown relentlessly. Oil use continues to be measured in barrels, and each barrel contains 42 US gallons, or 158 liters: world usage is measured in millions of such barrels of oil a day (mbd). To give some context to what growth levels have been, the IEA's 2009 *World Energy Outlook* noted that in 1980 the world consumed 64.8 mbd: by 2008 that figure measured 84.7 mbd.[26] By 2017 oil demand measured 95 mbd, and in 2019 global oil use measured 99.2 mbd. Taken visually, as one title of a popular book put it, those totals start looking a lot like "*A Thousand Barrels a Second*."[27] Some more aggressive forecasts have put demand growing to 130 mbd by 2040: more moderate forecasts put the final tally at between 104 and 106 mbd by 2026.[28] In the space of forty years, oil demand has increased by about 40 mbd, roughly an additional 10 mbd each decade.

Clearly even the best forecasters differ significantly on how much oil the world will need in the future. The paths of technological development and consumer preferences are difficult to predict. As for governments – in particular, democracies – planning and executing consistent policies over decades seems like a near impossible thing to do, particularly with regard to measures designed to lower oil use. Governments switch frequently, have different ideological approaches to solving problems, and have to keep their eyes relentlessly focused on the ballot box. In the realm of lowering oil use, even if they do meet their pledged carbon-reduction commitments – and historical experience indicates not all of them will and that they may fall short in fulfilling the carbon-reduction promises they have made – carbon use still rises until approximately 2040.[29]

Who Is Doing the Consuming?

For decades, the United States led the way in overall energy consumption, holding the twin title of being both the world's largest consumer and its largest importer of oil. Its massive and robust economy, large landmass, high standards of living, and prevalence of cars as a primary transport mechanism combined to make its thirst for oil gargantuan. In the not-so-distant past, US consumption totaled one-quarter of world demand all by itself. It has dropped a bit: in 2018 that consumption measured 20.5 mbd, which was but a measly one-fifth of the world total. For most of the past seven decades, the developed markets in Europe and Japan consumed much of the rest of the world's remaining global oil production. In 2019 they hovered around 14 mbd and 4 mbd, respectively.[30,31,32] Those regions are even more reliant on imports as a percentage of their total oil consumption than is the United States. Japan possesses few indigenous oil reserves, and Western Europe's are also insufficient to meet its oil needs, which necessitates a high level of collective imports for both. Both have made significant efforts in pursuing non-carbon-based energy sources, and today both Japan and Western Europe consume less carbon per capita than do citizens of the United States. But they still need a steady supply of a lot of oil.

Next we consider China, whose economy has demonstrated massive growth over the past several decades. China has been the world's major player in energy demand for a while now. In 2009 China surpassed the United States in its overall demand for energy. Much of it was for coal to fuel the electricity production grid that continues to power its sprawling economy. Oil is on the same growth trajectory. In 2018 Chinese overall oil demand measured approximately 13 mbd, and in 2017 China surpassed the United States in the absolute amount of oil it imported.[33]

China is hardly alone. The statistics of emerging market demand are revealing and typically point only in one direction. Developed economies belonging to the Organization for Economic Cooperation and Development (OECD) might see their demand collectively swell to 49.4 mbd by 2020 and to 70.4 mbd by 2040. However, overall demand for oil in the broader Asia-Pacific region is growing at seven times the rate it is in North America.[34] India, with a population of well over 1 billion people, consumed only 3.7 mbd in 2013: its projected need is set to rise to 10 mbd by 2040. By 2030 Latin America's consumption will grow from 4.8 mbd to 7.1 mbd. Africa's overall consumption will within a decade also grow from 2.8 mbd to 4.8 mbd, and that continent is just beginning its industrialization rise.[35] Even the Middle East – long identified as the world's key source of export supply – saw internal oil demand levels almost double between 2000 and 2015, growing from 4.3 to

7.9 mbd. Those internal demands will likely rise due to the effects of rapid industrialization, rising incomes, and expanding populations.[36] Unless those Middle Eastern oil producers increase production, become more efficient, or convince their populations to use less oil, this will leave less of their oil for export, a gap that must be filled from elsewhere.

This shift in demand patterns means that emerging markets now grapple with the same reality of import vulnerability long afflicting developed markets. Most emerging markets cannot supply their oil needs with domestic resources: they need imported oil, and that dependency is only going to grow. In developed markets that has been true for decades. In the United States import dependency grew steadily between 1973 – the year US regulators abandoned limits on domestic US production, believing the country would consume all the oil it could produce and would still require hefty imports – until 2010, when the fracking revolution began to produce in earnest. During that forty-year period, US domestic production struggled to maintain a steady-state level hovering around 6 mbd.[37] Because its economy grew and its ability to procure more domestic oil did not, import dependency climbed steadily and reached nearly 14 mbd by 2010.[38] What was then true in the United States is now true elsewhere. Given current consumption and demand patterns, oil demand and import dependency for rapidly growing emerging markets is larger – and perhaps much larger – than the reduction in demand developed markets might see.

Is There Enough? Revisiting and Updating Peak Oil Theory

The most pernicious geopolitical fear historically haunting oil market supply is that demand will someday outrun available supply. The fear is understandable. The earth's reserves are presumably limited, and we are using ever more of them with each passing year. Peak oil theory is therefore simple to visualize and explain: if oil-dependent economic growth continues, we will start consuming known reserves faster than we are finding replacement fields, which are themselves becoming harder to locate and more expensive to access. Logically there will therefore come a time when we will have consumed more than what remains, and supply capacities will no longer be able to keep up. When that happens, we will have reached the fabled point of "peak oil," and the countdown to running out will accelerate, forcing countries to then scramble in a headlong rush to secure whatever supplies may be left.[39]

Such warnings tend to surface when oil prices are high and supply capacity pressured. At such points present shortages are equated with increasing "scarcity," and from there it is but a short imaginary leap to "the world is running out"[40] narrative. That generates frightening, conflict-laden future scenarios that can become the stuff of Hollywood movies and popular culture. However, before the world succumbs to a *Mad Max*–reminiscent, gasoline-deprived wasteland, it is perhaps worth exploring the reality of whether such fears are really justified.

Peak oil theory represents but one boundary of an interpretive spectrum about how much oil the globe has and how much it can produce. Those endorsing it argue that global supplies are finite, they will become exhausted sooner than we think, and that all manner of dire consequences are going to follow. They cite the scientific legacy of Marion King Hubbert, an American geologist who gained fame via a paper he published in 1956 forecasting that US oil production would reach maximum output somewhere around 1970 and would thereafter decline. His prediction proved prescient: US production did more or less peak in 1973 at 8.5 mbd, and then it began to drop, reaching a low of 5.5 mbd in 2005 before the modern fracking revolution began and production levels rose once again. Contemporary peak oil adherents argue that what was true for the US must inevitably be true for the rest of the oil-producing world. The earth's reserves have a presumable limit. Only so much can be produced, irrespective of the additional expense and engineering talent thrown at the problem of extracting out ever more. The only questions were when, and how rapidly, global supply decline would happen and how severe the economic consequences would be when it did.

The opposite pole represents those believing that worrying over oil shortage is unwarranted. "Copernicans" argue that the earth has plenty of reserves left. Though admitting that extracting additional reserves will become progressively more difficult and expensive, explorers can overcome the challenges. History, they argue, is on their side. Fears of shortage occurring in the past have always subsided, and the oil market has repeatedly proven its production resilience.[41] Periods of shortage inevitably morph into periods of glut, as intrepid oil explorers, return-seeking financiers, and ambitious engineers invoke their collective production wizardry to coax more oil from the ground. Copernicans may grant that finding new so-called easy oil – plentiful fields located in relatively hospitable and easy-to-access terrain – is unlikely. But higher prices provide enough economic incentive to extract oil from the harder and more expensive places, and improved engineering and production efficiency lowers the production costs from these fields, making yesterday's "hard" oil easier to find and less expensive to extract.

To Copernicans, shortages and supply constraints do not happen because of any inherent limits on recoverable reserves. They happen because people get in the way. Put more technically, "significant non-geological obstacles" impede new production. Perhaps too much political risk accompanies exploration and production in a given area. Maybe opposition based on environmental concerns or landownership disputes is enough to stop exploration and drilling efforts in others. Capital markets may be stingy and increasingly picky, proving unwilling to provide the funding necessary to develop new sources, either because the returns are too low or, more recently, because they prefer not to provide capital to carbon-intensive businesses. Production cartels may allow too much oil into the system: that drives down price, making other fields uneconomic (but not necessarily unproductive). It is these artificial barriers that impede resource development more than does any limit on the amount of oil that is there. Explorers can handle the geology: solve the human problems and more supply will flow.

Copernicans also have faith that improving technologies will open up new sources of oil or will allow more oil to be recovered from existing ones. After all, there are two primary ways of increasing oil production: finding new fields or extracting more oil from fields we already know about. Today's technology holds great promise for both. For example, enhanced technology (if allowed to be imported) might perhaps increase recoverable reserves in Russia's West Siberian oil fields by as much as 30 billion barrels.[42] Moreover, it was the improving, not the initial, fracking technologies that made the technique cost-effective and ended up boosting overall daily output in the United States by over 10 mbd. Additional examples of enhanced recovery through advanced technologies could fill its own chapter.[43]

Meanwhile, companies continue exploring, scouring for new oil deposits in diverse geographies. Perhaps the likelihood of finding true "elephant" fields is low – like their pachyderm namesake, such fields are now endangered – but finding significant fields is itself fairly common. There is also a lot of supply left we already know about. The Alberta oil sands, for example, have 175 billion proven barrels that carry virtually no exploration risk. It is its operational and technical complexity, high and sometimes prohibitive cost, and strong environmental opposition that ultimately hinders its production.[44] Other new and/or non-conventional sources of oil include those buried underneath the ocean floor[45] or buried under Arctic ice,[46] which admittedly carry their own extraction challenges. But the oil is there.

Long-term supply estimates give confidence to the Copernican position. The IEA estimates that the world holds 2.2 trillion barrels of proven conventional crude oil reserves, and if one considers all the unconventional sources as well, that total rises to over 6 trillion barrels.[47] "Proven reserves" – oil that can be extracted profitably at current price levels and technologies – will rise if prices rise and/or technology improves. There remains significant additional production capacity in Iraq, Iran, and Saudi Arabia that could be unleashed quickly if political barriers were removed. In the latter's case, officials have claimed that an additional 200 billion barrels of proven reserves could conceivably be added to the already proven 260 billion barrels of reserves.[48] Both Iraq and Iran have the potential to produce between 6 and 8 mbd reliably if their endemic political barriers could ever be overcome.[49] The technology of fracking unleashed new output from the United States, and similar shale rock formations exist around the world. If accessed in the same way, new volumes of oil and gas will be released. Today the oil market is well supplied, and if there remain any die-hard peak oil theorists, they are staying quiet.

Claims about shortage and residual fears about running out should therefore be taken with several proverbial bags of salt. At this writing, the world is awash in a plentiful supply of relatively affordable oil. Multiple reputable sources of energy statistics reassure us that known existing supply will meet demand for decades to come, and those estimates do not take into account the additional oil that exploration efforts will likely add. It is difficult – but not impossible – to envision a future where fears of peak oil once again grip imaginations the way they have in the past. Such fears have been repeated features of the oil world. But right now those fears are dormant, which may or may not be a good thing. Having inexpensive and plentiful oil might lower the economic incentive to stop, or least reduce, its use. Environmentally that could be problematic and may inhibit solutions when talk turns to "transitioning" or "bridging" the global energy system away from carbon-based fuels. But more on that later. For now, suffice it to say that, though the earth's supply of oil is not limitless, running out is a problem for the very long run and, as John Maynard Keynes argued, in the very long run we are all dead. Fears of future peak oil help us little in analyzing the choices companies, governments, investors, and individuals are making today.

The earth holds enough proven hydrocarbon resources that will be sufficient to meet projected demand. Indeed, the reader may wonder why, in a world flooded by oil and when bunkers are full and price is low, we are talking about peak oil at all. Talk of potential shortages seems trivial and off the mark when compared to the more pressing needs of preventing the environmental Armageddon our internal combustion engines are driving us toward. That catastrophe seems virtually assured if we burn the oil reserves companies are still spending billions of dollars each year trying to find. But fears of peak oil may reemerge, particularly if exploration spending and investment slows and prices shoot upward. They have before and caused the financial and economic problems explored later. When and if peak oil reasserts itself, it would be well to remember that the Stone Age did not end because we ran out of stone. The Oil Age will not end because we run out of oil.

The Economics of Oil

The economics of oil can also be impressive. After all, justifying all the expense and effort needed to bring new oil to market was, and of course is, the promise of profit. That profit can be enormous, immensely rewarding those controlling access to oil reserves. When prices are high, having oil reserves generates perhaps the closest thing to a private right to print money that exists in the global economy. That goes for people, companies, and governments. Oil revenue generated some of history's largest personal fortunes, perhaps most famously that of John D. Rockefeller, discussed in the next chapter. In the late nineteenth century Rockefeller parlayed control of the Standard Oil Company into massive personal net worth that in today's figures would measure in the hundreds of billions of dollars. Today's oil revenue also enriches a select number of individuals the world over. These range from the "frackers" operating in the US shale deposits to the Russian oligarchs who survived the bloody post–Cold War scramble in the Russian energy sector to the modern princes governing the sands of Saudi Arabia. Given the promise of profit that high oil prices provide, there has never been a shortage of available capital and ambitious people willing to do what it takes to bring more oil to market.

The companies doing the producing can also become immensely flush, particularly when oil prices are high. During the first half of 2008, oil prices were averaging over $100 a barrel and eventually reached a one-day peak of $146 a barrel. That year the profit levels of the world's major oil companies reached record highs. Exxon-Mobil, the world's largest private-sector oil company, recorded in 2008 a US$45.8 billion profit, setting a record for a US corporation at the time. Its competitor Chevron, another US-based oil multinational, recorded a net profit of $18.7 billion that same year. Even low prices can still generate impressive profit and revenue levels. At the end of 2014 – after having endured several months in which oil prices had fallen by half – ExxonMobil still recorded profits of several billion dollars. So did Chevron, who in the fourth quarter of 2014 – again, one of its least profitable quarters in the previous five years – still recorded $3.5 billion in profit.[50]

Moreover, those companies keep spending and earning whether oil prices go up or down. In 2017, three years into an extended oil-price slump, ExxonMobil still earned $19.7 billion, spent $23 billion in capital and exploration expenditures, and held a market valuation of $354 billion.[51] It would take the massive hit of the 2020 COVID-19 pandemic to significantly damage the supermajor's profits, which are likely to rebound once the pandemic eases and more travel and transport activity resumes. The impressive resiliency of oil company profits is not a big mystery. Oil companies provide a product upon which current economic activity is more or less utterly dependent. Substitutes for it either do not exist or are in their deployment infancy. The price paid for oil is typically above production costs, and sometimes well above. Profitability explained.

Governments make money from oil, right alongside companies and individuals. Governments of oil-producing countries often take ownership positions in their country's domestic oil fields and often even field a national oil company that controls those fields' production. The economic attractiveness of state ownership over oil production is apparent: the sums generated by a productive oil industry can be enormous. If oil garners $100/barrel, and a government controls a company exporting millions of barrels a day, that government might conceivably then enjoy hundreds of millions of dollars of daily free cash flow into its treasury. Its financial coffers may expand rapidly when oil prices rise, and it can come to rely on those oil revenues to fund large portions of its budget. That dependency eventually comes to be all but total: having substantial oil revenues can lessen incentive to cultivate other industries or develop the internal willingness or capacity to collect taxes.[52] By one measure, taxes on oil revenue now comprise 50 per cent of Russia's state budget,[53] and oil revenues are similarly dominant in the budgets of Iran, Iraq, the United Arab Emirates, Saudi Arabia, and Venezuela, among others. Countries can build expansive fiscal plans based on the assumption that such oil revenue largesse will continue: they can get into severe financial trouble if it ever stops. Even countries producing smaller amounts of oil find the revenues generated or lost with price movements can have an immediate impact on their economies.[54]

The political consequences of all this are many and are examined later. The economic consequences are immediate. Clearly the global oil game is played for very high stakes: the industry spends hundreds of billions of dollars in investment capital each year, funds engineering projects that may take over a decade to complete, employs millions of people, and provides countries the fiscal wherewithal to modernize rapidly. The production and transportation of refined oil products utilizes a massive associated infrastructure that took a century and a half to build. The network of pipelines, container ships, refining facilities, railway cars and tracks, transport vehicles, and gas stations required enormous effort to create and still more to maintain. Companies continue to look for and extract oil from diverse geographies, a task requiring advanced engineering techniques, sophisticated financing, and management practices capable of handling the associated environmental, political, financial, and technical risks. It also requires intrepid individuals and companies willing to take those risks on. Plenty of them seem willing to because the potential rewards are so immense. To them, anything is possible – if the price is right.

The Oil Production "System": What Does It Look Like?

There are further oil market puzzles we need to decipher. Consider the production profiles of the world's three biggest producers of crude oil: the United States, Saudi Arabia, and Russia. Beginning with the US, in January 2020 – before COVID-19 hit – the Energy Information Administration forecasted that US production would average 13.3 mbd for the rest of the year.[55] That production came from literally all over the place: seventeen US states do not produce any oil, but the remaining thirty-three do, to a greater or lesser degree. Five states – Texas, North Dakota, California, Alaska, and New Mexico – collectively produced 63 per cent of the country's output: another 18 per cent came from offshore drilling operations in the Gulf of Mexico.[56] Each drilling site has its own particular topography, associated drilling technology, and engineering challenges, which the US has apparently been able to solve.

The US also has many different types of companies doing the producing. It is home to several of the world's largest private oil companies – ExxonMobil, ConocoPhillips, and Chevron, to name just three – that are household names, have massive production capacities, and operate all over the world. But it is also home to hundreds of smaller companies that extract oil from more specialized or limited fields, as well as an equally impressive network of thousands of subcontractors that provide specialized engineering and technical services that fulfill the operational needs of this diverse array of producers.

All these firms rely on a sophisticated domestic financial system that provides credit, floats securities, and creates tailored financial solutions that suit the financial profiles and needs of all of these different kinds of companies. There is an active market for publicly traded company stock: companies so listed must comply with stock exchange listing requirements and are subject to the ferocious demands US shareholders inflict. There is a vibrant venture capital community willing to fund innovative efforts in all manner of industries, including energy. Regulators exert significant control over private and publicly traded companies alike, both in terms of how they operate and in the financial requirements they must meet before their stock is publicly traded.

The various US governments (federal and state) do not take ownership positions in oil companies: they regulate and tax them. Government attitudes toward oil and gas development vary significantly and usually are divided according to electoral party, Republican or Democrat. The former generally endorses policies favoring domestic oil production, while the latter generally puts more emphasis on renewable and alternative energy. Politicians may praise or criticize the industry depending on their ideological stripe and whether they currently hold the reins of legislative power. Consequently, oil companies cannot count on consistent or predictable policy from their government, still less any form of overt support. Indeed, US government–business relations in the oil sector mirror those generally existing in others, where latent hostility is only interrupted by periods of more open hostility.[57] To oil companies, the US government is as often an obstacle as it is an ally. It is as likely to oppose what a company might want to do as support it, and given the time major oil projects require, companies may see several reversals of policy between the time they begin a project and when the oil begins to flow. Taken together, the US oil-production beast absorbs vast amounts of investment capital: between 2009 and 2019, oil production consumed over two-thirds of net industrial investment and was responsible for 40 per cent of the growth in new industrial production.[58] The US industry is complex, has many moving parts, is built into the fabric of an advanced, sophisticated, robust, and diversified economy, and remains enormous in scale.

Contrast that with the Kingdom of Saudi Arabia, which in the fall of 2019 produced on average 11 mbd. That impressive production level actually reflected a deliberate production cut they had enacted three years earlier to prop up price. Saudi Arabia is capable of producing several million more barrels per day, should opportunity or necessity strike.[59] It does things differently. First, its geography and field structure are well suited to oil production. Saudi Arabia draws the bulk of that production from relatively few but comparatively massive domestic fields, where the country houses three of the world's ten most productive fields. They include the famous Ghawar field: discovered in 1948, which still reliably pumps out close to 4 mbd, decades after its production started. The Abqaig and Shaybah oil fields complement Ghawar: both also are decades old yet still reliably produce hundreds of thousands of barrels of oil per day. Fields of this size and long-term production capacity are rare: the odds of having several within the confines of a single country's borders is the geological equivalent of winning the lottery.[60]

Oil production in Saudi Arabia is done by its national oil company Saudi Aramco, which is owned by the Saudi government and is the world's largest and most valuable oil company.[61] Saudi Aramco's executives do interact regularly with Saudi government officials who are, after all, their owner. The company's affairs are of deep interest to the Saudi state. However, operationally the company largely sets its own objectives and priorities.[62] Aramco's executives can, at least theoretically, plan and execute focused strategies over a longer period than what Western capital markets would likely tolerate.[63] This governance structure also allows the country to manage oil-production efforts with a goal of maximizing the recoverable volume Saudi fields generate.[64] That involves careful monitoring of field output, as well as a program of continuous investment that builds significant spare production capacity should there be need for it.[65]

Saudi Aramco has developed advanced drilling and extraction technologies suitable for its topography. It also invests considerable amounts in employee training, technology, and education: its management capacities are consequently strong.[66] But it does not possess – nor is it apparent that it needs – as wide a range of engineering capacity as that possessed by large private companies, who must drill in a variety of topographies. The vast revenue Aramco generates provides the monetary backbone not only for the company's own investment needs but also the Saudi state budget as well. That revenue is also the feedstock for its massive sovereign wealth fund (SWF). Aramco does not typically rely on capital markets for financing, nor does it publicly disclose all of its corporate information.

It is difficult to get a full picture of Saudi Aramco's financial position, as the company is not well known for financial transparency. Even its own employees rarely have a clear view of the company's finances, and external observers have even less. Part of this is the legacy of oil wealth, as one Saudi manager put it, "What right do people have to know when they pay no taxes and when the government provides all needed services?"[67] This has consequences. Recent efforts to float a percentage of Saudi Aramco stock on Western markets fell short, as investors could not get as full a picture of the company's finances as they wanted.[68] It chose instead to float that stock on the Riyadh market: the crown prince himself encourages wealthy Saudis to take an ownership stake, pushing the company's value to well over the $2 trillion mark. Saudi Aramco remains highly professional in operation and is a virtual cash machine, continuing to draw its oil out of the world's most productive and cheapest fields.

Finally, consider Russia, which in 2020 fed another 11 mbd into the global supply system. Russia has massive natural resource reserves, which is perhaps not surprising given the size of the country. It has 80 billion barrels of proven oil reserves,[69] while also holding the largest amount of proven natural gas reserves in the world. Many of its most productive oil fields lay in western Siberia: it also holds significant production capacity off its eastern border of Sakhalin Island, as well as huge volumes buried under its northern border and under Arctic ice.[70] The distance of these fields from major export markets, as well as the harsh weather and difficult topography, requires massive amounts of extended transport and refining infrastructure to bring that oil to market, not to mention enormous engineering effort.

Ownership in Russia's domestic oil production and transport and refining capacities remains mixed. It features a number of nominally independent private oil and gas companies intermixed with heavy doses of state involvement. Russia has particular strengths in natural gas production: Gazprom, the massive Russian state-controlled natural gas giant, controls that production and is the largest natural gas company in the world. In the oil sector, government control is also present. The Russian government has shareholding interests in many of the country's oil and infrastructure companies, and even the fully private companies are ultimately reliant on Transneft, the state monopoly pipeline company that controls internal oil and gas transit around the country.

If Russia is a "riddle wrapped with a mystery inside an enigma,"[71] then its oil industry seems to represent the country well. Oil companies have heavy doses of private and public ownership, depending on the company. Unlike Saudi Aramco, which is almost completely government owned but largely operationally separate, Russian companies are neither completely private nor completely separate. Even the most independent-minded of them remain heavily attuned to what Moscow, and in particular Russia's leader Vladimir Putin, may be thinking. Where government interest ends and private-sector decision-making begins is sometimes hard to demarcate in Russia. But the sector clearly features a mix of private- and public-sector interests where a high degree of mutual dependency exists.[72]

These three countries produce about the same amount of oil every day, but they do it very differently. They have different production profiles and place more or less strategic importance on the domestic production of oil. In the US case, oil is produced by a highly decentralized system, one driven primarily by market incentives, whose industry players may view its domestic government as often as an adversary than as a partner. It relies on ambitious entrepreneurs, venture capitalists, and a mixture of established companies both large and small to build that industry. Those entities in turn require enough financial return before taking the plunge to develop new fields or to fund new technologies. Its industry, reliant on markets, is therefore subject to the vagaries those markets generate, particularly a boom/bust cycle driven by price and the desire for profit. It has watched its companies gain enormous size, revenue, and profitability: it has also tolerated many of them plunging into bankruptcy if oil prices suddenly fall.

Saudi Arabia's system emphasizes stability, predictability, and coordination. Its economy, and indeed the national interests of the country, are deeply intertwined in the operations of its state-owned oil company. Saudi Aramco's production generates enormous revenue when prices are high, and its low production costs allow it to survive price downturns better than just about any other company. Russia's political fortunes are also deeply tied to the production of natural resources and the revenue it generates. Energy revenues fund government budgets and, as we will see, provide the foundation for the country's broader geopolitical aspirations. Taken together, the world's oil-production system is a hybrid featuring both state and market interests that differ depending on the country. Oil producers the world over fall somewhere on a spectrum between those allowing markets free rein and those where governments exert strong, perhaps absolute, control and ownership. Some endorse markets filtered by prices, others are loath to give the market such free rein, still others adopt some kind of mixed approach, allowing markets to decide some things and government officials others. The devil is in the individual country details, but political and economic interests are always at play.

Consequently, the oil system can sometimes generate difficult-to-understand, even bizarre, outcomes, particularly to those schooled in the textbook definition of efficient markets. They would likely assume that a product's output and price is determined completely by some combination of supply and demand, minus perhaps a little bit of market friction. Buyers want to pay as little as they can, sellers want to charge as much as they can, and the market clears transactions at the point where willingness to buy meets willingness to sell. Moreover, under standard theories of market competition, the only way companies gain a sustainable competitive advantage is through the roads of price or quality. They either offer products similar to competitors but at lower prices – thereby increasing their market share – or they offer a better product for which customers willingly pay more. Those routes allow companies to gain market advantage by offering some combination of cost or differentiation not easily replicated by competitors.[73]

That is hard to do in the oil business. The product is largely undifferentiated, and demand is inelastic. While some fields certainly offer higher grades of oil – meaning they contain differing levels of sulfur or other impurities, making them more or less easy to refine – the differences are not enough to justify a too-hefty price premium for individual types of oil. If a given source becomes too expensive, refiners simply switch to other sources of cheaper, if dirtier, oil and willingly suffer the extra refining costs less pure sources might require. Secondly, demand historically does not and cannot easily or rapidly change due to price fluctuations. Customers may complain about prices at the pumps, but it is difficult to change the necessity of the daily commute (though this may change after the pandemic). If prices fall, companies still have to pump oil out to meet debt obligations. People need the products oil provides and will shoulder escalating costs if necessary to get them, while companies themselves also have bills to pay.

If customers alone dictated things, they would want the lowest oil prices they could get and would therefore expect oil to be sourced from the cheapest places possible. For their part, companies desire to maximize profits and would also likely want to produce in cheap places, while of course selling as dearly as they could. That would mean sourcing oil from the lowest-cost production sites first and managing their investments such that they collectively do not overproduce, a problem taken up in the next chapter. Over time, as cheaper fields ran low, companies would then progress to the more expensive fields that would drive up costs. Prices would then naturally have to rise: if they did not, returns would be insufficient for capital providers to invest in new production, and new fields would not be developed. A lack of new investment would eventually generate supply shortages that would then drive the price up, restoring the necessary profitability that would fund new exploration. If markets were all that mattered, cheaper fields would receive the bulk of initial investment: subsequent fields would be developed later.

Yet even a casual observer of the oil market knows that is not at all how things work. Private oil companies are not free to invest wherever they want. Most of the world's proven oil reserves – approximately 80 per cent – remain under the purview of state-owned national oil companies (NOCs). Their home states often exclude foreign investors, or at best allow foreign companies limited access to upstream investment, usually because only foreign private companies possess the necessary drilling expertise to extract the reserves. State treasuries certainly want the money that comes from oil sales, but they also want to watch their reserves carefully and certainly have no interest in having their reserves drained first just because they happen to be the cheapest. Doing so would be selling out their biggest economic strength for a fraction of what might have been generated if a way could have been found to keep those prices high. Some set limits on their own production levels, and if they can, they will use production-control arrangements to collectively enforce limits on the production of others as well. That acts as an artificial boost to global prices. It also helps private companies, whose more expensive fields then become financially viable when they likely would not have been had such supply control measures not been in place.

This system only works by balancing state, market, and company interests. But it creates a convoluted economic story that is hard to disentangle. Moreover, economics is only half the story: political and geopolitical interests also season the oil market stew, given the centrality of oil revenue to the political and geopolitical calculations of importers and exporters alike. The oil market therefore sometimes generates strange results. Private companies today spend vast sums extracting oil in expensive, geologically challenging places to add to their production reserves. Meanwhile, vast quantities of cheaper known oil remain locked in the ground, oil that is doled out by parsimonious governments looking to manage their supply and keep prices elevated. This system serves the interests of state-owned and private companies and keeps revenue flowing to governments and shareholders. But it is hard to see how consumer interest and buyer preference are in the driver's seat: in some cases those interests seem not to matter at all.

States continue to manage most of the world's oil production, and that control will be ideologically opposed by those championing a market-based system. But even market purists in the oil industry might want to think twice about their preferred solution. Cheap oil might enhance consumer welfare, at least in terms of lowering the cost required to produce oil-based products. But if that oil is sourced from cheaper foreign fields, it might drive domestic oil producers out of business. Cheap oil might also lower incentives to develop industries around alternative energy, in itself a huge potential future market. It would also likely depress investment return and raise energy dependence and import vulnerability issues, all of which governments do not like. The current system, though admittedly neither fish nor fowl, delicately if awkwardly balances contending elements. If it generates puzzling outcomes, we should probably not be surprised. War is too important a matter to be left to generals, and oil clearly is too important a commodity to be left to the market.

A Deeper Look at Oil Companies

What about the actors within that system that actually do the oil exploration and extracting – the companies themselves? They clearly matter. After all, public discussion (and often criticism) of oil often focuses on the large, publicly traded, well known oil companies that are often household names and – until recently at least – have been staple stocks for investment portfolios and mutual funds. They carry with them the impressive title of "supermajor," and the names include such corporate titans as ExxonMobil, Royal Dutch Shell, Chevron, Total, and BP. To many, these companies epitomize the essence of what the oil industry is and how it operates. They are big, employing tens of thousands of people. They each produce millions of barrels of oil a day, earn tens of billions of dollars a year in revenue, and spend billions of those dollars each year looking for new fields or upgrading current ones. They do it all: exploring for and extracting oil, refining that oil into fuels and feedstock products, and delivering those products downstream to gas stations and distribution terminals. Their marketing and brand presence is ubiquitous: people certainly know who they are, even if they are not always clear about what they do.

The supermajors are technologically sophisticated and boast impressive engineering capacities, being able to find and extract oil from barren, remote, and geologically difficult places or from under thousands of feet of ocean water or seabed. Millions of individuals, institutional investors, and pension funds have historically bought and sold their stocks and bonds and continue to monitor their financial performance closely. They have been around a long time: the US-based oil giants trace their roots back to the nineteenth century: the European supermajors go back almost as far. Their corporate presence continues to loom large over the psyche of the global economy and condition the images popping to mind when discussion turns to oil.

The supermajors are also financially very large. Of the ten largest publicly traded companies in the world by revenue (pre-pandemic), four are in the oil industry.[74] Like all publicly traded companies, their primary management priority is to increase shareholder value. That can make them appear cold and ruthless in the rigor with which they manage their operations and pursue additional cost efficiencies. They may be grudgingly admired for such efficiency and managerial discipline,[75] but they are rarely well-liked. Consumers are suspicious of their accumulated size, power, and suspected political influence. They are resented for making so much money by providing one of the staples of modern life, one for which customers have no real alternative. Strong and repeated criticisms are thrown their way: customers may accuse them of gouging, collusion, the buying of politicians, the flouting of regulatory restraint, and all manner of corporate malfeasance, particularly when oil prices are high and profits balloon. Moreover, money is not all that matters. Their operations are criticized along non-monetary fronts as well. Oil companies are pilloried for the environmental damage oil operations inflict, the displacement of indigenous personnel drilling sites may demand, the pay oil and gas executives receive, and the greenhouse gas emissions the burning of their product generates. A host of unpalatable adjectives often consequently follows this invective: destructive, uncaring, greedy, and corrupt are some of the nicer ones.

Rarely does the adjective "small" make that list. But it could, because they are, particularly when compared to the state-owned oil companies that do the bulk of the world's producing. NOCs are often significantly larger than the private companies and are more prevalent in the oil-producing world. In terms of people employed, they are some of the largest companies in the world: their workforce may total in the hundreds of thousands. Yet they can be small as well, working primarily as a joint-venture, revenue-absorbing entity. NOCs vary a lot: each such company developed differently according to the circumstances of the country. In some cases, the NOC was there at the beginning: oil production began with state oil companies and stayed that way. In others, domestic governments undertook a sustained and relentless effort to wrest control over their domestic fields from the foreign oil companies who had already set up shop. That nationalization may have been immediate, as a result of a political event or revolution. Or it may have taken time as nascent NOCs who initially lacked drilling expertise partnered with investing private companies to build the required capacities. Ownership structures can vary considerably between NOCs, even for those descending from similar circumstances and having similar geographical distributions of oil reserves.[76]

What unites NOCs is a shared belief that states owning both the resource and the means of production will extract the greatest economic benefit for the country while also protecting economic sovereignty.[77] Many NOCs are respected, if not revered, by their domestic citizens, who view them as symbols of independence and vanguards of domestic economic prosperity.[78] Moreover, this choice of organizational form is often largely also a political story, one detailed in the next chapter. But its economic purpose is simple enough to convey. State ownership and operation of oil companies, done effectively, allows states to get the most benefit out of their resources. Countries can use the companies to generate domestic jobs and can concentrate whatever geopolitical influence oil production has through the focus of a single company. Consequently, few countries employing this form are looking to privatize them anytime soon.

Today state governments directly control most of the world's known resources and monopolize all the truly inexpensive ones. The biggest of them are significantly larger than their private-sector counterparts in terms of production, number of employees, and amount of reserves under their control. Depending on extraction costs, they can be extremely profitable. By most measures Saudi Aramco is the most profitable company in the world. Other large NOCs include the National Iranian Oil Company (NIOC), the Abu Dhabi National Oil Company (ADNOC), and the massive Chinese state-owned oil companies that include the Chinese National Offshore Oil Company (CNOOC), the Chinese National Petroleum Company (CNPC), and Sinopec. To give a graphic sense, Table 1 gives a comparison of size, in terms employees, crude-oil production, and revenue of some of the world's largest oil companies, both private and public.

There are other differences between IOCs (international oil companies) and NOCs than just size, revenue, and reserves under control. They also differ in how they are run, the pressures they face, and the operational challenges they must overcome. The NOC form does generate advantages. It shields such companies from the demands of private capital markets. Their government is the sole, or at least majority, owner, providing a measure of potential financial and political cushion that can also in theory help moderate financial performance expectations while providing other forms of state support. Operationally, NOCs can adjust production levels and investment targets based on their government's preferences. In terms of corporate strategy, NOC's production decisions may be linked to state objectives. In some instances, the NOC's

Table 1. Largest Oil Companies by Ownership Type, Home Country, and Daily Production Volume (Thousands of Barrels/Day)[a]

Company Name and Ownership Structure	Country	Crude Oil Production (bbl/d)[b]
Saudi Aramco (NOC)	Saudi Arabia	10,963,091
Rosneft (Mixed)	Russia	4,217,780
Kuwait Petroleum Company (KPC) (NOC)	Kuwait	3,412,203
National Iranian Oil Company (NIOC) (NOC)	Iran	3,256,486
China National Petroleum Company (CNPC) (NOC)	China	2,981,246
ExxonMobil (Private)	United States	2,294,701
Petrobras (NOC)	Brazil	1,987,950
Abu Dhabi National Oil Company (ADNOC) (NOC)	United Arab of Emirates	1,973,135
Chevron (Private)	United States	1,830,537
Petróleos Mexicanos (Pemex) (NOC)	Mexico	1,813,360

a 2019 Fortune 500 Global List (https://fortune.com/global500/2019/search/)
b Ali, Umar. 2019. "Top Ten Companies by Oil Production." *Offshore Technology*. https://www.offshore-technology.com/features/companies-by-oil-production/.

senior executives report directly to or indeed may even be members of, the government itself. In others, executives are truly an arm's length away and make decisions based on market metrics.

There are some peculiarities, if not disadvantages, to the NOC form as well. Governance within some NOCs may utilize an elaborate model in which state policy, bureaucratic procedure, and corporate strategy all contribute.[79] This produces a complicated, idiosyncratic decision-making culture that outsiders find difficult to penetrate. For example, in many Middle Eastern NOCs there may be a web of social and familial connections that permeate management structures that, though not formalized on organizational charts, must nevertheless be navigated before significant decisions are taken.[80] Their decision-making may appear slow, and it is sometimes difficult to identify the locus of power. Different governments demand different things from their NOCs. Some have diversified economies that provide governments with alternate sources of revenue. In others, the domestic economy and state revenues may be almost solely dependent on the revenue the state oil company provides.[81] NOCs may act as a social insurance mechanism, maintaining employment levels even during economic downturns to aid domestic stability. Some NOCs maximize production levels in times of high prices, generating revenue when the getting is good. Others are more restrained, pursuing disciplined investment and production targets irrespective of price fluctuation. Some act simply as joint-venture partners for investing companies, others are as operationally advanced as any private-sector company.[82]

Given all this, the supermajors can claim with some justification that they operate in a more competitive environment than their critics often grant. The do not enjoy market dominance, far from it. They face entrenched competition from NOCs with large reserves and cheap production costs. That is in itself a formidable-enough challenge, but it is not the only one. Some state governments can and do extend advantages to their NOCs, ranging from cheap loans to state subsidies and other kinds of political help.[83] IOCs, by contrast, derive their economic advantage from paying minute attention to market conditions, maintaining a diverse production profile, and monitoring expected price levels carefully. If they sometimes clamor or advocate for help from their home governments, it is easy understand why, even if one is not inclined to give it to them.

The (Potential) Game Changer: Fracking and the Resurgence of US Domestic Production

The phrase "game changer" is thrown around a lot today. The term conjures up images of a supposedly revolutionary new phenomenon or technological event that somehow remakes the world as we know it. The term may also be used simply as a marketing ploy to hock the latest and greatest technical widget whose acquisition will somehow make everyone's life far better. However, it is rarely a term used for an activity as old, ponderous, sclerotic, and as seemingly entrenched as is oil production (which incidentally is clearly not a game). Yet no other term really suffices to describe what has happened to domestic US oil production capacity as a result of fracking. It is hard to visualize what "fracking" actually is: the term seems like an adjective, verb, and half-formed expletive all at the same time. At the very least, it conjures up images of breaking something solid, which for oil production is not a bad way to describe what the technique has done.

Unlike drilling, which taps preexisting fields, fracking effectively creates new pools of oil by injecting a slurry of chemicals, water, sand, and solvents into shale rock formations to "crack" those formations. That releases the volumes of oil and natural gas trapped within, which may be substantial. The technique itself is not new and dates back from at least the 1860s.[84] However, it took the determined efforts of an inspired entrepreneur to finally make it financially viable. Most credit George Phydias Mitchell as being that key entrepreneur: his determined efforts, undertaken over a period of decades, eventually proved the technique viable. Labeled the "determined tinkerer,"[85] Mitchell spent tens of millions of dollars, and decades of his life, trying to find the right combination of fluid components and drilling technologies that could unleash the gas and oil volumes he knew shale rock held.

The US government helped. It had endorsed research on the technique for decades, largely in response to overall declining US production and the consequent political worry about increasing dependency on foreign oil. Yet it took a prolonged period of rising prices, combined with engineering persistence, to find the right combination that could increase the oil and gas extracted from shale formations at a commercially viable price. Once discovered and widely deployed, however, shale extraction techniques improved rapidly, in some cases increasing the oil flow rate by a hundred-fold over what previous attempts had achieved. As the technology spread and became increasingly profitable, legions of oil explorers began deploying it over ever-greater amounts of shale acreage located in the Texas Permian basin and in the Eagle Ford shale rock formations. They succeeded in turning the declining US production picture completely around: fracking output vaulted the country into one of the top three oil producers in the world.

Fracking is unconventional, and not just in the ways that it extracts oil from the ground. To begin, it is comparatively cheap, in direct contrast to the supermajors' massive exploration efforts. Large oil companies may spend hundreds of millions of dollars drilling individual wells in remote or seaborne locations, with the hope of finding large enough fields to make the expense incurred worthwhile. In comparison, it takes but a few million dollars to drill a fracking well; consequently, many fracking wells can be built quickly. Once proven, variations on Mitchell's techniques were rapidly copied, modified, and deployed by hundreds of small companies, as much of the upfront costs of developing the technology had already been borne. Exploration risks were low, as knowledge of where the fracking rock formations were remained widely shared. Gaining access to those formations was also easy. In the United States, owners of land situated on shale rock had incentive to grant drillers access because they owned the rights to the oil and gas extracted from their property and are compensated handsomely by those doing the extracting. Such factors created the perfect storm that unleashed US fracking production capacity.

The subsequent production results were astounding. As the drillers deployed the technique, US oil-production levels began to climb steadily and relentlessly. In 2000 the United States produced its expected 6 mbd. That production level was, if anything, trending downward, despite continued upward pressure on demand.[86] The US was consequently importing the rest of what it needed, which measured around 13 mbd. Then US production began to grow, a trickle at first, then a flood (it never even bothered establishing a mere river). By 2008 US production had climbed to slightly above 6 mbd; by 2012 it measured 6.5 mbd. Then came the flood: by 2016 US production measured 13 mbd,[87] and projections of continued US production increases became common and increasingly grand. Some projected domestic production totals would soon top 20 mbd,[88] a point at which the US, for the first time in decades, would achieve the hallowed status of "energy independence." Within a decade, the US had more than doubled its domestic production: it now produced at levels matching those witnessed in Saudi Arabia and Russia. It seemed to have solved, or vastly reduced, its oil import problem. It also had generated an energy production boom that lifted the country out of the post-2009 financial crisis economic doldrums.

Fracking has changed the oil game in ways other than just the volume of oil it unleashed. It was flexible and nimble and could adjust rapidly to market price movements. Smaller companies could bear the lower exploration costs necessary to access fields and could therefore get in on the action of a price rise quicker. Improvements in fracking technology and efficiency came quickly, and as the volume of oil it produced went up production costs per fracked barrel went down. Fracking operations became progressively better able to withstand price declines, and overall US domestic production capacity became much more resilient. Fracking operations could start or cease relatively quickly, depending on oil price movements. Unlike large capital projects that might take a decade to come onstream, fracking production came as close to "turning a tap on and off" as one was likely to find. Suddenly, what had been largely a price-inelastic commodity – where price increases did not result in demand drops or generate immediate supply increases – was now much more responsive.

Fracking of course generated opponents and critics. Environmental groups also raised concerns, arguing that the techniques' impact on watersheds were at best unknown and at worse borderline catastrophic. Reports of fracking operations that created minor earthquakes or having "fracked" oil and gas seep into groundwater located above the shale rock beds created publicly disturbing headlines.[89] YouTube videos of people lighting tap water on fire, with the attributed cause being leaked oil and gas that fracking had released into their groundwater aquifers, became fodder for Internet clickbait and scrolling. The industry, and some state regulators, denies any link between fracking and such episodes, arguing that naturally occurring methane was responsible.[90] Nevertheless, environmental fears have limited, but not stopped,[91] the techniques' deployment around the world. It is already more or less banned entirely from Western Europe, and some US politicians have echoed calls to ban it or severely slow it down, including president Biden. The productivity of shale rock is also unpredictable: most wells generate a lot of oil for the first year or two of being tapped, but their production rates fall off quickly, necessitating yet more drilling to keep the oil flowing. It is therefore difficult to judge how long and productive individual fields will be.

Despite these objections, the fracking revolution has nevertheless changed the production profile of the United States. The US has large basins with the right kind of rock, a permissive regulatory environment, and highly liquid capital markets that allowed fracking operations to grow very quickly. The last two of these can change, and perhaps change very quickly, but the first one will not. Moreover, the technique's success portends much for the future of oil production. Other places also have the same kind of shale rock formations as the US, and if import concerns are real, they are likely to also embrace the technique. Teams of engineers from around the world have made pilgrimages to the Permian rock basin to study fracking's secrets and to think through how they might apply it in their home geographies. As technological, capital, and political constraints are overcome, other places certainly can produce oil using similar techniques. For all these reasons, fracking deserves the label "game changer" often applied to it.

Summary

Economic and population growth continues to drive global energy consumption, and both are on an upward trajectory (though the former may be momentarily slowed during the pandemic). People want their standard of living to improve rapidly, and governments want to ensure they get it, if only to enhance their electoral prospects or at least enhance their domestic support. Raising living standards requires a steady supply of low-cost energy, which allows people to create, move, and learn, which correspondingly leads to investment and economic growth. The accumulated infrastructure built to find and transport oil striates the global economy: building an alternate infrastructure of sufficient scale will require a similarly extended and consistent investment effort also carried out over decades. Oil's features as a fuel feedstock remain unmatched:

oil-based fuels are easily transported, deliver and release a tremendous amount of energy per unit volume, and are readily available. It is a tough combination to beat.

Worldwide oil demand is likely to continue increasing before it begins decreasing. It will do so for decades yet. There is enough oil in the system to meet foreseeable demand, if political barriers are overcome. The composition of who is doing the demanding will change: developed markets will remain important ongoing sources of demand, but their portion of global oil consumption will level off and even decrease. However, the reductions they achieve will likely be significantly less than the increasing oil demand emerging and developing markets will witness. As developed markets demand less oil, the political and geopolitical significance of oil in emerging markets – both in terms of demand and supply – will grow. The United States developed a technology that now generates enough oil and gas to render them much less dependent on the international oil market.

Operationally, the modern oil market combines state and market interests. To be sure, there are several consistent incentives at play in determining how that market works. The economic returns provided by high oil prices can be enormous, but that money must then be plowed back into additional exploration and production that keeps the oil and its associated revenues flowing. Oil companies usually typically become proficient at extracting oil once thought almost impossible to access. But high prices may provide incentive for others to join in the production game, which brings more supply to market and sets the stage for price falls. For private companies what matters over the long term is not the prosperity brought by high prices but who is best positioned to survive when low prices inevitably hit. The better oil producers become at discovering oil or extracting new supply from known fields, the less stress there collectively will be on global oil supply.[92]

There remains debate and considerable latitude about how the international oil market will function and evolve over the next few decades. The state remains particularly powerful in the oil industry. It may feature intense competition between NOCs and IOCs vying for resource access, or a deliberate attempt to strengthen an international market-based system that will soften this competition, or an ongoing combination of the two. Countries will remain interested in securing oil and in the success of their companies. New technologies will evolve that force market participants to adapt. In short, while much remains the same, much is also changing. As the IEA notes, the most significant factor affecting how the oil market develops is "whether – and how – government policies evolve."[93] Politics matter a lot in the oil industry and will continue doing so.

The next chapter guides readers to a better understanding of what these politics are. It traces the history of oil politics and helps readers understand the choices governments and companies have historically made to address them. The political issues associated with the extraction, refinement, selling, and use of oil can be limiting factors on meeting production. Maintaining a robust global oil market that can meet demand, not aggravate domestic political problems, enhance national security, confront the problem of climate change, and meet rising consumer social performance expectations will present ongoing challenges that are political. While some are new, and are dealt with in later chapters, many of them are longstanding and are revealed by looking at the industry's history. We turn to that task next.

chapter three

The Legacy of Oil: 1858–2000

Summarizing 150 years of oil history in a single chapter is challenging. Other adjectives might also apply: impractical, ambitious, and perhaps even a bit hubristic. Yet it still must be done. The industry as we know it today came from someplace, is structured in a particular way, and has established roots that will condition where new growth might go. If that history teaches anything, it is that the oil market did not evolve the way that economic theory describes, where markets dictated a process of creative destruction and only the fittest survived. It is instead a product of political as well as economic choices, of protection and government help, as well as of market competition. Governments began caring about oil early in the industry's history and made choices influencing, sometimes even dictating, the direction that market would go. Governments have always intervened, watched, commented on, and shaped the oil market: it therefore seems reasonable to think they will continue doing so. Understanding what governments did in the past should provide insight into what they might do now.

This chapter is not and cannot be exhaustive.[1] Though it proceeds in a rough chronological order, it focuses on identifying and discussing a discrete set of economic and political challenges or issues repeatedly afflicting the industry as it grew, internationalized, and evolved. Those challenges emerged as often out of a political calculus as they did an economic one and were created and shaped by the way the world bought, sold, and consumed oil. They have appeared repeatedly over the course of the Oil Age and the mountain of evidence that has generated. We should therefore not be surprised if and when they rear their heads today.

Reality #1: Price Volatility and Industry Boom/Bust

Oil is a commodity. Theoretically, it should be produced, bought, and sold according to the same marketplace signals that govern any other. The primary market signal is price, which supposedly matches buyer and seller inclinations. Price provides the primary indication used to decide whether it is worth investing dollars to bring more oil to market or whether those dollars should be deployed elsewhere. So, it makes some sense to look at the history of oil prices. We therefore examine why prices measured what they did and to extract from the first 140 years of commercial oil exchange insights that might tell us something meaningful about what happened during the last 20 or what might happen over the next 10.

We begin by tracing those prices. Figure 2 charts the price[2] that a barrel of oil commanded, on average, every year between 1859 and 2019:

Figure 2. US Crude Oil First Purchase Price (USD), 1859–2019

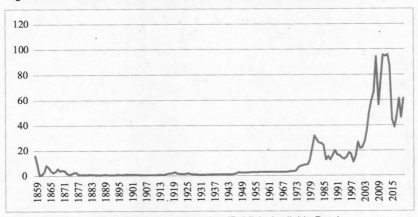

Source: US Energy Information Administration (Publicly Available Data).

Later chapters examine in detail what happened during the first two decades of the twenty-first century, or the approximately one-eighth of the graph stuck on the right-hand side. That part shows huge volatility and significant price increases, a pattern that differs markedly from what went on during oil's first century and a half. Oil prices began with a short period of volatility that was then followed by almost a century of persistently low and predictable oil prices. Volatility and price rise only reentered the equation during the last quarter of the twentieth century and accelerated rapidly during the first two decades of the twenty-first. For much of oil's history, prices remained stable, more or less cheap, and predictable. How and why did that happen?

We begin at the beginning, which is usually attributed to Colonel Edwin Drake's discovery of the oil fields buried beneath the scrublands near Titusville, Pennsylvania, in 1858. Volatility was present at creation, as was luck. On the eve of his discovery, Drake had largely run out of investment capital, and it was only his final drilling efforts that proved successful in tapping the bounty laid below. But any celebration on his part would prove to be brief: his discovery yielded competition, and a lot of it, very quickly. Word about it spread rapidly, and other drillers descended on the Pennsylvania landscape in droves, setting up oil derricks of their own practically overnight and thereby launching the world's first recorded oil boom.

All sought the "black gold" that they thought would yield immense and almost instant fortune. Yet, in their collective excitement, they could easily ignore an uncomfortable reality: if all were successful, more oil would be brought to market than what it needed or could bear, resulting in a supply glut that would cause prices to collapse and potentially drive them all into bankruptcy. At the time, demand for oil was limited. Coal-fired steam continued to power most factories and oceangoing vessels, and the automobile revolution remained decades away. So busy were the Titusville drillers kept in finding oil that few asked themselves where they could sell it or at what price.

The reckoning came. Supply exploded, prices collapsed, and sites previously hosting frenetic drilling activity became littered with half-built derricks whose operators had run out of capital and who subsequently abandoned their drill sites as quickly as they had built them. Successful drillers fared little better, being unable to sell what oil they managed to produce. Expected profit turned into catastrophic loss as prices fell: at the height of the Pennsylvania oil boom, the oil derived from new discoveries was worth less than the wooden barrels carrying it to market.[3] Bankrupted producers stopped dumping oil onto the market, and no financier proved willing to bankroll further exploration. Of course, that was exactly what was needed to restore balance to supply and demand, but it proved to be a painful way to go about it.

The cycle inaugurated by Drake's discovery – seemingly unprecedented boom through to the misery of widespread economic ruin and loss – heralded the first episode of market "madness" that would repeatedly infect the oil market ever since.[4] Much as a recessive gene waits for the right conditions before blossoming, so too can the eruption of oil fever break out, given the temptations black gold can offer. The lure of oil discovery as a route to fortune can take very rapid hold when prices are rising quickly. Rumor compounds established fact: momentary shortage can be crafted into a believable story of the fortunes to be made remedying it, leading to an exploration boom. That boom brings too many explorers – and too much oil – to the market, thereby engendering a rapid fall that bankrupts all but the financially strongest players and burns caution into the psyche of erstwhile swashbuckling wildcat drillers.

More rational and patient investors quickly recognized that pattern for what it was. To them, the cycle of boom and bust appeared unnecessary, silly, caused more pain than profit, and ultimately served no one's interest. It certainly did not appeal to someone as astute and monetarily ruthless as John D. Rockefeller. Rockefeller disdained both the chaos high prices unleashed as well as the undisciplined ambition and greed those prices ignited among inexperienced and individualistic drillers. He had witnessed how efforts to limit drilling activity, either by persuasion or by regulation, had proven fruitless in the aggressively capitalistic United States of the late 1800s. The desire for riches, stubborn independence, and inherent rebellious instincts against mandated limits shown by entrepreneurial oilmen meant that it proved impossible to corral their drilling activity even when logic dictated that it made sense to do so. Realizing that they would not be tamed, Rockefeller crafted a coldly rational response, built on the premise that dampening price volatility would moderate, perhaps even eliminate, the nausea-inducing boom/bust pattern plaguing the industry even then.

If drillers could not be constrained, perhaps what they produced could. Rockefeller's strategy, enacted through his Standard Oil Company, was to relentlessly target and build a dominant position in the bottlenecks limiting how much oil ultimately reached the market: transport and refining capacities. If one could control the amount of oil moving on tracks or being refined into products, prices could be managed indirectly by limiting the supply so moved and products so refined. He set about that vision with relentless determination, acquiring refining capacity as fast as he could, using his accumulating mass to absorb those willing to sell their operations and smothering competitors who would not. His strategy proved wildly effective: at its peak the Standard Oil Trust controlled upwards of 85 per cent of the domestic oil refining in the United States and had extended its interests to the rail lines servicing those refineries. Standard Oil became his instrument for calming and managing the oil market, and his success at doing so became the stuff of business legend.

For four decades, Standard's efforts to induce exploration restraint, ensure predictable supply, and moderate prices worked. By century's end oil delivery indeed had become "Standardized": stable, predictable, and boring. Standard's control bordered on the absolute, and Rockefeller's personal fortune ballooned. But customers did not often complain: prices were low and supply predictable. The rapidly accelerating US economy gained momentum, largely due to its being able to count on predictable energy supplies to power its increasingly oil-fueled factories. The boom/bust problem seemed to have been solved: prices remained stable and supply assured. Absent massive price gyrations, there was no incentive for drillers to descend like locusts on production sites whenever prices ticked up or rumors of a new field spread.

That control generated immense and sustained corporate profit over a period of decades. It also made Rockefeller one of history's richest men. Yet, in a hard-to-swallow, you-have-got to-be-kidding kind of irony, Rockefeller often claimed that his personal enrichment was only a by-product, rather than a primary goal, of Standard Oil's strategy. That strategy could even be likened to a public service. His company kept the oil market in balance and gave oil consumers a predictable supply at stable prices. That helped a booming, increasingly oil-based US economy invest and grow at a rapid clip.[5] The fact that it also made him immensely rich was almost an afterthought; even his vast wealth remained tiny compared to the economic growth Standard Oil helped generate. It was but a small price to pay in exchange for the prosperity his company fueled.

Rockefeller was also anything but naïve. He knew that not everyone would buy his monopoly-as-a-public-good argument, still less endorse Standard Oil as any kind of public benefactor. A monopoly's logic may seem clear to its members and even justifiable in the abstract, but those arguments are unlikely to win over a public believing deeply in the value of entrepreneurialism and competition, as the American public did, or one that distrusts the very idea of centralized corporate or political power, as that public also did.[6] Rockefeller correctly judged that few of his fellow US citizens would be convinced that Standard Oil was good for them or the country. If his system ever became widely understood, it would likely generate outrage and resistance rather than support.

The answer of course was to keep that strategy hidden. One way of maintaining a monopoly for an extended period is to ensure that the consuming public does not know about it. At that he proved masterful: even at the height of its power, US consumers remained largely in the dark about the scope of Standard's reach, still less of its mode of operation. Rockefeller kept details of the company's operations shrouded from prying eyes via a system of interlocking trusts that were almost impossible to decipher from the outside. Those trusts concealed the centralized ownership control he and his top lieutenants wielded and camouflaged how deeply Standard Oil's capillaries wove through the fabric of the entire US economy. That system saw oil flow out of Standard's refineries and transport facilities, funneled money back to corporate headquarters, and did so successfully for decades.

That system might have continued for even longer than it did were it not for the relentless efforts of industry critics determined to expose what was going on. In Standard's case, Rockefeller's nemesis came in the form of journalist Ida Tarbell. Suspicion of Standard had certainly percolated among other industry watchers, but it was her damning exposé of the company that revealed the ruthless lengths to which Rockefeller habitually went to eliminate unwanted competition and to stop prying eyes from discovering what was really going on.[7] Her book certainly penned a damning personal portrayal of Rockefeller and his lieutenants, but it struck an even deeper chord in the American public that went beyond the indictment of individual personalities. The idea of a managed monopoly cut against the grain of a deeply held US economic and political ideology, which professed belief that open markets and competition best enhanced consumers' interests. Entrepreneurs should be given rein to challenge established industry players: the process of competition eliminated inefficient companies, created new industries, and propelled the economy forward. Monopolies crushed all of that. They gouged customers, destroyed entrepreneurial drive and opportunity, and created small numbers of very rich people who used their wealth to build political influence, make it more difficult for competitors to survive, and keep the common folk ignorant and in their place.

The reaction to Tarbell's work ignited a latent but deep public antipathy toward entrenched corporate power. The revelation of Standard Oil's tactics helped generate waves of popular criticism that propelled so-called trust busters into positions of political power. The US government subsequently launched the Sherman Anti-Trust case against Standard Oil, which in 1911 generated a ruling that broke Standard Oil up into several subsidiary companies, the forerunners of today's large US oil companies.[8] That landmark case proved so significant that it remains in the curriculum in many US law schools today.

Yet, even after its breakup, the echoes of the Standard Oil saga can be heard today. Its breakup shaped the development of the oil market in ensuing decades, as its descendant companies struggled for influence. It also forged and hardened a popular mistrust of large integrated oil companies in the United States as inherently untrustworthy entities that often worked against, rather than for, the interests of consumers and sometimes even the country.[9] Standard's breakup vindicated the company's opponents and created at least the appearance of a public victory over corporate interests.[10] It did more than that: it also cemented distrust and suspicion of large oil companies within the American popular psyche. As Anthony Sampson notes: "In the next six decades (after the breakup of Standard Oil), there were to be successive duels between the oil companies and the Justice Department, and most often the oil companies would win. But the duels were played out before a public opinion which could never be fully reassured about the giant combinations. Periodically, in sudden gusts of anger ... they would turn on the oil companies as the symbols of everything that was sinister and secretive in modern industrial society."[11]

Standard Oil had also set a precedent of what was possible if one could control the oil supply hitting the market. There were clearly huge advantages to be had if it could be pulled off. Not only did supply control generate enormous profit for insiders, it also solved the problem of volatility witnessed at the industry's creation. The logic of moderating price movements by controlling supply proved compelling enough that other combinations would in the future try to repeat it. Individuals, consortiums, and later even combinations of countries have all made similar efforts to manage supply.[12] They would adopt some of Standard's proven tools, particularly those of secrecy, internal discipline, and wherever possible keeping a low public profile. The temptation to try to control supply remains a built-in feature of the oil market.

Reality #2: Oil, National Security, and Foreign Policy

A second major reality permeating the oil market is its importance to, and link with, national security and foreign policy. This was a largely inevitable by-product of the technological progress and industrialization experienced primarily in North America and Western Europe in the late nineteenth century. As those econo-mies grew, and as factories and armed forces became more mecha-nized and oil-dependent, governments would start viewing oil as more than just a commodity. It became a strategically important resource: procuring it became a matter of national security. Gov-ernments proved willing to use whatever instruments they had to ensure their own supply and in wartime denying that supply to adversaries. In terms of foreign policy, particularly in peacetime, how a government chose to procure oil said much about the type of international economy it wanted to foster.

The crucible of two world wars forged the biggest links in the oil–national security chain. Technological developments had rap-idly changed both how advanced economies worked as well as the nature of the military forces protecting them. Oil folklore com-monly credits Winston Churchill as being among the first to recog-nize the strategic necessity of procuring oil and to use instruments of state power to further that goal. Acting as first lord of the British Admiralty shortly before the First World War, Churchill authorized the transition of the British Navy – then by far the world's largest and most dominant – from coal-fired to oil-fueled warships. He had his reasons. Britain's Navy had dominated the seas for centu-ries and had been the instrument allowing it to create and police its massive empire. The country also relied on naval mastery to safeguard the island nation's security and to guarantee its ongoing geopolitical heft and relevance. Consequently, in 1900 that mastery rested upon an arsenal of coal-fired battleships that formed the backbone of the British fleet, warships that could be comfortably refueled at home with Britain's ample coal supplies.[13]

Yet technology marched on. Newer and better battleship designs emerged that carried bigger guns, were sheathed with thicker armor, and could move faster, all obvious tactical advantages that Britain's adversaries were eager to exploit.[14] The catch, of course, was that the more powerful engines needed to power such ships ran on oil, which provided greater energy output per unit of weight than did coal. Britain had plenty of domestic coal, but at the time had no known oil reserves. Embracing the new designs would in effect trade one security risk for another: more advanced warship design could only be purchased with the loss of fuel security and the consequent strategic need to procure foreign oil.

That fact probably gave Churchill and the British government significant pause: it was not an easy choice to make. In effect the decision was made for them: Britain's main naval rivals, primarily continental Germany, had no reticence in embracing the newer oil-based designs and began building them at an alarming rate, effectively forcing Churchill's hand. His resultant directive authorizing Great Britain to modernize its battleship designs came with it an explicit admission that the government now had a strategic interest in procuring oil supplies.[15] In practical terms, that essentially meant that the British government was now going to go into the oil business. It could not leave its oil procurement issues to the whims of the market and would use government instruments to ensure oil would flow.

Those instruments proved formidable. Fear of oil shortage occupied British military thinking, and its leaders were not above using state resources and government power to secure necessary supply. In 1912 it authorized the formation of the Anglo-Persian Oil Company (later renamed Anglo-Iranian, which eventually would become British Petroleum), in which it took a majority ownership position. That company continued to strike further concession deals in the colonial possessions in the Persian oil fields[16] and waged continued contests with its European rival Royal Dutch Shell to gain footholds in emerging new oil fields.[17] The aggressiveness and confidence with which Great Britain used state power to protect its interests and procure oil gave others pause. The game was now going to be played by governments.

US officials certainly took note. They were in a quandary of their own: their domestic companies had no immediate commercial interest that compelled them to immediately match the British moves. There was plenty of domestic supply: and after the breakup of Standard Oil, US companies were initially more worried about shoring up their domestic positions than they were with incurring the bother and expense of international exploration. But that would not do. Having foreign state-owned companies going around the world securing concessions – and potentially shutting out American companies from prolific fields – did not at all serve US interests. The US government consequently began turning attention to helping secure concessions for its own companies and to actively encourage their internationalization,[18] particularly in Latin America. It coaxed, prodded, and sometimes outright dragged its companies to take advantage of the foreign opportunities US diplomacy began opening up.

It seemed quite a switch, given that this was the very same US government that had proven such an implacable adversary during the Standard Oil fight. Yet, when viewed through the lens of national security and foreign political interests, it was not so surprising. Even with a robust domestic US production capacity, government officials were already worrying about long-term potential shortages and thought it made sense to seek out a diversity of suppliers now rather than relying on domestic resources for the indefinite future.[19] Moreover, such efforts also fit more broadly with general US economic interests. Though remaining ideologically committed to allowing free markets to sort out who would do what in the world of oil production, the US and others quickly realized that the oil market was not always going to work that way. European governments were willing to use what instruments they had to secure oil access. They had access to their colonies, some of which were proving to hold significant oil reserves. They had established preferential economic agreements with those colonial networks, networks outsiders found difficult to penetrate. They clearly were not above using state direction, ownership, and investment into private companies to secure oil resources.

Given this, a more aggressive US diplomatic and security posture in the oil business was perhaps inevitable. It was in the US interest to have its companies and diplomats at the table when concession discussions were going on.[20] They expected their companies to shape, rather than react to, global markets in a number of industries.[21] Promoting US oil interests abroad became part of a broader US economic strategy to break down existing trade and investment barriers that had been constructed by European colonial powers. National economic interests began permeating the thinking around oil on both sides of the Atlantic.

If security considerations influenced oil markets in peacetime, they dominated those markets in wartime. Evidence of oil's national security importance accumulated during the First World War, which proved a potent precursor to the mechanized battlefields of the future. That war began with combatants still using horse-drawn carriages to ferry supplies and move personnel, which might have been sufficient had the war only lasted its anticipated six weeks and involved armies numbering in the mere tens of thousands. Yet, as it ground through its four-year agony that eventually saw fielded armies measuring in the millions, oil became ever more critical to the acts of moving, supplying, and fighting. Combatants waged increasingly mechanized battles on sea, land, and air. Battleships, merchant ships, and submarines all required oil. So too did the tanks that eventually broke the stalemate of trench warfare, the aircraft being produced in ever-greater numbers, and the motorized supply chains necessary to service all those machines and men. Combatants began consuming massive and increasing amounts of petrol: by wars' end, having access to better and deeper oil supplies proved almost as key to victory as was military prowess.

The combatants drew lessons from the experience of the First World War that would eventually condition how the Second World War would be planned for and fought. It was now beyond doubt how vital oil supplies were to military efforts, that wartime shortages were possible, and that if they occurred, they would cripple strategic plans. It was therefore necessary to create surge capacities to supply military forces if and when they were employed and to keep a very close eye on available sources of supply. In the United States both oil executives and government officials clearly saw the importance of international oil markets for the future and the need for government support in accessing those markets. In 1919 the American Petroleum Institute (API) issued a report on the threat foreign state-controlled oil companies might pose to American petroleum interests. Ominously titled *The Menace of Foreign State Monopolies to the American Petroleum Industry*, it argued that, although the US endorsed a free-enterprise market system to govern international oil flow, other countries might not. It further noted that, if those countries extended official aid to their companies,[22] the US government should consider doing the same thing for theirs. Other oil executives wrote letters to public officials advocating for greater US participation in global oil markets: one such letter envisioned a "world-wide exploration, development, and producing company, financed with American capital, guided by American engineering, and supervised in its international relations by the United States Government." Government officials got on the bandwagon: secretary of the Navy Edwin Denby proposed federal support in expanding the US merchant marine fleet, which would require "fueling stations on world trade routes, preferably under American control and developed by American business interests."[23] Both government officials and oil executives supported the creation of strategic reserves and the bunkering of fuel.[24] The buildup and conduct of the First World War demonstrated that governments would insert and assert themselves in the oil business. That made soliciting government aid in international expansion efforts an expected rather than a rare thing.[25]

If securing oil had proven important in the First World War, it proved overwhelmingly critical during the buildup and conduct of the Second World War. Both Germany and Japan internalized the importance oil had for prevailing on the battlefields of the future: particularly as both lacked domestic sources. In the interwar period they pondered the problem of oil procurement as they amassed their strength and took significant steps to ameliorate it. Japan built its vision of a "Greater East Asia Co-Prosperity Sphere" on conquering new territory holding the oil and other resources their island nation lacked.[26] Hitler's prewar strategy and conduct during the Second World War also reflected the constraints Germany's lack of domestic oil supply placed on his military strategy. He knew that, without oil, the Third Reich's armies, no matter how well led, would grind to a halt. The course of the war proved that judgment right and showed how crippling oil shortages could be for both the Axis and Allied powers. In Germany's case, after the German Blitzkrieg had garnered its initial victories in the relatively constrained geographies of Western Europe, it proved less effective in dealing with the vastness of Russia. The decision to invade Russia, though likely inevitable given Hitler's prewar thinking, eventually generated an Eastern Front hundreds of miles wide, creating a protracted conflict fought over great distances. As the war dragged on and the Eastern Front continued to spread out, procuring necessary oil supplies became central to an increasingly oil-desperate German strategy. Fuel availability dictated where and how far German forces could move and what objectives they could seize. In that Germany was hardly alone: generals from both the Allied and Axis powers often lamented that a lack of petrol prevented them from doing what they wanted.[27] Having greater and more secure oil supplies gave advantages to the Allied powers and eventually proved vital in securing victory. The modern battlefield now was a fully mechanized one, and victory depended upon the number of well-supplied internal combustion engines – surrounded by armor, weapons, and trained people – that a country could put into the field, ocean, or sky.

By the end of that war, the need to procure oil had been permanently etched on the easel of national security. It created a series of concerns requiring attention even to this day. Countries vulnerable to oil shortage had to craft national security strategies to minimize that vulnerability.[28] Military forces needed oil to ply their trade, and some additional supplies needed to be secured if the civilian economy supporting those forces was not to grind to a halt. Not everyone had oil, and importing governments therefore were increasingly reliant on the international supply system to provide them what they needed. Bunkering oil became important, as countries had to ensure enough was on hand to provide the surge demand wartime might require. Finally, given that governments had already proven willing to support their oil companies – by investing in them, using diplomacy to secure oil concessions, and giving them preferential access to various markets – others might be expected to do the same thing. How far would that support go? What would a country do, or tolerate, in the name of accessing oil? How could a country balance its need to procure oil with other national security interests? Such questions would continue plaguing the national security considerations of oil procurement and linger with us even today.

Reality #3: Overproduction and Supply Management

The companies had also responded powerfully to spikes in wartime demand and had proven quite capable of finding new oil. While fears of shortage had animated public discussion during wartime, they rapidly abated in the postwar world due to the flood of new oil wartime exploration efforts began bringing to market. Global oil production doubled between 1919 and 1923, and proven industry holdings of crude oil reserves went from 136 million barrels in 1920 to over 400 million barrels by 1924.[29] That would create a problem afflicting both the interwar period and the post–Second World War environment as well: the problem of supply glut. Massive and successful wartime investments in finding new oil reserves had built up a potential supply overhang that extended into the postwar civilian oil markets. How was that going to be managed?

Exploration success created problems of its own. Investing companies had found the new oil they were looking for: but once resources had been found, host governments expected them to be developed, which an investing company felt obligated to do lest they lose that government's favor and perhaps even the drilling lease. Yet if everyone did that, more oil would once again be brought to an already saturated market, further flooding the world with cheap oil indefinitely. After both the First and Second World Wars, the oil market would face the same problem Standard Oil had tried to solve in the United States seventy years earlier: over-supply and a consequent depressed price that was destructive to company balance sheets. It would be up to the companies to sort out the resultant supply overhang, and governments would have to live with what those companies did.

Potential supply sources kept ramping up. In the United States, US oil executives certainly were aware of the emerging international competitors and the productive fields being found in Russia and the Middle East.[30] But they saw no initial need to counter them, choosing instead to capitalize on their entrenched position to serve the lucrative US market. Yet, after Standard Oil's breakup, its descendants no longer had the advantages a near-monopoly provided[31] and had to adapt quickly by seeking new resources and filling other kinds of competitive gaps. Those descendants all consequently developed distinct corporate personalities, operating cultures, and strategies and began looking abroad.[32] Smaller independent producers – the very kind Rockefeller had so ruthlessly sought to destroy – now found the competitive field reopened. Their derricks began peppering the fields in Texas, the Midwest, and California, thereby ensuring oil's political influence would grow, eventually impacting elected officials throughout the country.[33] An increasingly robust domestic competitive market began reemerging in the US, and production increased.

As the US continued sorting out the Standard Oil drama, Europe had witnessed Henri Deterding and Marcus Samuel busy themselves in creating the Royal Dutch Shell (RDS) oil company. They amalgamated their two trading and oil-exploration companies in 1906 and quickly proved adept at launching an international oil-exploration program. They did so largely out of necessity: neither of their home countries of Great Britain and the Netherlands possessed significant known domestic oil resources.[34] Oil field discoveries in Russia and the Far East beckoned, where initial drilling results revealed immense potential reserves, and Royal Dutch Shell began investing heavily. The Anglo-Persian Oil Company continued its exploration efforts as well: its additional exploration motivated by the potential needs of wartime demand unlocked potentially vast fields in the Middle East. Taken together, these forces created a global market for oil that began tapping new sources of supply.

Private companies made investment decisions according to what the markets, not geopolitics or military strategy, dictated. The markets' instruments – companies and financial houses – secured and produced oil with an eye toward maximizing and stabilizing financial return. Company executives had understood the wartime politics, but they were paid to worry about the economics and the geology, about finding oil and bringing it to market profitably. The prospects of doing so looked difficult, particularly after the surge of production capacity forged in wartime. A larger number of increasingly capable companies competed for reserves and to build other kinds of industrial advantage. That market was also an ever more international one as more companies entered the oil-exploration game. The global market became preoccupied with the problem Standard Oil had tried to solve in the United States: overproduction among individualistic producers and the need to manage oil flow so companies remained profitable.

Businessmen consequently began realizing that there might be some collective benefits in imposing a semblance of structure and control upon the oil market. European governments had already set precedent informally by allocating colonial authority in what would become the world's most prolific oil-producing area. In 1915 the Sykes-Picot Agreement divided up much of the modern Middle East into French and English spheres of influence.[35] The oil companies would eventually follow that with the infamous 1928 Red Line Agreement, which structured concessions to the participating consortia of companies across the similar stretch of land that comprised all of the former Ottoman Empire.[36] That agreement forbade participating companies from seeking additional oil interests outside their demarcated areas, in effect apportioning to the major oil companies the productive capacity of distinct parts of the Middle East. Other concessionary agreements followed over the next two decades, as more regional oil-producing areas were explored and collective worries about oversupply spread.[37] Some measure of management of the emerging Gulf production output seemed a necessary thing.

At the end of the Second World War, major oil companies would continue crafting a system of informal supply management. That system came to be known as the Seven Sisters oil cartel, which managed the oil market between 1950 and 1970. The Seven Sisters was a group of five American and two British oil companies that effectively parceled out the production rights and oil flow emerging from the Middle East. Their names – Exxon, Chevron, Mobil, Gulf, Texaco, Shell, and British Petroleum – remain familiar today, and this period marked the height of their international power. Each company managed production in its demarcated areas while collectively reinforcing an elaborate system of interlocking concessions, ownership structures, and production limits that was all but impenetrable to outsiders. Companies were careful to tread only in their area, continued brokering informal production agreements, and kept a collective eye on avoiding supply glut, a problem companies feared as much as governments feared shortage.

That system emulated Standard Oil's strategy in the sense that it was well understood by participants but remained obscure and difficult to decipher by outsiders.[38] Unlike Standard, however, what really made it work was the system's capacity to serve multiple political and economic interests and constituents. First, it enabled oil companies to maintain their profitability. Second, the deals companies struck with local governments generated steady and increasing revenue flow for domestic political leaders, revenue they could then use to consolidate power. Third, that steady revenue made those domestic governments even more amenable to other Western commercial interests. Fourth, Western investment and revenue flow made it less likely that regional governments might succumb to any potential Soviet communist expansion, the prevention of which was then the dominant foreign policy concern of the US government.[39] Stable emerging oil production kept the region calm, and importing countries felt confident that their energy needs would be met.

The Seven Sisters also served other interests. Stable prices helped keep domestic US producers remain marginally profitable, in itself a major achievement in the face of a potential flood of cheap imports. Consumers certainly liked cheap oil and did not much care where it came from, but sourcing oil abroad threatened to destroy the viability of the US domestic industry. The clash between consumer interests and the need to preserve a viable domestic US industry created an extended political fight[40] and an imperfect domestic policy response consisting of a complex system of price and import controls that proved difficult to administer.[41] In managing supply and price level, the Seven Sisters cartel indirectly served US interests in keeping a reasonably robust US domestic production capacity while also avoiding the politically unpalatable outcome of having that industry destroyed by cheap foreign oil. Such an outcome would banish to electoral oblivion any US politician that allowed it to happen.

There were political problems associated with having too much oil, as well as too little. Though surplus was a better problem to have than scarcity, it still created real concerns, particularly if countries came to rely on cheap imports at the expense of domestic sources. The positive characteristics of supply management continued to wield an attractive logic, especially when that system served all these contending interests. It worked well for a quarter of a century in managing supply levels and maintaining profitability.[42] Indeed, the era of the Seven Sisters became emblematic of the dominance the large oil companies could exert over oil-producing countries; it was perhaps the heyday of "big oil." Yet it was also a delicate system, one balancing several competing political and economic forces. It was open to disruption along a number of fronts, and one force capable of doing a lot of disrupting was resource nationalism.

Reality #4: Resource Nationalism

Countries care about their natural resources, viewing them as their national birthright, and often do not like having to rely on foreign companies to extract them. They may need the foreign company's expertise but often do not like soliciting it or admitting it. If not carefully managed, the resentment against foreign owner-ship can build, even if operations appear steady and profitable and everyone is smiling. Even with that, the "liability of foreignness" is rarely shed completely:[43] citizens may rarely believe a foreign investment company has their nation's domestic interests at heart, a suspicion never fully eased. The potential revenues associated with oil production make those liabilities particularly heavy. By mid-century, governments had already shown how aggressive they could be in reclaiming what they had always considered theirs. Mexico nationalized its oil industry in 1938 and in doing so had refused to compensate companies for the full worth of the appropriated assets.[44] Similar oil nationalization trends had spread across Latin America, particularly in Venezuela,[45] and Soviet Russia also had shown no qualms at all about taking state control over oil production after establishing its communist government. Companies knew that nationalization of oil resources was and is a reality with which they must contend.

The Seven Sisters knew this threat lingered and never fully went away. It was therefore crucial to maintain and constantly cultivate host government support in the burgeoning fields of the Middle East. That had been simple enough in the beginning: colonial relationships and the drilling sophistication of the oil companies themselves meant investing companies had considerable bargaining leverage. They crafted comfortable arrangements with local leaders to manage nationalization through an easy-to-explain bargain. Companies provided local governments oil revenues and would support their right to rule: in return those leaders left the companies largely alone and shielded them from domestic criticism. The initial revenue-sharing agreements struck by the Seven Sisters had proven sufficient to keep their end of the bargain up. They had generated a vast increase in those governments' wealth, and most of it flowed directly to the ruling families that dominated the region's governance structures. The US government also tacitly supported that arrangement. Oil revenue provided by the companies to host governments meant there was no need to transfer aid or extend official monetary assistance to the region. The richer Gulf countries became, the less likely they were to embrace communism and would resist Soviet expansionism. Moreover, as those countries became wealthier, they became increasingly attractive customers for US industrial goods, in particular military and security exports. All in all not a bad US bargain, strategically.

Yet such a cozy relationship did not last. Over time, the delicate balance making it work eroded. Investments in local oil fields began creating pockets of opposition to foreign control over those fields, and an increased willingness to challenge the system the Sisters had crafted. The first termite in that system came from an increasingly adept and knowledgeable domestic public service, one that began deciphering how the oil industry worked and how the inflow and outflow of cash was managed. The more they learned about the transfer-pricing mechanisms companies used to maximize profit, the more they realized how little of the take they were actually getting. Second, domestic technical knowledge bred confidence as well: local personnel developed intricate engineering knowledge of their own reservoirs and of the extractive techniques needed to access them. Technically, they could perhaps eventually manage these things on their own. Knowledge and confidence led to a third component of resource nationalism: resentment. As they learned and knew more, local citizens became indignant about a system in which boardrooms in New York, Houston, and London privately rationed out their economic lifeblood. Eventually that confidence motivated them to start pushing back against the system bequeathed to them by the Seven Sisters.[46]

Some of the more ambitious challengers engaged in a frontal assault on that system, wishing to overthrow rather than reform it. The passion of postwar anti-colonial sentiment helped: broader nationalist movements began erupting literally all over the post–Second World War world, where the desire to shake off colonial ties or foreign subjugation began animating domestic politics.[47] In the oil-producing world, a prominent test tapping into that nationalism came in 1950, when Dr. Mohammed Mossadegh began invoking resource nationalism as an additional political tool to end broader colonial domination and to begin pursuing social reform in his home nation of Iran. His call for greater Iranian independence found a receptive initial audience eager to embrace his nationalist vision, giving him the domestic support necessary to overthrow the ruling Pahlavi royal family. His opposition to royal rule emerged at least in part from their willingness to work with and tolerate foreign oil interests, whose revenue-sharing arrangements funded their lavish lifestyle. Upon gaining power, Mossadegh called for an immediate nationalization of the oil industry, expropriated the Anglo-Iranian Oil Company in 1952, and called for the withdrawal of the oil majors, not just from Iran but from the region generally.

Mossadegh's example proved powerful but premature. The oil companies certainly feared it, but so too did the neighboring monarchs who saw in Mossadegh's triumph a potential threat to their own rule should their domestic populations get similar ideas. That fear motivated collective action: an alliance between the regional monarchs and oil companies emerged wielding enough collective strength to crush the Iranian example. One main tool doing the crushing was the blockading of transport networks out of Iran. By refusing to move its oil to refineries and international markets, the anti-Iranian consortium created in effect a reverse blockade. Unable to sell its oil, Iran rapidly ran out of cash, people grew increasingly desperate, and with it much of the revolutionary fervor that had propelled Mossadegh to power began dissipating.

Yet that was not enough: it would take more than an oil blockade to topple Mossadegh. His political opponents also received help from the US government, who thought the Pahlavi family more reliable oil partners, as well as stronger opponents of communism, than what Mossadegh was ever likely to be.[48] Starved for oil revenue, and facing a domestic coup financed and aided by the US Central Intelligence Agency (CIA), Mossadegh eventually lost power. Upon reassuming control, the Pahlavi family had Mossadegh tried in an Iranian court, where he eventually was confined to house arrest where he would remain for the rest of his life. The example, however, had been set. Mossadegh had proven that a powerful Iranian nationalism existed, and a key symbol around which its citizens could rally was opposition to foreign control over its oil. It had taken the combined efforts of the oil majors and the regional and US governments to quell it. Iranian resentment of the US-inspired political coup would grow and fester for another two decades, just waiting for the right time to reignite.

Other nations took a different tack against the oil companies. Domestic governments began exerting ever-greater pressure on those companies, demanding higher prices and more revenues than what the Sisters were delivering. One particularly assertive force in this trend was a young Libyan Colonel named Muammar Gaddafi, who had been part of a group of army officers who had seized power. Upon gaining control, he began almost immediately to pressure the oil companies, arguing that Libyan oil was priced too low.[49] The companies proved unable to mount the kind of united response with which they had confronted Iran, and began a series of independent negotiations with the increasingly assertive Libyan government. This resulted in the Tehran Agreement of February 1971 and the Tripoli Agreements of 1971, which saw the companies agree to significantly increased prices. The psychological effect of these agreements rippled through the oil world: for the first time, the companies had buckled under the demands of an assertive local government. Producing countries started seeing they could get a far better deal than what they had been receiving by increasing the pressure on investing companies to give them better terms or by developing their indigenous capacity to produce oil.

Another factor aiding the nationalization process was a new breed of confident and aggressive oil entrepreneurs who chafed at the output restrictions and cozy club atmosphere evinced by the Seven Sisters and were more than happy to break the established rules. John Paul Getty became the most famous of these independent producers. He struck deals with Gulf producers, giving them much better terms that what the majors had set while still leaving himself plenty of room for profit. Word spread, and regional business leaders began pressing the larger companies for ever-better terms, while showing no small bit of anger at not having been granted those terms in the first place.

The secrecy and opaqueness of the Seven Sisters consortium began breaking down. Local officials gained knowledge and experience and began realizing how pricing mechanisms did not work in their favor. They pushed hard for better terms. Libya had been first off the block in demanding and receiving increased revenue from investing companies.[50] Witnessing the successful Libyan example, others joined in with fervor, demanding greater control over their oil either for its own sake or as a pledge against US foreign policy actions in the Middle East.[51] Others took more time, instead choosing a calibrated but relentless approach that was less confrontational but nevertheless moved in the same direction. They partnered with investing companies and mandated the transfer of technical knowledge as a precondition of continued investment. This more moderate approach enabled local oil companies to gain operational capacity: as they did they would need the majors less and less.

A final factor weakening the Seven Sisters' control was the growing capacity of oil-producing states to act in concert in pursuing their collective interest. An ominous sign had come in 1960, via the formation the Organization for Arab Petroleum Exporting States (OAPEC), which would become the oil producer's cartel and forerunner of the OPEC cartel. The organization began innocently enough: its initial meetings barely warranted headlines and heralded little about the potent force it would eventually become. Its formation did not worry either the companies or the governments of importers, who thought the participating governments too individualistic and fractious to exert the discipline a successful cartel required. Geopolitically, Western politicians thought OAPEC unity would be shaky at best and would crack under economic or political pressure. Its creation had no discernable initial effect on oil prices or flow, and as long as that was the case there was little initial cause for worry. Yet, over the next decade, the cartel's solidarity strengthened: it continued their meetings and expanded their membership to include non-Gulf members (hence the change of name to OPEC). It increasingly became a potent united force that eventually was able to wield significant political and economic impact.

The system the Seven Sisters created worked well for almost three decades because it did several things. It provided oil, plenty of it, at low and predictable prices. It helped manage the problem of accumulated oil-production surplus and helped preserve the profitability of those companies who could not match the production costs of Middle Eastern reserves. The oil producers appeared initially to be politically stable and enjoyed predictable inflows of revenue, allowing leaders to bolster their domestic position while also appearing amenable to US foreign policy interests. As long as prices were low, the oil kept flowing, and producing governments appeared placated, consuming governments had little reason to intervene or seemingly to worry.

Trouble, however, continued brewing. Home nations came to realize that extracting their own oil and collecting all the associated revenue would generate more funds than anything the production schemes concocted by the oil majors would ever grant them. OPEC unity grew, and the Seven Sisters' unity weakened. Resource nationalism proved to be a relentless force capable of breaking the control exerted by the private companies. Taken individually, the forces of nationalist passion, economic ambition, increasing technical competence, and growing producer political will might have been manageable. When combined, they produced a force powerful enough to disrupt the entire industry. A spark of assertiveness against the oil companies by the major oil-producing governments set off a reaction that broke the shackles of the Seven Sisters control. Their "system" of interlocking partnerships, protected by an armor of complexity that outsiders could not penetrate, began breaking apart. Local governments grew resentful, wanted more control and revenue, and drew on the nationalist sentiment brewing in their own populations to help build the case against the majors. Taken together, the fiery politics of resource nationalism combined with the cold economic logic of national control forged a force powerful enough to push the Seven Sisters out of the Middle East and wrench production control away from companies and into the hands of producing governments.

Reality #5: Oil Price Shocks and Import Vulnerability

By 1970 the process of ceding control was well underway. Consequently, importing nations were becoming increasingly vulnerable to the production decisions that producing governments made. Initially, this caused little reason for concern, or even awareness that the vulnerability was building. Interests seemed aligned: producing governments appeared to have as much interest in selling oil as consuming governments had in buying it. Cheap imported oil had helped give an economic boost to importing economies: yet as their reliance on that imported oil grew, so too did their vulnerability to supply disruption. The Seven Sisters had managed to keep cheap oil flowing smoothly. However, that comfortable predictability was about to evaporate with a series of price shocks oil producers began inflicting on the economies of the developed world. The producers' ability to coordinate production and make collective decisions stick, combined with growing import vulnerability, set the stage for the first significant global price shock in over a century.

Initially, simple economics drove the decision to raise prices. Exporting countries realized they could exploit import vulnerability if they could collectively mandate and administer a higher price floor for the purchase of their oil. The first effort came in an initial OPEC effort to collectively "administer" prices that were far above prevailing market rates. Between 1973 and 1974 OPEC was able to orchestrate a series of price jumps that were both significant and repetitive. OPEC-administered prices saw the price of Saudi Arabian light crude jump from $1.80/barrel to $11.65 – a sixfold increase.[52] This engendered howls of protest, but there was little importers could initially do. Moreover, OPEC seemed successful at managing production levels of its members, displaying a degree of unanticipated collective discipline.

Many of those price increases were simply products of economic calculation: OPEC had control of supply, and importers could do little immediately to change that. Western protest turned to fear as the next series of price shocks had at their core geopolitical objectives. Producers began thinking that by manipulating or withholding oil output they could influence the political and geopolitical decisions those importing countries made. They could, in effect, play the oil card in the geopolitical poker game. An important test case came in 1973, when the Arab oil-producing world invoked an embargo of oil exports on Western countries to protest their support of Israel's actions against Egypt in the Six-Day War. Shipments to Western Europe were sharply curtailed: exports to the United States and Norway, Israel's strongest supporters in that war, were halted entirely. The embargo caught the US and others by surprise: the cartel was thought too fractious to pull off such a collective enterprise and that its cash-hungry members could not long withstand the political and economic consequences if they did. Western governments held to these judgments despite strong signals from Arab leaders that an embargo was not only possible but indeed likely should the US not modify its position.[53] The US did not, and the embargo happened.

The embargo generated an ensuing oil market panic. Oil prices jumped quickly and reached unprecedented heights: a barrel of

Arab light crude commanded six times more at the end of 1973 than what it had in 1970:[54] in 1972 a barrel of oil cost $2.80, by 1974 it cost $11.[55] To more rational minds, the ensuing reaction seemed overblown. By itself, the embargo was hardly catastrophic to supply. It only took about 4 per cent of globally produced oil off the market, and there remained plenty of alternative sources, as well as the oil that could be pulled from supply bunkers.[56] The economic costs of the embargo were not particularly drastic.

Symbolically, however, it was scary. The reality of import vulnerability crashed into the imaginations of advanced industrial economies and their citizens and often generated reactions born out of fear and ignorance rather than economic reality. Consuming customers thought the oil crisis to be worse than it actually was and that it would last longer than it actually did. Panic-stricken people lined up at gas stations for hours, even when their tanks were three-quarters full, to ensure they obtained gasoline before gas stations ran dry. Rumors grew: private citizens floated conspiracy theories about this being the first step in a nefarious plot Middle Eastern oil producers had hatched to bring down Western civilization. Private international oil companies were assumed to be in on the plot: they were often accused of colluding with Middle Eastern governments to advance the shared goal of jacking up price. Politicians began clamoring for new domestic drilling, became increasingly willing to authorize new exploration efforts, and began to at least think about the pursuit of alternative energy sources. The embargo's actual economic impact may have remained small, but the psychological impact was not. The fact that OPEC could pull it off at all brought home the consequences of import vulnerability. It left scars on the consumer psyche, who suddenly realized that unstable and not-always-friendly Middle Eastern governments had what looked like a chokehold on global oil supply.

Those scars would be reopened and amplified six years later by a political revolution in Iran. That revolution witnessed the final overthrow of the royal Pahlavi family, who had never quite recovered their domestic standing even decades after Mossadegh had lost power. Indeed, insecurity over his domestic standing fueled Shah Reza Pahlavi's often brutal repression of his domestic opponents. His purchase and subsequent use of US military and security hardware in doing that repressing steadily increased domestic resentment both toward him and toward the United States. That resentment grew, fueled by the fiery rhetoric of the fundamentalist Muslim figure of Ayatollah Khomeini, eventually creating a domestic revolution and the imposition of a fundamentalist Muslim government in Iran, headed by Khomeini himself.

The installation of such a regime in one of the world's preeminent oil producers rattled oil markets and inflamed and frayed the nerves of oil traders. Once again, prices shot upward, the price of a barrel of oil measured around $12/barrel in 1978: by 1979 it measured $29/barrel, and by 1980 it would measure $35/barrel.[57] Once again, the economic worry seemed overblown. Iran's revolution-inspired withdrawal from the oil market removed 2 mbd off that market, which measured about 3 per cent of global supply, an amount easily replaced by other sources. Yet the revolution helped generate a whopping 126 per cent increase in price, despite the existence of ample spare capacity and inventories that had accumulated after the 1973 shock.[58] Initially traders and governments again appeared flat-footed, seemingly unaware that this could happen and unsure of what to do once it did. They began scrambling to make up lost inventory, found alternative production sites, and worked to ensure a momentary shortage did not turn into a full-blown financial panic.

Politically, the effect seemed more significant. Not only had the revolution been generally unanticipated, its ferocity and widespread support also caught many by surprise. The displayed anti-American fury, evinced by the taking and holding of hostages in the American embassy in Tehran, and the continuous anti-Western vitriol emanating out of the Iranian regime's top lieutenants, boded poorly for the political future of US–Iranian relations. It made observers wonder how widespread that feeling might be among the other regional oil producers. The West, and the US in particular, now had what looked to be an implacable fundamentalist enemy ruling one of the world's preeminent oil-production countries. Now oil supply, once something taken for granted, vaulted once again into the realm of a national security interest.

The shocks afflicting the oil market during the 1970s demonstrated a mixed bag of lessons. First, it demonstrated how vulnerable advanced economies were to oil price disruptions and how politically and economically unprepared they were to combat it. Consuming nations had built economies and lifestyles dependent upon cheap oil. Those economies would now be more expensive to run, and those lifestyles more costly to lead, because the oil powering them had quadrupled in price from what it had been at the beginning of the decade. Second, by most accounts high oil prices looked like they were going to stay that way. Consumers worried that there was little preventing the oil cartel from continually jacking up prices more or less at their whim and that there was little anyone could do to stop them. Third, consuming countries seemed surprisingly incapable of coordinating their responses in dealing with the threat of oil embargo. In the US, domestic supply could not be easily or quickly ramped up. Neither Europe nor Japan had significant domestic sources: both eventually struck independent deals with alternative oil suppliers, including Soviet Russia, to make up for their domestic shortfall. In short, the developed world seemed to be unable to enact a coordinated response to match what the exporters appeared capable of. From that point on, the oil market would be subject to the shocks of perception and fear along with day-to-day economic reality.

Reality #6: Oil, Money, and the Resource Curse

The increase in oil prices generated economic effects beyond the world of oil producers. As oil prices rose, money began flowing from consuming to producing nations, resulting in an enormous and rapid transfer of wealth. Trade deficits in developed markets ballooned, as the value of the oil they imported began to swamp the revenues domestic exporters generated. Pressure on the US dollar increased[59] and, as oil procurement costs absorbed more capital, less remained to spend on other things. It became more expensive to produce goods, and the purchasing power of American consumers dropped. This contributed to the dreaded phenomenon of stagflation – high inflation with little growth – that emerged by the end of the 1970s. Rising oil prices contributed to the onset of one of the worst recessions to afflict the United States since the Great Depression, which helped doom the reelection bid of incumbent president Jimmy Carter.

Rapid price increases infused oil exporters with new financial clout. The power of oil spread beyond the commodity itself and began infecting domestic expenditures as well as global financial markets. The steady stream of income oil producers had been receiving rapidly turned into a flood. In 1975, after the first oil shocks had run their course, earnings from oil royalties generated US$50 billion in Saudi Arabia alone, and other oil-exporting Gulf states experienced enormous wealth increases as well.[60] This provided them the fiscal resources that allowed rapid increases in all manner of domestic expenditures. Oil-rich states began to simultaneously modernize their infrastructure, create new and expansive social programs, and enact domestic construction projects symbolizing great optimism and ambition for the future. Middle Eastern countries historically populated by nomadic tribesmen, coastal farmers, and local traders suddenly began constructing modern cities, replete with skyscrapers and a cosmopolitan sheen. They could also afford to purchase the very latest in military hardware, which they did in ever-greater amounts. The potential uses of that money were endless, particularly if high prices persisted, as many thought they would.

The rapid influx of cash into domestic governments created the potential for such blessings. But it also could cause problems, and the degree to which local governments and citizens actually benefited from the increased resource revenue became a matter of intense debate. Suddenly rich governments often could not absorb all the money flowing in no matter how much they spent domestically. The excess money created by oil revenue became coveted by those either simply wishing to aggrandize themselves or who wanted to use that revenue to gain political power. A sudden inrush of oil money could hinder entrepreneurialism, particularly in the developing world.[61] Some argued that oil revenue made states more aggressive, perhaps more prone to war,[62] more rather than less repressive of their domestic citizens, and less rather than more democratic.

On the monetary side, the effects of oil revenue were almost as pernicious. Oil exporters could suffer from what is known as the "Dutch Disease," an economic phenomenon in which a booming export-led commodity sector inhibits growth or development in other economic areas.[63] In the case of oil, so attractive were the potential returns in developing that one commodity that other economic sectors could become starved for capital and ambitious entrepreneurs willing to develop it. Over time some economies could become overwhelmingly focused on the production of oil to the exclusion of all else, particularly if they were small economies to begin with.[64] Other countries identified the problem of export diversification earlier and managed the problem better.[65] The academic debate around the "resource curse" became reinvigorated with the rise in oil revenues the oil shocks provided, and that debate continues to this day.[66]

The international financial system also felt the impact of the massive transfer of oil wealth. Oil-exporting countries, despite their best efforts, could not domestically absorb all the revenue pouring in. They consequently turned to the international capital markets to help them invest the excess and found a community of international bankers more than willing to provide such aid. Deposits in Western banks swelled, and the activity of what is now called petrodollar recycling commenced. That phenomenon looked simple on paper: banks, flush with the cash deposited in their vaults from oil exporters, now had to find outlets for those deposits. Having that capital cushion allowed them to make increasingly large and often more risky loans, particularly to emerging and developing markets that appeared to offer the highest returns. Those markets found banks more willing to loan them money: in many cases their overall debt skyrocketed and left them vulnerable to a swelling debt burden that could be crushing if they were ever unable to make the requisite payments.

Oil-producing states also became active investors in the equity, as well as the debt, markets. Flush with oil revenues, private investors or government-run SWFs began taking increasingly large ownership positions in Western stock markets, and even directly into many blue-chip companies. The excess investment certainly helped prop up stock markets, but it also raised eyebrows and even a few alarm bells in regulators. Some saw in the emerging financial power of oil exporters almost as great an economic threat as the one they exerted through their capacity to influence oil supply. Oil producers now had garnered geopolitical leverage not only from their ability to produce oil, but also from the financial power they could wield on global investment markets.

For oil consumers and their governments, the world certainly looked different in 1980 than it had in 1950. The consuming public was now very aware of the problems the modern oil economy had created. Much of their economic outlook now rested in the hands of national governments lying half a world away, of whom they knew little and over whom they could exert even less control. Oil producers seemed wracked by a complicated and dicey struggle between political and religious elements for authority: the outcome of that struggle was unpredictable. Some of those oil producers seemed intractably hostile. The Iranian Revolution featured a fervent anti-Americanism whose terrifying intensity left US citizens bewildered and afraid. The world of oil production, previously stable, was now volatile and unpredictable. There was a lack of consensus about the direction the oil market would take and what if any role US companies could play to shape it.[67] Conflict between suppliers and consumers seemed inevitable, and no one could now take the procurement of oil for granted. It had to be cultivated and, if necessary, secured.

Reality #7: Oil and US Foreign Policy

The previous events of the 1970s forced the United States to reevaluate its oil security strategy and its broader foreign policy generally. It had found it convenient, and politically expedient, to let the problem of oil procurement be managed by the Seven Sisters. With the oil companies taking care of that problem, US foreign policy could concentrate on other things, of which there were many. The

US remained embroiled in the quagmire of the Vietnam War, began pursuing a measure of détente with the Soviet Union, and also made overtures toward opening relations with Communist China. Politically, faced with many external challenges and a domestic US Congress increasingly weary of foreign expenditures, worries about the Middle East were sometimes put on the back burner.[68]

Once the reality of oil nationalization set in, the US crafted a foreign policy response designed to protect its political aims in the Middle East. It was entitled the surrogate strategy and involved building strong relationships with regional powers who could be entrusted with helping protect US interests. The terms of the bargain were straightforward and were phrased in political terms: the chosen partner would adopt a moderate position toward the state of Israel, would resist communist incursion, and would support US interests in the region more generally. In return, it received ongoing US economic support, regular endorsements, public statements of gratitude, the sale and transfer of advanced US military hardware, and muted if any US criticism for how they ran their country. That strategy had mutual advantages: it advanced US interests, avoided entanglement in a volatile region, created markets for US arms manufacturers, and seemed to enhance Israel's security. As long as the surrogate did its job, US foreign policy could keep its attention focused on other things.[69]

Iran had been one of the first proxy partners the US chose. After the US had helped expel Mossadegh, the Shah became progressively confident in his political bond with the United States and believed US support would be forthcoming no matter what he chose to do. Unfortunately, and as noted earlier, a regime chosen by the US for its perceived stability, predictability, and amenability to US interests proved to be anything but. The Shah's behavior became increasingly erratic and despotic, and the rift between him and his own population widened. He employed aggressive measures to counter domestic opposition, including jailing dissidents, inflicting severe human rights abuses, ongoing spying of political opponents by internal security forces, and ever more grandiose statements of personal achievement. Despite these increasingly repulsive and worrisome behaviors, US presidents continued doubling down on their professed support, further emboldening the Shah and making it impossible for the US to curb his problematic behavior. As domestic resistance to the Shah's rule grew, so too did an anti-Americanism and broader anti-Western sentiment that blamed the United States for propping up a reviled leader,[70] which culminated in the Iranian Revolution of 1979.

After that revolution, so worried was the United States about threats to oil flow out of the Persian Gulf that it made a formal national security commitment to protect that flow. President Jimmy Carter made that commitment in his State of the Union Address in 1980, which stated the following: "Any attempt by outside force to gain control of the Persian Gulf region will be regarded as an assault on the vital interest of the United States of America, and as such will be repelled by any means necessary, including military force."[71] It is hard to make a foreign policy commitment any clearer than that, and the necessity to protect oil flow was one of the few areas in which Carter agreed with his Republican successor Ronald Reagan, and indeed with every subsequent US president, each of which has made similar guarantees that the global economy would not be "choked" off from oil imports.[72]

The so-called Carter doctrine would be supported and enhanced by his successors, who would successively place ever more emphasis on reinforcing the other proxy relationship it had been crafting, the one with the ruling Al-Saud family in Saudi Arabia. That relationship, in Rachel Bronson's phrase, was indeed "Thicker than Oil."[73] It served mutual political interests that went beyond oil procurement. Like pre-revolutionary Iran, Saudi Arabia had become a proven export market for the US defense industry and had invested much of its newfound wealth in US financial markets. Yet it had done more than that. It had sometimes acted as a "bridge" for US interests in the region, helping US diplomatic efforts in managing the fallout from the Iranian Revolution. The US–Saudi relationship took on a personal flavor, in which friendship between the Al-Saud family and select US presidents flourished and appeared to influence much subsequent policy.[74] In the oil market, Saudi Arabia proved especially helpful. It pledged to help manage the production output of OPEC and to build significant additional domestic production capacity that would allow it more flexibility to add or withdraw supply to keep the market in balance.

The Saudi relationship, however, also subjected the US to the same risks and criticisms that its previous relationship with Iran had generated. The US seemed willing to tolerate Saudi governance practices that likely would have drawn criticism had the kingdom not been so key to the world's oil supply. The Saudi government pressed its position, using its monetary resources to obtain similar sales of advanced US weaponry that Iran had enjoyed, while also building a powerful internal security structure that could also police potential dissidents. That structure enjoyed funding boosts taken from the profits of oil sales. The weaknesses in the surrogate strategy was that it appeared to be based on mutual expediency rather than an agreement or alignment on goals and values. The US had now conflated its need to procure oil with other foreign policy interests in the region.

The primacy of procuring oil began at least appearing to dominate other foreign policy principles the US traditionally espoused. Taken together, the US–Saudi relationship was a case in point. Both shared political and geopolitical objectives that "established a strong foundation that supported close relations at the highest political level for decades." But that proxy relationship was bought "at the expense of democratization, human rights, and the promotion of religious freedom, goals animating American politics elsewhere."[75] The disconnect between what the US said its values were and what it proved willing to tolerate in the name of preserving oil security now infused and seemed to pollute other regional policy objectives and eroded global confidence in statements of US foreign policy values.

One consequence of that disconnect was that it became possible, even easy, to interpret every US action in the region as having less to do with principled foreign policy interests and more of being simply one more move to secure oil. Opponents of US foreign policy have not hesitated to make that claim. A case in point was the Gulf War of 1990, in which Iraq's Saddam Hussein invaded neighboring Kuwait to supposedly "repatriate" former Iraqi provinces that Kuwait had purportedly illegally seized. The veracity of this claim was doubtful, but likely immaterial. Most found it far more believable that getting control over Kuwait's oil-rich provinces was Saddam's real objective. He needed the money oil sales would provide to pay off the massive debt he had incurred, primarily in fighting an eight-year war with Iran. The Iraqi invasion prompted a massive international response, one Saddam seemed not to have anticipated. US diplomatic efforts rapidly forged a coalition of nations that committed military forces to liberating Kuwait.[76] It was done first by launching Desert Shield – the buildup of forces designed to protect Saudi Arabia from further Iraqi aggression – and then Desert Storm, an offensive operation designed to push Iraq out of Kuwait. That second operation made short work of Iraq's defenses and forced the invaders back over the Iraqi borders. At war's end, US troops remained stationed in Saudi Arabia, purportedly to enhance stability and ensure the protection of the kingdom from any further Iraqi incursions. US security policy had now apparently entrenched itself in the Middle East and had firmly committed itself to the goal of ensuring oil procurement for itself and its allies.

The planning for, conduct of, and aftermath of the Gulf conflict exemplified the complexities of oil politics, made the US and allied' motives even more difficult to dissect, and raised disturbing questions among critical observers. Would the US have moved so rapidly to counter Saddam Hussein if his aggression had occurred in someplace other than the world's main storehouse of oil? Would platitudes over protecting Kuwait's sovereignty been enough to motivate similar levels of military effort for someone else, located somewhere else? Indeed, even calling the Gulf War an effort to protect such cherished US values as "democracy" and/or "freedom" seemed a little rich, given that Kuwait was not particularly well known for either. It was perhaps more honest to name the conflict for what it was: a national security–motivated effort to stop Saddam Hussein from controlling yet more of the world's oil supply.

The developed nations had watched their dependency on oil imports rise and consequently began paying very close political attention to those doing the supplying. They devoted political capital to developing relationships with key oil suppliers and committed security resources to protecting the flow of oil from the

Gulf. That commitment was both real and perceptual. Not only did the US develop increased military capacities to deter, contain, and reverse key threats to oil stability, other nations also increasingly believed that the US could and would directly exert its military strength to protect oil stability.[77] Critics argued that it had become difficult to identify other US motives from this supposedly central goal, or to disentangle what interest drove what action. For Middle East oil suppliers, these questions also raised doubts and questions. Did they only matter to the West insofar as they could continue to supply the international system with oil? What would happen if and when alternative sources of oil were found, or if the world moved to another form of transport energy? Would anybody care about them then?

By century's end, the geopolitics of oil production had become powerful and obvious. Sovereign national governments now controlled oil production in the world's most prolific fields. Those governments did not always inspire confidence in their stability or friendliness. Iran had already experienced a revolution. Its neighbors worried that similar fundamentalist drives might spread to their own populations, threatening their stability and tearing apart the delicate process of economic modernization they had undertaken. Oil dependency certainly worried the oil-importing world as well: even supposedly moderate governments had proven capable and sometimes willing to disrupt oil flow should their political interest call for it. Those disruptions could cause serious economic pain in consuming countries. The resulting US response was to commit both its diplomacy and its military assets to the broad objective of preserving oil flow from the Gulf region. Ensuring stable flow was not simply part of the list of foreign policy priorities for the region: it now probably topped that list.

Reality #8: The Resiliency of the Supply System

The final reality we note in this chapter is to illustrate the resiliency of the oil market, and the oil companies themselves, in adapting to a volatile price environment. Oil nationalism and ensuing price shocks certainly generated plenty of political problems, but they also motivated a series of market responses as well. The first was a dramatic competitive overhaul in the major oil companies necessitated by the loss of their entrenched position in the Middle East. That freed resources that could be turned to other areas of exploration opportunity, areas that now were potentially profitable. The higher prices OPEC had managed to create suddenly made it economically feasible to extract oil in more difficult and expensive places, thereby diversifying global oil supply. Companies began looking for and finding new discoveries and increased their production capacities in newer, more expensive fields. Efforts to explore in Alaska, in the North Sea, and various other offshore locations began to grow. Having been largely expelled from the Middle East, oil companies began scouring the globe for new resources and began meeting significant success.

A second bright spot, at least from an oil security standpoint, was that the overall supply system had proven more resilient than many had initially feared. Fears of permanent shortage, running out, and ensuing economic chaos that populated headlines and watercooler discussions during the oil shocks of the 1970s never actually materialized. A lot of new places began sourcing oil, emboldened by the higher prices that oil now commanded. The United States, Great Britain, Norway, and others began developing their oil bounty, ranging from the Prudhoe Bay development in Alaska to North Sea exploration off the coast of Norway and Great Britain to production in the Alberta oil sands. After the tumult of the Iranian Revolution, other Gulf states also began investing more in developing their resources to provide spare capacity and to fill the gap created by less Iranian output. Finally, as the Cold War drew to a close, Russia's oil fields began contributing more to the global production scene, and those fields held enormous producing power.

The oil crisis had also tested global trading and spot markets, which had functioned reasonably well and eventually found ways to garner supply from various sources. Traders may have had to scramble to reroute oil to make up for looming shortfalls, but they were generally, if eventually, successful at doing so. Oil taken off the market due to political events in one region could increasingly be sourced from elsewhere. It was now possible to buy and sell oil from a variety of locations, and to do so increasingly on a spot market rather than a long-term fixed contract basis. Existing supplies and tanker traffic could be rerouted to make up for unexpected shortfalls at any particular node in the production system. That system began gaining a greater diversity of suppliers and more robust mechanisms for matching demand with supply.

Initially, this served OPEC's interests as well as those of the new suppliers: having a diversity of suppliers avoided excessive drain on their own fields and would lend an overall robustness to the market. But it also meant that their ability to manage global supply, and thereby keep garnering ever-inflated prices, would weaken if too many additional suppliers began entering the market. High prices turned that possibility into a reality: by 1990 successful new production sites started to once again flood the market with new oil. The world once again had an oil market in surplus, and eventual glut. The oil glut drove prices lower: they remained subdued for most of the 1990s.

Private-sector companies, in particular the majors, had to respond to persistently low prices with increasingly drastic action. They began with internal cost-cutting measures that included reducing staff, refocusing exploration strategies and geographies, and improving internal efficiencies. But these could only achieve so much. The only way to achieve the even-greater efficiencies the market demanded while also maintaining funds for exploration was to merge with other companies, thereby gaining the presumed "synergies" larger companies could garner. Investors liked the economies of scale large companies could provide, and at the end of the twentieth century, the topic of "merger mania" began populating the business literature, as scale and size were thought necessary if one wanted to be successful in a globalized world.[78] Scale economies were particularly compelling in the oil business: large companies could better attract exploration capital in an era of flat prices, thereby boosting their stock price.[79]

The merger logic compelled increasingly audacious responses, and the period 1998–2002 witnessed the mergers that created the modern supermajor oil company. First off the block was British

Petroleum, who in August 1998 targeted Chicago-based Amoco Corporation with a US$53 billion merger offer that shareholders approved. That was followed up four months later with a US$26.8 billion bid to buy Atlantic Richfield Company (ARCO), which when approved created the modern colossus of BP. Once started, merger mania gained traction and resulted in even bigger deals. In 1999 Exxon proposed to merge with the Mobil Corporation for approximately US$79 billion. That proposed merger gained shareholder support by May and federal regulatory assent by November, thereby creating the world's largest publicly traded corporation in the form of ExxonMobil. Not to be outdone, Europe too soon got in on the action. France's Total purchased Belgium's Petrofina and later merged itself with Elf, France's former state-owned oil giant.[80] The resultant company, rechristened Total, became continental Europe's primary supermajor.

The mergers kept coming. In October 2000 US-based Chevron merged with Texaco, and in November 2001, the mid-sized US companies of Conoco and Phillips merged to become ConocoPhillips. The lone holdout of the Seven Sisters, Royal Dutch Shell, was by structure a holding company that could not easily integrate a merger partner. However, it already possessed the scale to compete with the newly minted supermajors, having some 100,000 employees all by itself. Proposed mergers still had to clear regulatory hurdles and fears of overt collusion or centralization,[81] but economic realities proved compelling, and eventually all the mergers received regulatory approval. By 2002 only four of the fabled Seven Sisters oil companies were left standing,[82] and they were among the very largest companies in the world.

Fear, ambition, and financial logic drove the merger mania. Smaller (comparatively) companies worried that they would be starved for capital if investors flocked to the larger companies, who could claim to better control costs, achieve "efficiencies," and thereby boost shareholder return.[83] With OPEC continuing to exert much production influence, oil prices remaining low, and ongoing expensive exploration projects to manage, size gave the merged companies a better chance at survival. Moreover, the supermajors would be attractive partners for host governments due to their size and technical ability, and they could compete for drilling rights in new exploration areas if and when oil prices rose in the future.

Large companies claimed other advantages. Low oil prices demanded more efficient management of these multibillion-dollar investment projects, and larger companies could do that better than could smaller ones.[84] Size and integration remained key to the supermajors' success: their ability to produce and sell refined fuels, chemicals, and other types of products compensated for the lower revenue generated by the sale of oil itself. Offering a diversity of products, and reaping profits where they could, became key to surviving a prolonged downturn and gave the supermajors staying power that smaller companies did not have. The lengthy price downturn and increasingly globalized market forced a competitive reckoning, out of which emerged large, ferociously competitive companies managed by grizzled oil veterans who had proven their ability to survive.

Summary: The Enduring Political and Economic Problems of Oil

The first century and a half of its history created market and political realities that would condition the oil market as it entered the twenty-first century. Oversupply had repeatedly bedeviled the market, and supply management systems had been enacted to manage the flow of oil making it to that market. Each of those systems enjoyed a period of success, yet all had eventually been broken or seriously weakened by a combination of public criticism, government regulation, or market developments. Though it carries a tempting appealing logic, it was and is hard to create and execute supply control indefinitely.

Private companies had learned that governments could act as either friend or foe, depending on the circumstance. Producing countries could be counted on to assert their interests, and by century's end those countries had taken away from companies the strategic control over most of the world's oil and had created formidable competitors in their nationally owned companies as well.

For private companies, this power shift permanently altered how they saw the world and the strategies they would enact to survive in it. They had lost the ability to manage supply and had to adapt to a world where prices were volatile. Consequently, they became increasingly competitive beasts, relentlessly pushing for new sources of oil to replace the concessions they had lost or the fields they had drained dry. Their competitive environment, once managed and perhaps even comfortable, was now as unforgiving as any other.

Geopolitically the oil market now played a central role in how consuming and producing governments calculated their national interest. National security now depended on access to oil, turning it from just another commodity into a strategic resource. The experience of two world wars provided additional proof of oil's centrality to national security calculations. Price shocks, revolutions, and supply flow disruption in the latter half of the century caused further economic pain and security concern. They jolted consuming governments into paying much greater attention to the problem of import dependency. Cultivating diversity of supply mattered: too great a reliance on any single source of oil supply was dangerous. Finally, the need to ensure supply could pull governments into the domestic politics of oil-producing states, forcing them to make unpalatable foreign policy choices.

Supplying large volumes of excess oil both helped and hurt developing country exporters. Oil wealth provides exporters with bargaining leverage and geopolitical clout. But they too had vulnerabilities. For their oil to be of any use, they had to sell it. Many oil exporters had generally underdeveloped economies, and state treasuries therefore became almost totally reliant on the revenues oil exports generated. If prices plunged, or their market share dried up, so too would their main, and perhaps sole, source of domestic revenue. Price drops were at best destabilizing and could even be catastrophic for the political survival of those in power, who often depended on the distribution of oil revenue largesse to maintain their domestic base of support.

Finally, the oil market had proven resilient, even after all the twists and turns the twentieth century threw at it. Its production capacity was certainly capable of undershooting or overshooting the mark, and boom and bust characterized much of its history. Without effective production discipline, the appeal of potential profit brings new producers to the market that caused a supply overhang to develop. The subsequent price plunge forced private companies to do what they had to in order to survive. At the end of the twentieth century prices and supply overhangs had created some of the largest, but also the most cost-conscious, companies in the world. As the twenty-first century loomed, little could they know that within a few short years prices would start to skyrocket, bringing new and old political and market challenges. It is to those we turn next.

chapter four

The Oil Market, 2000–2014: Rising Prices and the Perils of Profit

The first two decades of the twenty-first century reflected the established challenges afflicting the oil industry, while also creating a few new ones. One challenging factor came in the arena of price volatility. Oil prices fluctuated dramatically during those twenty years. After a brief period of stagnation, prices rose steadily and then skyrocketed, flooding company balance sheets, state treasuries, and global capital markets with money. Elevated prices attracted new producers, anxious to capitalize on the revenue windfall, and motivated established producers to spend ever more money looking for oil. OPEC's ability to control production and manage supply appeared to weaken but also seemed unnecessary, as an increasingly oil-thirsty world seemed poised to consume all that could be produced and then some. Debates over peak oil reemerged: doomsayers issued warnings that the world could not meet the predicted required oil production and that economic calamity might very well follow.

Just as those warnings gained popular traction, the fracking revolution in the United States began in earnest, unlocking vast new supplies of oil. As US production grew, few paid heed to the warnings emanating out of Saudi Arabia that too much supply was starting to enter the market. Unable to engender any collective will to restrain that production, the Saudi kingdom chose in 2014 to keep their own production high, thereby augmenting global oversupply. That resulted in a massive price drop persisting through 2020, a drop that compelled industry exit among many producers and theoretically restored some semblance of market balance.

This chapter focuses on the economics driving the 2000–14 oil market bull run. During those fourteen years, prices oscillated but generally moved up, and sometimes dramatically. Upward price movements compelled correspondingly drastic reactions in companies and oil-producing countries alike. After the previously lean decade, one characterized by mergers and cost control, oil companies released their pent-up exploration effort and energy and reignited their search for new reserves, often in the world's most expensive and remote regions. Fear and investor demand cheered those efforts on, as scenarios of ever-escalating prices made even the most expensive fields economically feasible. Companies spent unprecedented sums expanding the frontiers of oil production, pushing into new countries and exploring unconventional sources of oil. National oil companies and their associated state treasuries benefited from high oil prices but fretted about whether and how much they should increase production capacity. Established producers upped their output, and important new producers entered the production game. The fracking revolution took hold in the United States: Russia, Canada, and others all increased their production, while developing-country oil multinationals, particularly from China, added to the production mix.

If the oil market is subject to episodic cycles of "Market Madness,"[1] then this period qualifies as one. It also generated questions. Why did prices move as rapidly and as dramatically, both up and eventually down, as they did? How did companies, both private and state-owned, react to these price movements? Why did the idea of peak oil and limited global supply achieve such widespread endorsement? In the wake of the 2008 financial crisis, why did oil prices recover so much faster than the rest of the economy? Why did oil producers and investors not anticipate the fall in price that occurred in 2014? Finally, what did that price fall ultimately mean for oil production, and would new producers leave the market or persist?

In addressing these puzzles, we divide those fourteen years into eras defined by discrete price movements. The years 2000–2 witnessed the continued subdued prices prevailing during the previous decade, as well as a series of economic and political shocks that damaged economic growth and kept prices low. Next, between 2002 and 2008 price levels began to rise, and rise dramatically, reaching unprecedented heights. Oil prices unsurprisingly plunged in the wake of the financial crisis of 2008 but recovered rapidly. By 2010 they measured $80/barrel, and by 2011 they once again topped $100/barrel. Prices would remain elevated until September 2014, when they were more or less cut in half by the Saudi production decision, forcing many companies back into survival mode. This chapter focuses on understanding what the market did and what it meant for the companies and countries doing the producing. Understanding the oil market's price movements generates insights into the political puzzles that market also generated. Tackling those is the task of chapter five.

What Did Oil Prices Do?

We begin this section with a visual of what oil prices did in the period 2000–14. The most common global measures for oil prices are Brent Crude and West Texas Intermediate (WTI), and we will use those benchmarks in our discussion of oil prices. Figure 3 shows what West Texas oil prices looked like during that fourteen-year stretch.

Even a cursory glance at that chart reveals some obvious things about oil prices. First, the new century began much as the old one had ended. The world continued to witness low levels of overall economic growth.[2] Oil market observers thought their strong global reserve production capacity, combined with low growth, meant the market was likely in for a lengthy period of supply glut.[3] OPEC had significant excess supply capacities, and Russia continued investing more in oil and gas production to buoy its shaky economy. Indeed, the end of the Cold War had not been kind to Russia and had placed it onto a very bumpy, prolonged, and incomplete transition to a capitalist economy. By 2000 selling oil and gas onto foreign markets was the country's primary if not only source of generating foreign exchange earnings.[4] Russian oil production rose from the 6 mbd it had produced in the early 1990s to 8 mbd by 2000, and it continued to make investments to allow it to produce even more. Consequently, the depressed price environment and stagnant overall demand facing oil producers seemed likely to persist.

Figure 3. Monthly Oil Prices, USD, February 2000–June 2014 (West Texas Intermediate)

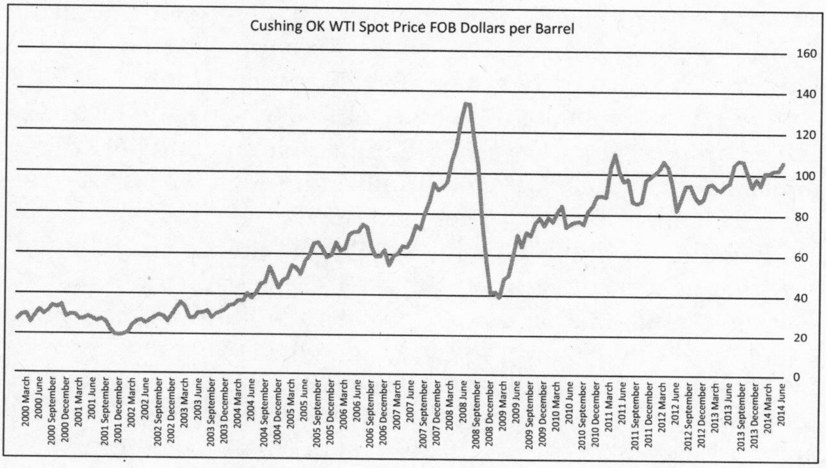

Source: US Energy Information Administration.

Oil prices therefore remained subdued: indeed, they even initially declined. In January 2000 WTI commanded $28 on the spot market, and then prices fell even further, bottoming out to a low of $21/barrel by January 2002. Then oil prices began to rise, slowly at first, then unmistakably, then rapidly. The seven-year period between 2002 and 2008 witnessed a sustained and consistent price rise that eventually looked more asymptotic than linear. They reached $33/barrel by January 2004, $63 by January 2006, and by January 2008 spot oil prices closed in on the mythical $100/barrel. They soon cracked, then shattered, that barrier: as the ascent continued during the spring and summer, oil reached a height of $135 a barrel.

The period 2008–10 witnessed a rapid plunge, but then a strong recovery, of oil prices. The financial crisis of 2008 not surprisingly caused the price plunge: the failure of the investment bank Bear Stearns created panic in financial markets not seen since the Great Depression. That fear rapidly infected the rest of the US economy and spread quickly around the world. Only massive and coordinated government intervention and the extraordinary financial measures provided by central banks and finance ministries prevented the economic skid from turning into a catastrophe.[5] The crisis put tremendous stress on the international economy: it all but destroyed global growth, which collectively dipped into negative territory for much of 2008 and 2009. Not surprisingly, oil prices suffered significantly: by December 31, 2008, they had plunged to $40 a barrel, a fall of almost $100 from their summer peak. They remained subdued as the crisis rumbled through the global economy: by January 2009 oil prices has settled at $46/barrel.

They did not stay subdued long. Prices stabilized in 2009, and then began a recovery that outpaced the rest of the economy. During the first quarter of 2009 oil prices of both WTI and Brent Crude vacillated between $35 and $50 dollars per barrel. But then they began an erratic but relentless upward climb throughout the remainder of the year. By late December 2009 both measures were approaching $80 per barrel. In 2010 oil prices swung between $60 and $90 per barrel but were building momentum toward the latter by year's end. By early 2011 prices for both crude benchmarks had recovered to their pre-crisis average levels, again regularly topping $100 a barrel in daily spot trading.[6] They would more or less stay there until the fall of 2014, when looming oversupply created the conditions for the price collapse chronicled later.

During each of these periods, there were specific reasons why the oil market moved as it did. We trace them and draw out implications for what they meant for producers and consumers. We detail how oil producers reacted to the price gyrations, what decisions they made on exploration expenditure, and how they, like everyone else, tried to discern what was really going on in the increasingly roller-coaster ride of the oil market.

2000–2008: Price Stagnation and Then Rising

At the beginning of the century the global economy continued performing sluggishly and oil prices remained subdued. Parts of that economy continued to stagger in the aftermath of the East Asian financial crisis that had ripped through the global economy in 1997 and whose aftershocks could still be felt years later. In the United States, the strong growth experienced during the early years of the "roaring" 1990s[7] – growth fueled in part by cheap oil – slowed, and then came to a screeching halt due to a series of damaging economic shocks. The stock market took a body blow via the bursting of the "tech bubble," in which the valuations of Internet-based companies had proven wildly inflated, motivating investors to flee equity markets generally. A second shock came via a series of accounting scandals and corporate bankruptcies that obliterated what had been some of the world's largest companies. Prominent corporate titans, such as Enron, Worldcom, and Tyco, collapsed as investigators uncovered massive and long-standing financial and accounting frauds buried deep within their financial statements. Such revelations shook corporate confidence and compounded investor timidity.[8]

A third shock turned the gloom already infecting an anemic US and global economy into a practical panic: the terrorist attacks of September 11, 2001. Those attacks generated fear and confusion that stunned governments and societies and further depressed global economic outlook. The attack rocked the very foundations of the international economic and security system and motivated a massive political, military, and economic response. Militarily, the US implemented a broad counterterrorism strategy that entailed the launching of war in Afghanistan and would eventually include an invasion of Iraq.[9] Economically, the attack jolted the US financial and economic system and left many to wonder if the shock to consumer confidence would knock the US economy into a prolonged recession. The economic response therefore consequently mirrored the power of the military one. Policymakers took measures designed to reinject confidence into their skittish domestic economies, ranging from cutting interest rates, instituting tax cuts, injecting liquidity into financial markets, and creating other fiscal incentives designed to reignite and maintain economic confidence.[10]

The oil industry reflected the cumulative effects of weak economic performance and terrorist shock. Oil prices remained subdued and the market well supplied. For suppliers, these were difficult times. As already noted, cash-strapped Russia continued to increase its production capacity and sold whatever it could. Other suppliers, both within and outside OPEC, proved equally anxious to generate cash and strove to maintain their market share. Private companies, faced with what looked like plentiful supply and low prices, continued their cost-cutting measures, consolidated their mergers,[11] and scraped additional savings where they could. The benefits of size had initially helped: larger companies could better manage the multibillion-dollar investment projects committed for the next decade,[12] and size would allow them to better manage exploration risk with fewer people. Yet by 2002 the logic of "synergy" initially motivating the mergers had begun to lose its luster. The supermajors had undergone major staffing reductions, had refocused their core strategies toward proven profitable projects, and consolidated operations. Yet without higher prices there were limits to what more even they could do. Economic growth seemed poised to remain weak for a long time: financial pressures on oil companies therefore grew.

Little did or could they know that the price tide was about to turn. An oil company's operating environment might not be getting any easier, but their revenue picture was going to. Oil producers were about to reap the benefits of a sustained price rise that would swell their balance sheets and fill their state treasuries and would last for a surprisingly long time. The period 2002–8 witnessed one of the strongest sustained price rises in oil market history. Oil rose from a price in the mid-$20s per barrel, reached well over $100/barrel, and miraculously stayed there for a good long while. Moreover, the dynamics of this price rise seemed and felt different from those incurred in previous eras. This rise was not due to a "shock" akin to what had happened in the 1970s, where prices had jumped in response primarily to discrete political events. This one appeared powered by long-term economic trends that were not going to go away and that governments had little power or willingness to stop.

Generalized economic recovery helped launch the price rise. After the grim period of stagnation and shock noted earlier, global growth once again began picking up, and remained strong for six years, until the onset of the financial crisis in 2008. Economic figures continued to impress: annualized global growth between 2002 and 2007 varied between 2.4 per cent and 5.4 per cent.[13] Several factors fueled that growth: two key propellants were the ongoing and accelerating process of globalization, one now amplified by the stimulus measures governments provided in the post-9/11 environment. Manufacturing continued migrating to low-cost offshore locations, boosting company productivity and lowering consumer prices, while companies created intricate cross-border value chains that further integrated production activity across borders. Growing electronic connectivity now allowed product design and development to proceed across these dispersed production sites, further boosting efficiency and lowering costs of production.[14] Trade agreements liberalized international markets, lowered prices, and raised demand for consumables of all kinds. Moreover, the post-9/11 economic measures reignited a surprisingly resilient consumer confidence in the United States.[15] Housing construction began to boom, as did the stock market, initiating the investment wave and subsequent bubble that would later prove so disastrous in 2008. Taken together, growth recovered and then accelerated far beyond what post-9/11 projections thought possible, let alone realistic.

Oil prices and demand received additional boosts from the economic revolution going on in developing markets. The process of globalization, outsourcing, and the migration of manufacturing to offshore locations created an emerging market economic boom. China led the way. It gained manufacturing jobs measured annually in the hundreds of thousands and received enough foreign and direct investment to record the annualized powerful growth levels that eventually lifted hundreds of millions of people out of abject poverty. They were not alone. India benefited enormously from the global technology boom in software development and associated services, where its deep reservoir of engineering and programming talent continued to attract investment dollars.

The Russian and Brazilian economies also gained strength as prices rose, as both were significant oil and commodity producers. Their collective growing strength gained attention and generated a label that began animating broad economic discourse: BRIC (Brazil, Russia, India, and China), a term lumping their collective

economic weight into an easy-to-remember acronym.[16] The implication seemed clear: developing economies with large populations
that generated powerful growth rates would eventually wield
enormous consumptive and productive power that would drive oil
demand for decades to come. Their ascent provided a clear beacon
on the direction the global economy, and oil demand, would take.

To be sure, much of the BRIC's collective economic power
remained in the realm of the potential, rather than actual. In 2002
US GDP measured $10.5 trillion, while the collective GDP of the
BRIC countries measured $2.7 trillion, with China alone account-
ing for half of that.[17] Put visually, in 2002 the combined size of the
Russian, Indian, and Brazilian economies measured one-tenth
that of the US. But that reality did not dull the allure and imagery
emerging markets commanded. Rather than focusing on actual
size, pundits pointed to the robust and repeated annual growth
rates as the more telling indicator. Strong growth rates that, in
the case of China and India at least, consistently measured in the
double digits, would act as a form of compound interest, rapidly
increasing their economic size.[18] Simply extending those growth
rates into the future created an easy visual of an ever-expanding
economic colossus whose gravitational pull would inevitably shift
power from developed markets and implant it in emerging ones.[19]
The case seemed obvious and more or less ironclad.

To do all that growing and consuming, developing markets were
going to need raw materials and energy of all kinds, and they were
going to have to import vast quantities of those things they could not
source domestically. That meant a lot for the oil market. Although
Russia and Brazil had domestic oil resources, China and India did
not, and their expected growth pointed ominously to heavy new
demand. Their consumption would soon far outpace what their
domestic fields could produce, setting the stage for massive new
import requirement increases, confirmed by both private-sector
and public forecasters.[20] Optimism bordering on giddiness (at least
for oil producers) began surrounding those demand projections.
The IEA noted that, though the world consumed 76 million barrels
per day (mbd) in 2000, it would require 86 mbd by 2007, 98.5 mbd
by 2015, and by 2030 would potentially need 116.3 mbd.[21]

Further IEA projections noted that it was not going to be advanced economies doing that demanding. They forecasted that between 2005 and 2030, annual growth in European OECD energy demand would be a paltry 0.5 per cent. Energy growth in Canada and the US would average about 1 per cent per year, while some subsets of OECD countries, primarily in Western Europe and Scandinavia, would be below even that. Taken together, they did not inspire much optimism on the demand side. By contrast, China's expected energy demand growth measured 3.2 per cent per annum: growth in India would be 3.6 per cent, and as both economies grew, their need for new energy would compound as far as the eye could see, as those growth percentages would be built on an ever-larger economic base.[22] According to accepted forecasts, total global primary energy needs would grow by 55 per cent by 2030, and emerging markets would collectively contribute to 75 per cent of that overall energy increase,[23] dwarfing the energy reductions achieved elsewhere. By 2030, and perhaps even earlier, China would become the world's largest consumer of imported oil.[24] Private-sector forecasts echoed the IEA: they too issued outlooks similarly portraying energy's future as lying in developing markets.[25] Moreover, the optimism went beyond oil: emerging markets would also need coal, natural gas, hydroelectric power, renewables, and really any other energy source they could find. The implications for the oil market were immense and seemingly obvious, and the projections showed it. The largest emerging market economies were becoming import-dependent beasts that were the center of demand growth action.

That reality carried with it a tinge of foreboding as well as excitement. Oil, and fossil fuel demand generally, would increase dramatically over the next several decades, and it was not clear where all that new energy was going to come from. Those likely demands certainly far exceeded what established energy infrastructure could supply. The oil supply system alone would by 2030 need to deliver close to 50 mbd more oil than it did in 2000. It was not clear how, or even if, it could do that. Capital spending by large companies had been restrained during the low-price 1990s, and their projected increased levels of spending were far below what would be needed to build the new infrastructure required. In the early 2000s OPEC nations were often cutting back their investment efforts, and private companies had also been keeping a tight rein on investment. Private worry that projected spending would not be enough eventually became very public fretting. As early as 2003 the IEA began issuing warnings about the potential for significant shortage in the oil markets that would appear soon. Oil producers were not investing enough to provide what was going to be needed, which was estimated to be a staggering US$3 trillion.[26]

Economic growth, emerging market demand, and lack of capital spending proved a combustible combination. Price rise began reflecting not only supply and demand dynamics but also anxieties over potential future shortages and inevitable scrambles to procure what was going to be required. Historical experience had shown how even momentary shortage could turn pent-up anxiety into outright fear and panic. What would happen when shortages appeared structural and by implication unfixable? Moreover, fear of supply shortage came home in the form of a particularly intense supply "crunch" in 2002–3, when observers could claim that supply shortages were real because, at least at that particular moment, they were. Oil demand had begun to surge so strongly that the comfortable 10 per cent cushion between available supply and required demand that had existed in 2000 had by 2003 dropped to 2 per cent, a far more worrisome level.[27] Moreover, suppliers did not appear to be responding with the urgency forecasters had hoped, and even when they did increase investment spending, any additional supply generated might take years of field development work before emerging new supplies came onstream. The oil market might be tight for a while. If demand projections proved correct, the tightness might be permanent.

The Return of Peak Oil

When faced with an increasing supply crunch, fears of running out returned. Not everyone believed enough oil could be brought to market to satisfy demand, even if massive increases in investment materialized. Several often-repeated reasons seemed to justify this outlook: known production fields could not supply enough, newly discovered fields were not big enough, expected demand was too large, additional exploration efforts too late, and there was simply not enough oil left[28] to fill the gaping hole new demand had blasted in the global supply picture. A more perfect stage could not have been set for a return of the theory of "peak oil." As price rises continued, ever more analysts proffered what looked like believable evidence that oil was running out.

Books and articles started emerging warning about ever scarcer and ever more expensive oil. One detailed analysis of the global production capacities of Asia, Europe, and South America argued that their fields were mature and were only going to decline in output, no matter how much investment capital they received. If they declined as predicted, they would subsequently inflict a very heavy strain on the world's remaining producers, particularly those from the Middle East.[29] That was also worrisome because some believed the Middle East producers themselves were hitting the wall of the maximum they could produce. OPEC's apparent reluctance to increase production reflected as much a matter of limited capacity as it did any reluctance to turn on the taps. Anomalies in their reserve reporting had led some to question the official reserve figures listed by these member states,[30] and that suspicion extended even to Saudi Arabia, the fabled "swing producer" the world relied upon to keep the oil market in balance. One analyst argued that "Twilight" was coming to the Saudi Arabian oil fields and that the country contained far less oil than what Saudi officials had publicly portrayed.[31] This might indicate less a wariness about overproduction and more a structural inability to increase production significantly at all. Some suspected both: in terms of capacity, few OPEC countries had invested significantly in new production and refining capacity since the mid-1980s, when low oil prices had prevailed.[32] It now became plausible to question how big its reserves were and whether they could or would continue tapping those resources to enhance supply and market stability.[33]

If one accepted the peak-oil premise, it was possible, even easy, to construct scenarios showing the dire impact oil shortages were going to have on the global economy. Energy would become progressively costly and would consume gargantuan portions of disposable income, leaving less money for anything else. High oil prices would drive inflation up[34] and, as prices soared, so too would panic about procuring new supply. This might even drive desperate countries to take drastic actions to secure supplies, up to and including engaging in resource wars.[35]

Even less-alarmist portrayals were still pretty drastic: as carbon became scarce and expensive, investments in alternative energy would dominate government budgets to the exclusion of all else, and energy desperation would drive those same governments to issue draconian measures curbing the energy waste endemic in consumer lifestyles. Globalization would stop, as manufacturers repatriated production from developing markets because increased energy costs destroyed whatever cost advantage low-cost labor markets had.[36] Geopolitically, oil producers had the developed world, in particular the United States, literally "over a barrel" in terms of oil dependence.[37] Depleting existing fields, a supply crunch, limited discoveries of new fields ... all of this made embracing peak oil not only plausible but intellectually difficult to resist. None of it was particularly appealing.

A final propellant of the oil price rise came from financial markets, which added a financial steroid to the anticipated looming supply shortage. Financial markets compounded the supply and demand realities witnessed in the physical markets because they operate according to a combination of market fundamentals and "animal spirits."[38] When those spirits are quiet, physical markets and regular trading practices dominate price movements, and the tension between supply and demand governs price outcomes. Prices fluctuate, but the amplitude of price swings remain moderate and should not exceed predictable bounds. However, when spirits are animated, investor rationality plays less of a role, and the market produces extreme outcomes. Investors have repeatedly proven capable of believing that an asset is worth far more, or less, than what market fundamentals indicated. Global finance is therefore subject to asset "bubbles" – a vastly inflated price for the asset, predicated on perceived rather than actual value – in everything from gold to tulips.[39] Investor sentiment, rather than market fundamentals, can influence the direction prices of any commodity will take and the speed with which they will take them.

The financial markets matter a lot to the oil industry. First, they provide the capital to fuel exploration expenditure, and that capital always looks for positive return better than whatever alternative investment outlet that capital may have. If capital providers and general investors are convinced prices will go up and that current capital spending is inadequate, they will likely make more of it available to oil explorers. Second, financial markets are also charged with absorbing the growing oil revenues oil exporters enjoy. The petrodollars oil producers acquire have to go somewhere, and oil exporters consistently seek investment environments that featured both a return on, and return of, their capital. The US financial markets usually offer the best combination of both. Consequently, as prices rose, petrodollar investments into the US stock and bond markets rose along with them, contributing to one of the longest bull market stock runs in financial history.[40]

The final, and perhaps most powerful, mechanism by which financial markets influenced sharply rising oil prices came via financial speculation. The real tightness in global oil supplies, combined with imagined public fears of "peak oil," drew investors' attention and the oceans of investment money that came with it. The investment pitch resonated perfectly: a required commodity, in short supply, with demand ever increasing implied that investments tied to oil prices had nowhere to go but up. That belief meant that storehouses of financial capital, ranging from large pension and endowment funds to SWFs, all wanted in on the action, trying to find ways to capitalize on rising oil prices.

This was not money used for the commercial buying and selling of oil, nor was it investment capital directed at building extraction infrastructure. It was instead investor demand, looking to capitalize on increasing oil prices to generate portfolio returns. The response by the investment community was to begin employing in the oil market the same type of securitization processes that created the bevy of financial derivative products that were then also infecting the housing market. Such products "derived" their value from the price of oil and on the direction and magnitude that oil price movements were expected to make. As long as prices stayed high, and there was a collective presumption they would, investment houses could count on customers gobbling those financial products up as fast as they could be turned out.

The predictable result was a rapid influx of massive amounts of investor money into financial products somehow tied to oil. Barrels of oil began being traded literally dozens of times before they reached any real end user – a relentless trading and investing activity that helped drive up price. Each link in that trading chain believed they could sell their barrels for more than they paid for them. The accelerant of investor sentiment added to the perception the fundamentals of supply and demand had, and the two combined to launch oil prices into the stratosphere. During the price run-up, oil prices regularly jumped in multi-dollar increments, and sometimes tens of dollars, sometimes over the course of a single trading day. They skyrocketed right through the summer of 2008: peaking at an intraday high of $147.27/barrel on July 11. As oil price continued that meteoric rise, even seasoned market watchers became increasingly incredulous and had difficulty determining what portion of price reflected market reality and what portion reflected financial market "froth."[41]

Rising oil prices revealed the interdependence between the oil business and financial markets. Exporters needed avenues to invest their excess cash and proved willing to reinvest their oil profits back into US-denominated financial instruments, ranging from Treasury bills to broader stock market purchases.[42] This influx of investment kept stock prices high and helped amplify the pre-financial crisis euphoria then gripping the US economy in general. Stockholders felt wealthier every day and consequently spent and invested even more,[43] thereby accentuating an already intense consumer boom. Both consumers and the US government appeared unworried about mounting levels of debt, and investors appeared willing to buy unlimited amounts of US government securities even when they offered low yields. This made further US deficits easier to finance and gave the US government the fiscal flexibility necessary to increase expenditures and decrease taxes at the same time. Not surprisingly, that combination increased the fiscal deficit and accumulated debt even more.[44]

The financial system came under intense scrutiny during and after the 2008 crisis: its lessons are still debated today.[45] The run up in oil prices, and the financial markets' contribution to it, got its share of attention as well. One prominent critic of the role financial markets played in artificially inflating oil prices was Michael Masters, an investment banker specializing in the oil market and in monitoring the financial products derived from it. His Master's thesis argued that speculators, not demand, was responsible for the massive jumps in oil prices the market witnessed: only investor demand could explain rising prices in well-supplied markets even where demand was actually falling. His argument that speculation had pushed prices far above what the fundamentals warranted led some legislators to call for increased controls on speculative behavior both in oil and in financial products generally.

Of course, the devil in analyzing speculation and financial markets lies in the details: it is difficult to delineate the effects of financial versus physical markets in any particular commodity. Some analysts disagreed with the Masters' thesis. They argued speculation did not play the outsized role Masters believed it did. Moreover, some argued, even in the wake of the financial crisis, that speculation controls might do more harm than good. Speculation disciplined the market and provided necessary liquidity. Curbing it would require massive government intervention that would rob the market of its key attribute: the adaptability and flexibility to meet new financing needs across all industries.[46] Gains in price stability were not worth sacrificing the flexibility and robustness that speculation provided.[47] That debate would continue and remains a perennial one afflicting Wall Street to this day.

Even with this controversy, it still seems reasonable to argue that more than just the fundamentals of supply and demand propelled the historic price rise. Expectation, perception, belief, and popular psychology also mattered. Emerging market demand growth was thought practically limitless, the earth's available supply by definition limited. Shortage meant that oil prices should go only in one direction. That easily and convincingly justified narration at the very least helped drive an explosion of investor sentiment and financial market activity.

Whatever oil price tremors afflicting the oil market from supply constraint could easily become full-blown earthquakes by the collective weight of millions of investors whose portfolios gyrated along with every price rise and fall. Financial markets helped intensify the "perfect storm" of perceived shortage, peak oil, and endless future demand, even if their role in causing it remains debatable. Narratives and beliefs matter, as well as economic fundamentals.

The Oil Industry and the Financial Crisis

The industry, along with the global economy in general, was brought back to earth by the financial crisis of 2008. The oil industry proved no more immune from the shock of that crisis than was any other industry. The crisis inflicted enormous economic dislocation and distress across all aspects of the international economy. Financial markets plunged, in some cases by more than half. Growth in developed markets virtually stopped and then crept into contraction territory, and they would remain anemic for much of the next half decade.

Not surprisingly, oil prices dropped significantly during the financial crisis, as did every other economic indicator. Prices that had shot upwards during the first eight months of 2008 began an equally rapid descent throughout the remainder of the year. By December 31, 2008, oil prices had fallen by almost $100 a barrel from their summer peaks: they now measured around $40 a barrel. They continued to remain subdued as the crisis rumbled its way through the global economy throughout the next year. By January 2009 oil prices hovered at $46/barrel,[48] and during the first quarter of 2009 oil prices of both WTI and Brent Crude continued to vacillate between $35 and $50 dollars per barrel.

Oil prices did not remain subdued for long. Instead they then began an erratic but unmistakable climb back up throughout the remainder of 2009. By late December 2009 both WTI and Brent Crude were once again approaching $80 per barrel. In 2010 prices still showed a lot of volatility, swinging between $60 and $90 per barrel, and began approaching the latter amount by year's end. By

2011 prices for both had almost fully recovered to their pre-crisis levels, each again regularly commanding $100/barrel in daily spot trading,[49] and they continued to hover near $100/barrel up until the fall of 2014. Figure 4 show what oil prices in the three years during and after the crisis looked like.

The graph reveals some puzzles. First, why did oil prices recover more quickly than the rest of the global economy? There are several potential answers. First, OPEC proved capable, at least in the short term, of enforcing a supply cut amongst its members, an impressive feat given the budgetary hit they had all taken when oil prices fell. Saudi Arabia initially shouldered the bulk of that production cut: OPEC production fell by 3.6 mbd between September 2008 and January 2009, and Saudi output alone fell by 1.3 mbd during that period, which comprised 37 per cent of the OPEC cut.[50] Though this increased Saudi spare production capacity, it did serve to remove some production and thereby helped stabilize price. Not surprisingly, the decision to withdraw supply from the market to boost price angered Western consumers still reeling from the economic

Figure 4. Oil Price, West Texas Intermediate, $USD/Barrel

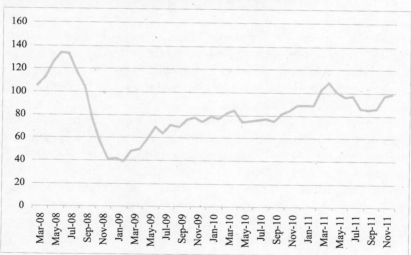

Source: US Energy Information Administration.

contraction the financial crisis had inflicted on them personally. Paying more for carbon fuels due to an OPEC-induced production cut in the middle of a deep recession rubbed consumers the wrong way. OPEC countered by arguing that, without higher prices, they could not justify making additional capital investments in new production necessary to meet the very-real longer-term demand that had so occupied the pre-crisis oil psyche.

Political risk also helped prices climb back up quickly. Political events removed some producers from the market and injected a significant "fear premium" into the price that a barrel of oil commanded in others. One key event was the launching of the Arab Spring, which after beginning in Tunisia rapidly spread elsewhere. In 2011 open revolution in Libya against its tyrannical leader Muammar Gaddafi also inspired a broader political movement spreading to other countries in the region. Revolution in Libya alone removed 1 mbd of production from that market, not a particularly large figure, but concerns of revolution spreading to other oil-producing nations added a further risk premium to oil markets generally. Other OPEC nations suffered from additional production constraints. Iran continued to operate under economic sanctions imposed by Western powers wary of the country's suspected pursuit of a nuclear weapons program. Those sanctions inhibited the capital investment needed to rebuild its oil-production capacity. Iraqi production output also remained constrained, as it continued to recover from the US-led 2003 invasion and ensuing internal civil conflict. Political events constrained some supply and added general overall risk to the market.

A third reason why oil prices recovered quickly reflected the general trends noted earlier, trends that had not really gone away despite the preoccupation with the financial crisis. A structural tightness remained in global oil supply: additional production and investment still lagged behind what the global economy was likely going to need over the long term. While growth in demand had slowed during the crisis, it did eventually begin to climb back, as economic recovery, particularly in emerging markets, took hold. Moreover, as oil prices advanced, fears of shortage returned, as did concern that high oil prices would stall an incipient economic recovery. Many of the market fundamentals that had led to previous increases in price remained.

Consuming governments began expressing worries that rapidly rising oil prices were outpacing, and might eventually stall, general economic recovery. So concerned were they that, in response to further OPEC cutbacks, the IEA authorized its member countries to release stocks from their collective strategic petroleum reserves (SPRs) in June 2011. US policymakers argued that high oil prices were holding back the rest of its economy. Releasing stocks from the US's SPR could affect short-term supply dramatically and quickly.[51] US pressure to release stocks proved difficult for the other members of the IEA to resist. In June 2011 the organization capitulated, authorizing the release of 60 million barrels of combined reserves: less than half of the IEA's current members contributed releases. Many members thought the market was, or was about to be, well supplied[52] and that these storehouses of oil were built explicitly for release in times of emergency supply disruption or need, which was not the case in the summer of 2011. Accessing them to combat rising prices seemed more a measure of disguised economic stimulus than it was any response to a supply emergency.[53]

Taken together, these factors created momentum that increased oil prices. The longer uncertainty and political risk fears percolated and the more production discipline OPEC could exert, the longer high prices would likely persist. Indeed, the years 2010–14 could be characterized as a "sweet spot" for oil producers: fear and supply shortage kept prices elevated, and OPEC proved able to exert enough supply control to buoy price. Of course, such a pleasant state of affairs for the producers could not last forever: by 2014, suppliers had once again responded, though not in the way many had predicted.

How Did Different Types of Producers Respond to Price Movements?

The oil market in the early 2000s faced a pressing problem: the world needed more oil, a lot of it, and informed people had expressed deep concern that the supply system could provide enough. That fear was shared by more than just pundits or opportunistic fly-by-night analysts. In 2008 the International Energy Agency also got in on the act. It appeared worried enough to write that, even with massive increases in investment spending, "the gap between what is being built and what will be needed to keep pace with demand is nonetheless set to widen sharply,"[54] and that "it was by no means certain that all of the necessary additional capacity will be forthcoming."[55] Where was the needed new oil going to come from?

Steve Yetiv has provided an answer on how oil markets would respond, one that characterizes the oil market as one featuring "complex stability."[56] Put simply, that means it has a lot of moving parts, with many different producers. Some producers are (loosely) coordinated, particularly in the OPEC cartel. Some are big and ponderous, reacting to market movements with all the nimbleness of an aircraft carrier. Other producers are smaller, more freewheeling, and look to capitalize on upward prices while the getting is good. This makes the market appear chaotic and sometimes generates head-scratching results. However, that diverse production gene pool actually generates a surprising amount of resiliency. Both state-owned and private oil producers decide independently on how they will react to the signals the oil market sends, and they do not all react to price movements the same way. They have different logics in terms of how, and how much, they can and will increase production. This section tracks what the major producers of oil – the large NOC and IOC companies – did in responding to price movements and the looming fears of "peak oil" and supply shortage.

A period of high prices, one would think, should solve the problem of supply shortage pretty quickly, as ever more investors and producers are drawn into producing a commodity that provides a very high financial return. The incentive to increase production seems powerful when prices rise, and the reasons for doing so obvious. Even if the problem of peak oil is a bit overstated, there still was practically unlimited demand that would consume all the oil produced. All companies have to do is increase production and watch their revenues rise.

Yet, strangely enough, that is not what either the OPEC nations or the big supermajors did. Some did increase production, but nowhere near as fast or as much as market dictates seemed to warrant, or what they seemed capable of doing. For others, oil production remained flat, or even declined, despite the high prices. Oil company executives, both in NOCs and IOCs, proved cautious about embracing those claims, even when the oil price boom was well underway. That skepticism was born of long and hard experience demanding that certain questions be asked first. How long would the price rise last? Was the giddiness around emerging market demand justified? How much did it mark a real shift in long-term demand and supply fundamentals, or did it just reflect a temporary "crunch" between rising demand and available supply? How much should be spent now to increase production versus conserving resources for a time when prices might fall, or perhaps even be sold for a higher price later? Even in an era of high prices and escalating demand, deciding what to do was no simple matter.

How companies responded to a period of price rise depended on the company's ownership expectations. The politics of oil production inevitably intervened. A good place to start is the OPEC cartel, whose member governments owned the NOCs having the most spare production capacity, the lowest production costs, and who still collectively held an overwhelming portion of the world's known and easy-to-access oil supplies.[57] As the decade began, the cartel's production remained consistent but subdued. Its members feared that the persistently low prices of the 1990s might continue for an extended period, which certainly curbed enthusiasm for expanding output. The market then seemed like it would remain well supplied: the worry was more about maintaining an established and reliable price floor, a worry that consumed more OPEC attention than did any desire to ramp up production. Having lived through a decade of low prices and constrained revenues: they were wary of taking on additional investment risk.

When prices did began rising, OPEC's initial response continued reflecting caution, for several reasons. First, they wished to gauge how permanent price rises might be, and how real long-term demand projections would prove. After all, talk of sustained price rises and of "running out" had animated oil discussions before: OPEC's members remembered earlier episodes where over-investment predicated on assumption of ever-rising prices, created oversupply, a buyer's market, and consequently ushered in prolonged periods of low prices.[58] Second, OPEC was also concerned that if it decided to increase investment and output, it would be giving as sure a signal as could be given that others should also follow suit. That would make fears of global oversupply more likely, as their investment would act as a signal that drew in a host of additional producers hoping to cash in. Ironically, higher prices may even have given OPEC nations a reverse incentive that would motivate them to constrain, rather than increase, production. Prices creeping toward $100/barrel, combined with low production costs, meant that they were literally swimming in cash: OPEC oil export revenues doubled between 2002 and 2007, reaching a record high of $732 billion.[59] That was far more than they could absorb or salt away in an SWF, and some of the major OPEC producers, including Saudi Arabia and the United Arab Emirates, thought it better to conserve production for future generations, rather than increasing extraction now. Of course, not everyone agreed, and differences of production opinion within OPEC remained powerful. Both Iran and Iraq remained debt ridden, and Iran was subject to increasingly stringent economic sanctions. Political and investment barriers meant neither could rapidly nor easily increase production: they wanted to maximize the revenue they obtained right now.

The bulk of OPEC production increases, if it was to come at all, was going to come from Saudi Arabia. Other OPEC members could not easily increase production to meet anticipated demand: they suffered from production bottlenecks, had smaller recoverable fields, or suffered from significant political risk inhibiting investment. Saudi Arabia by implication now lay at the confluence of contradictory internal and external pressures. If price crept too high, it would compel new production globally, thereby eroding OPEC's ability to manage the market. Yet some cartel members wanted, perhaps even needed, as high a price as possible and would likely break any negotiated production quota in the interest of generating more fiscal revenues.

In response Saudi Arabia chose a moderate course that balanced these contending forces. It reiterated the importance of price stability while also beginning to cautiously augment its production capacity. In 2006, for example, the kingdom announced a major capital investment program designed to raise daily production capacity by over 1 million barrels, while also preserving the country's spare production capacity.[60] Yet that new investment would take time to bear fruit. Meanwhile, Saudi production actually *decreased* between 2005 and 2007: in 2005 the kingdom produced an average of 10.9 mbd, in 2006 it produced 10.6 mbd, and in 2007 10.2 mbd.[61] Its production rose once again in 2008 to 10.8 mbd, then dropped to 9.7 mbd in 2009 and 9.8 mbd in 2010 as it cut production to buoy price levels during the financial crisis. Only in 2011 did that production rise again, hovering between 11 mbd and 11.5 mbd between 2011 and 2014.[62]

The reaction over the price rise reaffirmed Saudi leadership over OPEC, due to its large reserve and production capacity and comparative political stability. It acknowledged a need to increase supply but kept tight control over its own production. It used that leadership position to reaffirm and publicly state price targets as a means of guiding external observers about what it would likely do. What therefore constituted a targeted "fair" price became a matter of intense OPEC internal debate, as did the mechanisms for achieving it. Saudi Arabia proffered a price level of $70–$75 dollars as being such a price. Other members of OPEC were more desperate to maintain cash inflow levels. Many had built fiscal programs based on price levels that were much higher than that. Indeed, some OPEC countries required well over $100/barrel to meet their fiscal breakeven requirements.[63] Consequently, their incentive to increase production remained powerful as they lacked comparable fiscal reserves that Saudi Arabia enjoyed.

The divisions within OPEC nations were revealed in their collective response to the financial crisis. It seemed clear that the best way to stop prices from falling even further was to cut production levels. Yet who was going to do the cutting? OPEC meetings in the spring of 2009 were brief and acrimonious, particularly toward those countries wishing to produce at or even over their quotas,

which had already been parsed below their 2007 levels.[64] Most of
the cutting burden was therefore borne by Saudi Arabia: between
June 2008 and December 2009 Saudi Arabia reduced its oil output by over 2 mbd. Saudi Aramco also began contracting its previously announced capital expenditures, which declined by 15 per
cent during the years of the financial crisis. Taken together, this
brought some semblance of balance back to the market while also
reinforcing additional OPEC spare capacity, which in January 2009
measured 4.87 mbd.[65]

Post–financial crisis, OPEC countries continued to reveal divergent preferences. Some chose to increase investment and capacity. Between 2009 and 2010, Middle Eastern and African NOCs
collectively increased capital exploration expenditures by 15 per
cent, from US$55.2 billion to US$63.5 billion.[66] The NOCs ADNOC,
Kuwait Oil Co., Sonongol, and Sonatrach – owned by the governments of Abu Dhabi, Kuwait, Angola, and Algeria, respectively
– all increased their expenditures significantly.[67] Yet these were
comparatively small production areas: Kuwait added about half a
million barrels of new oil to global supply between 2009 and 2014,
Angola's production remained more or less flat during that period
at 1.7 mbd. Algerian production actually decreased from 1.7 mbd
in 2009 to 1.5 mbd in 2015. Iraq production went up less than a
million barrels, going from 2.4 mbd to 3.2 mbd between 2009 and
2015.[68] These were hardly the game-changing, peak oil–alleviating,
now-you-can-relax kinds of increases the global market was hoping to get.

The era of high prices, punctuated by the financial crisis, revealed
clear discrepancies between what OPEC said it could do and what
it actually could do. Its capacity to restrain its members' production was limited: the incentive to cheat may be powerful, and the
capacity to monitor or enforce limits is not one of OPEC's strong
suits. As prices began their recovery, a desire to pump out more oil
became powerful, and OPEC's constraining power often proved
more illusory than real.[69] Building a collective consensus about
managing either price upticks or economic downturns had proven
hard. Some members of OPEC could increase production but did
not want to. Others wanted to but could not, lacking investment

capital or stability. At the end of the day, overall OPEC cuts or additions to global oil supply was going to depend very much on the proclivities of Saudi Arabia. Taken together during the entire period of the price rise, the collective output of the OPEC countries went from 29 mbd in 2002 to just under 35 mbd in 2014, a cumulative rise of about 6 mbd. Not nothing, but not gargantuan either, and hardly the impressive kinds of growth the region seemed capable of and oil-thirsty countries wished they would do. Internal dynamics had proven difficult to manage, and the presumption and reality of high prices seemed to have provided less, rather than more, incentive to increase production. The new sources people thought the world would need were going to have to come from elsewhere.

Private-Sector IOCs: Unprecedented Profit and Expenditures

We turn now to the private-sector oil companies, where the newly formed supermajors also became important bellwethers of how the industry would respond to price movements and apparently growing demand. They had their own operational challenges to confront. First, they had to complete the amalgamation process that had created them. By 2002 that process had largely run its course: business integration, streamlining, and layoffs had created most of the efficiencies they were ever going to. However, the expected monetary payoff generated from these efforts remained elusive. The share price of most of the supermajors dropped, rather than increased, between 2000 and 2003: Chevron's stock measured $41.81 in January 2000 and dropped to $32.20 by January 2003: ExxonMobil's measured $41.44 and then dropped to $34.15; in the same time period Shell's stock dropped from $55.06 to $41.89.[70] Size and mergers were not going to be a panacea for ensuring shareholder return.

To be fair, this was hardly a problem unique to the oil industry. Similar mergers in other industries had also often failed to achieve the financial Promised Land that the merger road was assumed to lead. In addition, the oil industry, like all others, still reeled from the economic shocks of 2001/2, while managing all the collective challenges outlined in the previous chapter. Taken together, the vaunted gains of "synergy" that propelled the oil merger boom of the 1990s had not fulfilled their promise, and the companies remained in a difficult position. Oil market observers remained skeptical that things would soon improve. IOCs faced the relentless demands of financial markets, which had imparted harsh lessons during the lean years of the 1990s. Those markets may reward current production, but they reward the finding of new oil more, simply because only that new oil will generate the cash flows of the future. Private companies faced the constant problem of drawing down their proven reserves year after year to maintain current levels of production. If they did not find more oil – each and every year, regardless of prevailing prices, to replace what they extracted – they will over time simply run out of oil to bring to market. To remain viable, those companies had to spend a lot of exploration money every year and had to find new proven reserves with the money they spent. Merged companies by themselves did not solve that problem: the supermajors faced the same "finding new reserves" problem that the individual smaller companies did, they just faced them on a larger scale. The act of oil exploration remained difficult, expensive, and necessary. It had to be done even when oil prices were low.

Higher prices beginning in 2002 began providing welcome financial relief that made more tolerable their strategic and operational challenges. As oil prices rose, financial results began improving, and the integrated production structure featured by the supermajors allowed them to make money all along the value chain. Profits and revenue flow consequently grew, became large, then enormous, then unprecedented. Between 2004 and 2007 the supermajors collectively received an aggregate cash flow of US$397 billion. In 2008 ExxonMobil alone reported an annual profit of $48 billion, setting a record for profitability among US corporations.[71] Chevron followed that up by reporting a profit in 2008 of $23 billion.[72] These were some of the largest profits ever posted by publicly traded corporations, and their economic impact began to be noticeable, to say the least.

High oil prices provided IOCs a lot of cash, which led to the obvious question of what they should do with all that money. Stock prices and dividend payments grew, but so too did expenditures on oil exploration and infrastructure development. The capital markets and public expectations valued the exploration enterprise: it was advice the supermajors took to heart. In 2000 Chevron's capital budget expenditure for upstream exploration measured US$9.5 billion: by 2010 that budget had more than doubled, ballooning to $21.8 billion. In 2000 ExxonMobil's capital expenditures measured $11.2 billion; by 2005 they had risen to $17.7 billion, and by 2010 they measured $32.2 billion. Exploration expenditures took a significant but short-lived hit in the period 2008–9: in percentage terms, they declined 12 per cent in 2009 from 2008 levels.[73] However, even during the depths of the financial crisis, oil companies still collectively spent over $400 billion on exploration, and that short decline came after six years of annual double-digit percentage growth in investment and exploration expenditure.[74]

The dip did not last. Between 2010 and 2014, global exploration expenditures rebounded and then continued to accelerate. In 2012 all six IOC supermajors were among the top ten companies (including NOCs) in terms of exploration expenditure in the world,[75] and collective expenditures once again became staggering, measuring over US$600 billion per year. Indeed, it was the private-sector oil companies, supermajors, and other smaller competitors that were doing the bulk of the spending. NOCs maintained their share of investment expenditure of about 40 per cent of global totals. The supermajors alone accounted for 29 per cent of that spending; smaller private companies accounted for an additional 31 per cent. Annual investment by private companies was set to be two-and-a-half times greater between 2008 and 2012 than it was between 2002 and 2007, and they were set to increase their share of the total exploration budget even further.[76] As oil prices began rising after the financial crisis, private companies began spending ever more money.

For the supermajors, that posed challenges. The act of exploration involved more than just the deployment of money, in itself a formidable task. It also strained management capacities, as they increasingly had to direct ambitious exploration products from around the globe. The companies certainly benefited from a more welcoming investment environment. The higher prices went, the more anxious host governments were to extract what oil they could and the more welcoming they were to the companies that could help them do it. The supermajors also dispersed their investment dollars around the world. Offshore and continental Africa held significant production potential if the political risk could be endured, as did the oil-producing states of the Caspian basin region. Deep-sea drilling opportunities were available in the littoral regions surrounding the Gulf of Mexico, in the North Sea, and under the Arctic seabed. Companies also could not ignore the vast reserves held in the oil sands of Northern Alberta, which by some measures were second only to those of Saudi Arabia and had zero exploration risk. There were places where that investment could and did go, creating an economic boom in the world's oil frontier towns.

Even with the promise of high financial return and welcoming governments, there remained a number of production challenges and industry problems to overcome. Targeted investment areas often had smaller fields and/or held less recoverable reserves. They were difficult to get to, often required vast infrastructure investment to get the oil out, and sometimes were drenched in political and operational risk. Moreover, because all companies were targeting more or less the same places, the cost inflation for labor, materials, and supply services became rampant: $600 billion in investment simply did not buy what it used to. Inflation ate away at the real value of exploration budgets, salaries soared, costs for materials and basic supplies grew rapidly. It consequently was not all that easy to safely deploy all that capital in a way that managed risk effectively and that shareholders and critical outside observers would find tolerable.

Diversity and risk mitigation therefore became key concerns for the investment strategies of the supermajors. The capital they deployed went to a lot of different places, as they wanted to maintain a hand in all potential production sites. Sometimes they bought production assets others had developed: the supermajors often acquired many smaller companies that had become financial distressed during the financial crisis.[77] They also continued to acquire and hold new leases in areas ripe for future production potential. By the end of 2011 ExxonMobil alone had built up over 36.5 million acres of global acreage from which future oil and gas production could be drawn.[78] At that point the company held a total of 7 billion barrels of proven oil reserves: 2 billion were in North America, 1.4 billion in Africa, 2 billion in Asia, and rest were scattered around the world.[79] In 2011 Chevron held 11.2 billion barrels in proven reserves (oil and natural gas) in its acreages: they too were distributed geographically between the United States, Africa, Asia, Australia, and Europe.[80] IOCs scoured the globe for future production sites, spread their investment dollars around, and snapped up acreages like hungry piranha if those acreages even smelled like they might eventually yield something.

The production totals generated reflected some challenging realities. First, those totals increasingly reflected diversity. Domestic North American conventional production still featured prominently in many companies, but in some cases it even declined. But those production declines were offset by oil produced offshore and internationally. By the end of 2011 ConocoPhillips produced 46 per cent of its global output in North America: it drew the majority of its production share internationally.[81] Chevron's US annual production actually decreased from 667 million annual barrels (MB) in 2000 to 489 MB in 2010. That decrease was also offset by its increased international production, particularly from its offshore African fields that grew in production from 357 MB to 443 MB. Exxon Mobil also witnessed an overall US production decline from 733 MB in 2000 to 408 MB in 2010. They too increased their international production: their African production rose from 323 MB in 2008 to 628 MB in 2010.

By the end of 2014 the supermajors had collectively spent a lot of money, pushed exploration frontiers back, expanded drilling geographies, and advanced their production technologies. Yet despite all the drama of the merger process, the hundreds of billions of investment expenditure dollars spent, and the absorption of high amounts of political and economic risk, the one thing they did not do was expand production much. The output of the supermajors, even after consolidation and spending all that money, did not really increase. Looking at post-merger Chevron, which had acquired Texaco in 2001 and Unocal in 2005, is a case in point. Comparing the integrated company with the sum production totals of the three previously independent companies yields some sobering results. In 2007 Chevron's annual results showed that its combined oil and gas reserves were 9.4 per cent and 2.7 per cent lower, respectively, than were the separate companies' totals eleven years earlier. Oil and gas production totals were 16 per cent and 22 per cent lower, respectively.

In some ways the results were even bleaker: when taken together, the supermajors' output had hardly budged during the entire period of high prices. Despite all this effort and expense, production totals sometimes showed surprising and perhaps worrying results. Taken together, aggregate proven oil reserves were 8 per cent lower in 2007 than they had been eleven years earlier.[82] Private companies were certainly punching above their weight in terms of production: by 2008 the world's six largest IOCs – Exxon-Mobil, BP, Royal Dutch Shell, Total, ConocoPhillips, and Chevron – controlled only 3.7 per cent of the world's proven oil reserves, yet were collectively responsible for 15 per cent of global oil output.[83] Despite all their efforts at integration and gaining cost efficiencies, the supermajors seemed to be losing production output ground no matter how hard they ran. As the following graph notes, despite a period of very high prices and record exploration budgets, the actual amount of oil produced by the supermajors remained, at best, more or less stable.

High prices, at least in terms of the large private companies, did not necessarily cure output problems. Difficult facts remained that impeded their ability to rapidly increase production. First, the supermajors' investment horizon often took a decade to get new production on-line. Adding reserves and managing capital mattered as much to financial markets as did the increasing of actual output, and capital markets is what CEOs pay the most attention to. The supermajors therefore guarded against overinvestment in developing new projects and instead often focused on increasing the barrels generated from existing ones. New projects had to remain financially viable even if prices dropped, as their size and

Figure 5. Global Oil Production by Company, 2005–20 Thousands of Barrels/Day

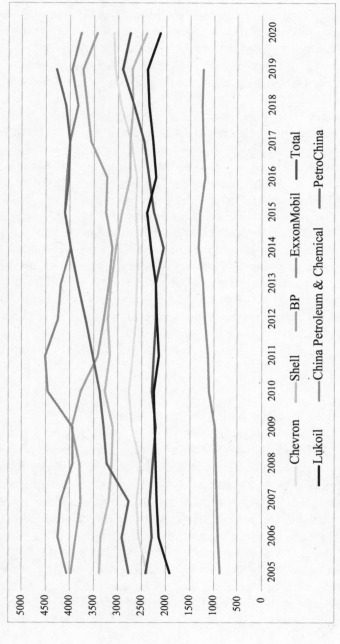

Source: Company Annual Reports.
Notes: Excludes Gazprom due to lack of company disclosure. PetroChina and China Petroleum & Chemical had not yet released 2020 production data at the time of writing.

scale dictated a constant flow of investment funds no matter what oil prices were doing.[84] Investing companies also did not always get a full bang for their investment buck due to cost inflation and competition for scarce resources. Simply increasing expenditures does not necessarily or quickly cause a jump in production. It may not do it at all.[85]

A period of high oil prices, though monetarily more rewarding, poses management challenges to IOCs every bit as real as those they face when prices are low. High oil prices and profit levels compel IOCs to invest more money in exploration, and quickly. That is no easy task: there are a limited number of areas carrying the required combination of potential oil reserves and manageable risk profiles they need before investing. Moreover, they had to deploy all that capital and make all those decisions while being uncertain of what OPEC and other suppliers would or would not do. Consequently, as the decade progressed, a strange scenario developed in which IOCs spent massive sums to acquire oil acreage in difficult and expensive terrain but did not produce a lot more oil. Meanwhile, a cautious OPEC often left vast reserves of cheaper oil untapped. Taken together, the actual production totals from these two groups were not going to make up the production shortfall driving the price rise.

So, Where Did the New Oil Come From?

If neither OPEC nor the supermajors either would or could increase production significantly, then who could and did? To begin, Russia helped: it was anxious to increase its production and did all it could to facilitate it. Russia had fashioned a production system featuring a symbiotic relationship between the centers of political and economic power. As prices rose, both government-owned and private companies wanted to maximize their respective. Neither the Russian government nor its companies had the incentive or discipline to limit production output the way that OPEC or the IOCs might have: indeed, incentives ran in the opposite direction. The government wanted and needed revenue, and the Russian oligarchic class who directed its oil companies proved willing to oblige by ramping up domestic production.

Russia continued pouring investment into its domestic industry. Its economy remained heavily dependent on natural resources; high prices generated fiscal strength and also generated incentive to keep producing more. Russian production grew from 6 mbd in 2000 to almost 10 mbd by 2010[86] and then grew to 10.8 mbd by 2014.[87] Initially most of that increase came from raising output in known fields. But between 2010 and 2014 Russian companies continued to pour money into increasing capital expenditures, collectively raising them by 20 per cent, which in dollar figures measured an increase of $30.9 billion to $37 billion.

There were other geographies also interested in increasing their production total. A further area that looked to increase its oil production was Latin America. The region's NOCs also raised their expenditures 9 per cent, from $41 billion to $45 billion, and began exploring in more technically challenging fields. Brazil's Petrobras became increasingly invested and active in deepwater exploration. Their investment efforts added another half-million barrels of production to global totals between 2008 and 2014.[88] Norway's Statoil became active in African and Middle Eastern growth areas.[89] This helped compensate for the significant drop in Norwegian domestic production, which went from 3.3 mbd in 2002 to 1.8 mbd in 2014.[90] As detailed in the next chapter, China's state-owned oil companies increasingly became internationally active players as well, particularly in Africa. Canada added approximately 2.5 mbd to the global production total: it produced about 2.8 mbd in 2000, and production measured 4.5 mbd by 2014.[91] Taken together, these production increases certainly helped but hardly constituted any kind of tidal wave.

The strongest source of new production came instead from the fracking revolution in the United States. That revolution began quietly enough: at the turn of the century, fracking accounted for a negligible percentage of US production, as the technique was not thought financially viable for large-scale deployment. Then fracking production began creeping up, along with price. In 2007 production measured about half a million barrels per day. Not small, but certainly not yet the game changer alluded to earlier. Yet, as prices continued to remain elevated and the profitability of the technique improved, more tight oil wells began dotting the US shale oil fields. Domestic oil production in the United States began to climb. Figure 6 shows what the increase in US production looked like.

As balance sheets grew, more drillers arrived to take advantage of the bonanza, amplifying fracking's impact. Oil production rate in the US began increasing at a rate not seen since the nineteenth century. Domestic US production that had measured 5–6 mbd in 2008 had effectively doubled in a decade, and more, potentially much more, was on the horizon.

Initially, the EIA stuck to offering conservative projections for fracking's potential. It argued that the technological and environmental uncertainties associated with fracking might limit production growth levels to an additional 3 mbd by 2019. However, even if only that

Figure 6. US Oil Production 1998–2018, Thousands of Barrels/Day

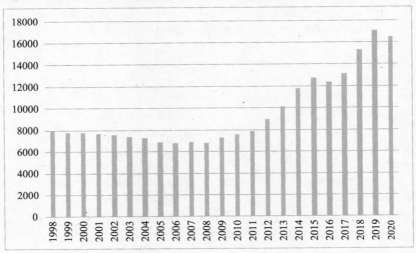

Source: US Energy Information Administration.

was achieved, it would still create a profound shift in the oil market by lowering imports down from a 2005 high of almost 60 per cent of total US consumption to a projected low of 34 per cent.[92] However, they admitted this could be a conservative estimate. Other potential scenarios envisioned even more aggressive drilling, which could in a few short years result in required import levels dropping to virtually zero.[93] As fracking production levels made steady progress and started surpassing initial estimates, observers began wondering just how high US domestic production might go.

Fracking recalibrated the entire production dynamics thought to typify the oil industry. It was cheap and flexible. At a time when oil companies collectively were spending over $600 billion annually in exploration (and making little progress in the way of increased output), the few million it took to drill a fracking well seemed like spare change. Fracking also carried strategic value: anything reducing US import dependency was a welcome change from the previous four decades, where import dependence had grown and strategic worries along with it. Fracking production could sprout up quickly if prices rose or shut down if prices tapered or fell. Fears of shortage began receding as this revolution in production took place, and all of that happened within the space of a decade, more or less an eye-blink in what was thought to be a rather ponderous industry.

Collective Lessons of the Long Period of the Oil Price Rise

The decade began much as the last had ended, with a period of low prices and gloom in the marketplace. Subdued oil prices motivated private-sector companies to field cost containment strategies in response. They ruthlessly managed costs in product exploration and delivery, created lean production mechanisms, conserved and refocused exploration budgets, and eventually merged. Companies had to prove they had staying power to continue operating and investing even when prices were low. Their consequent efficiency allowed them to survive a bleak price environment that did not appear like it would change soon.

But it did. The global economy shook off the century's early shocks and began growing rapidly. Oil prices rose and remained generally elevated throughout the 2002–14 period, interrupted relatively briefly by the financial crisis. The perception of scarcity caused fears of "running out" to seep into popular imagination. Books emerged issuing dire warnings of the imminence of supply shortfall and the potential calamities that might follow. Such views shaped thinking, investor sentiment, and popular consensus. During the price run-up, what people felt and believed about the oil market amplified the upward demand trend data the marketplace showed. Conditions prevailing between 2002 and 2008 created a "perfect storm": perceived supply shortage, ongoing political tension, new centers of economic growth, and popular imagination shredded more sober analysis and shot prices ever upward. The narrative proved powerful and difficult to break. It carried over into the post–financial crisis world as well, as prices resumed their upward climb.

High prices did create incentive to increase exploration and production. Oil companies did expand their exploration budgets: they had the revenue, and customers expected they would do what was necessary to ameliorate the supply crunch. However, predicating long-term investment budgets on permanently elevated prices was risky. As prices moved away from the fundamentals of supply and demand, the sustainability of individual investments became difficult to ascertain.[94] Despite the consensus of growing supply needs, neither IOCs nor OPEC's NOCs could, or perhaps even wanted to, rapidly increase production.[95] IOCs had to worry about the permanency of the price rise, while OPEC fretted about its conflicting incentives. Raising production too much may send the wrong sign to other producers and may even prove financially painful if prices then dropped. Initial responses to rising prices belied the industry's legacy of intrepid and bold risk taking: many NOCs and IOCs were careful about embracing the new price environment and proved deliberate and cautious in the decisions they made. It took convincing to inaugurate new spending, and time to invest, and even after doing that for a decade, overall production output did not rise all that much.

In terms of oil prices, it is difficult to tell precisely how much the speculative side of capital markets affected the price run up. Once started, investor enthusiasm is hard to stop: as Citibank CEO Chuck Prince famously observed, in financial markets, it is necessary to keep dancing until the music stops. Once a financial bubble starts artificially inflating an asset's price, it is hard to convince others that it is indeed a bubble.[96] That pattern happened in oil markets, particularly when prices rose as quickly as they did, which generated expectations that the good times would last indefinitely. Investor confidence leaped beyond what fundamentals justified and gripped markets with the "irrational exuberance" Alan Greenspan warned about.

As oil prices remained high, they brought new, but largely unexpected sources of production to the market, particularly from the US. Those increases in production helped calm fears about peak oil. Fracking's impact was nothing short of profound. Its capacity to rapidly increase production, along with the other alternate oil-production sites now coming onstream, eroded OPEC's capacity to control supply. As high oil prices persisted, OPEC worried about how it might maintain is ability to manage supply. The best it could do remained jawboning, in effect warning that individual efforts to maximize production would spell collective doom. OPEC also began consultations with Russia, which depended on high oil revenues and had at least a theoretical interest in preserving high prices through supply control as long as possible.[97]

Yet these responses proved unable to slow the increasing amount of money flowing to the global oil market, or the oil output flowing out of it. By 2014 the Saudi government had cause to feel both worried and aggrieved. They had done the most to restrain production during the financial crisis, incurring the wrath of international customers in doing so. In its perception, its OPEC partners did not do their share and were in effect free riding on the Saudi effort. Now, the US and others kept pouring new oil into the market. Attentive observers might have noticed Saudi Arabia's warnings about the measures it might take to remedy a supply overhang it saw building in the market. But that would not hit home until 2014.

Meanwhile, the era of the price rise and perceived scarcity had political consequences that were every bit as significant as the economic ones. Politics as ever mattered significantly in the course the oil market took in the period of rising price. We examine these next.

chapter five

The Politics, Geopolitics, and Global Governance of Oil: 2000–2014

In 2006 Thomas Friedman, foreign affairs columnist for the *New York Times* and author of numerous bestselling books on globalization and world politics, penned an article for *Foreign Policy* magazine that struck a familiar chord to students of the oil market. The article introduced and subsequently made popular his First Law of Petropolitics, in which "the price of oil and the pace of freedom always move in opposite directions in oil-rich Petro states."[1] Its premise was simple: for countries that exported a lot of oil and did little else economically, the higher oil prices went, the less evidence one saw of a modernizing economy, an increasingly free people, or a transparent and more or less honest government. Indeed, high oil prices seemed associated with the opposite of these things. Oil-rich governments often doubled down on increasing oil production at the expense of economic diversification, used oil revenue to further entrench their political positions by crushing opponents, stalling democratic movements, and sometimes conducting a more aggressive foreign policy that diverted attention away from domestic problems. Conceptually, Friedman's framework was simple enough to understand and seemed to explain much of what was then going on in the world.

As oil prices rose, a lot of those goings-on that Friedman and others saw did not seem good. Even everyday observers could easily link oil production and high oil prices to many of the geopolitical problems the world faced. As more countries became enmeshed in the oil-production game, accounts of corruption and civil strife became endemic in new oil exporters and began peppering even a casual scan of the world's news.[2] Oil-producing states seemed to suffer from their riches as often as they benefited, and empirical surveys and measures emerged that put statistical meat on those anecdotal bones. Surveys from the World Bank,[3] Freedom House,[4] and *Foreign Policy* magazine[5] seemed to confirm what many already suspected: most of the world's oil exporters did poorly across measures of governance, and their performance often worsened, rather than improved, as they garnered more and more oil revenue. To be sure, Friedman's assertion and these accompanying measures may have simply shown correlation: the how and whys of causation were a little trickier to demonstrate. But they did motivate further investigation and pondering over a hard-to-ignore reality: high oil prices enabled countries to do things Friedman thought they should not and allowed them to avoid doing the things he thought they should.

Such was and is the essence of the resource curse, one of the central political problems of oil markets, and one outlined briefly in chapter two. The enormous revenues oil production can generate are associated with some political and geopolitical opportunities, but they also pose challenges and can create problems. This chapter chronicles the most notable of the latter. All those challenges were longstanding, and different countries have better and worse records in managing them. But high oil prices accelerated and amplified them and often dominated how those problems were interpreted and what policy responses were possible. That was true for both importers and exporters, both of which had to manage their own versions of the resource curse.

We start with the big importers. Both the United States and China saw their foreign policy interests clouded and sometimes even defined by the need to procure oil. On the exporter side, we examine how oil revenues allowed Russia to centralize political power and reassert itself geopolitically. But it also made the country steadily more dependent on resource revenue the more prices rose. We examine the Middle East exporters, who had to manage massive oil revenues while also watching one of their major customers steadily march toward oil self-sufficiency. We also look at the global governance organizations and citizen groups attempting to instill more rules of the road for the oil system, as that system expanded, had important new players, and generated effects afflicting the globe's entire population.

The politics and geopolitics of oil became more complicated as the revenues and governance stakes rose. They came into ever-bolder relief for both importers and exporters during the extended price rise of 2002–14. High oil prices, and the perceived need to procure more oil, generated geopolitical currents that rippled beyond the oil market. It thrust issues of oil security back into the very heart of national security debates. Oil seemed to touch every major national security issue with which developed markets had to contend. The world had witnessed human rights abuses, massive expenditures on security and military items, terrorism, and bloody civil and regional conflicts before. But oil intensified these problems, and the need to procure more of it seemed to limit what, if anything, could be done about them.

None stated that reality or frustration better than former US secretary of state Condolezza Rice, who in testimony before the US Senate Foreign Relations Committee, stated that "I can tell you that nothing has really taken me aback as Secretary of State more than the way that the politics of energy is 'warping' diplomacy around the world."[6] Oil dependency diluted if not polluted other foreign and domestic policy objectives, and even if procuring oil was not the driving force behind a particular government decision, it often looked like it was. High prices and perceived scarcity meant oil was now a centerpiece of political and geopolitical life.

Oil, Politics, and Geopolitics in the United States

The politics of oil clearly mattered in what was, for the United States, the dominant geopolitical event of the decade: the terrorist strikes of September 11, 2001. Those events killed over 3,000 people and wounded 6,000 more, and responding to them would be the defining foreign policy challenge of president George W. Bush. The primary US response was to launch a "war on terror" that involved measures designed to bring retribution to the initial perpetrators and to prevent any further attacks other terrorist groups may have been plotting. The primary target remained the Al-Qaeda terrorist network suspected to have planned and executed the 2001 attack, and in particular its leader Osama Bin Laden, the Saudi Arabian national who now operated out of the mountains of Afghanistan. The US launched reprisals quickly and, by the time oil prices began rising sharply in 2002, was already deeply enmeshed in military conflict in Afghanistan. It also had its eye on Iraq, whose leader, Saddam Hussein, was suspected of both funding terrorism and of having a covert weapons of mass destruction (WMD) development program. By 2003 the US had laid the diplomatic groundwork for and had launched an invasion of Iraq to rid it of that suspected WMD cache.

The efforts the US made to fund and fight the war on terror were by any measure gigantic, and their effects reverberated economically as well as geopolitically. The link between oil production and terrorism came early. To begin, of the nineteen individuals involved in the 9/11 attack, eleven were Saudi Arabian nationals. How and why those nationals had become motivated enough to kill themselves in order to hurt the United States – especially after successive US administrations had cultivated such a strong political relationship with the ruling al-Saud family[7] – remained a genuinely shocking puzzle. It did not stop there. Osama bin Laden was also a Saudi Arabian national whose wealthy family had benefited enormously from the long-standing US strategic relationship with Saudi Arabia. Given this, what had motivated the terrorists to do what they did? How had they been funded, and where had they trained? How had the US's most reliable Muslim partner in the Middle East allowed such a powerful terrorist network to fester and grow, seemingly under its nose? Somehow, such questions seemed linked to Saudi Arabia's dominant position in the oil-production system and the US and its allies' continued reliance on it.

The words and deeds of Osama bin Laden personified the nexus of oil, terrorism, and security now facing the United States.[8] Bin Laden had spent much of his adult life condemning Western infidels for their supposed "theft" of Muslim oil. He had portrayed US military efforts during the Gulf War of 1990–1 not as a response to a strategic threat, still less as an effort to defend and protect a stable Muslim country from an aggressive regional neighbor. He instead portrayed those efforts as a not-so-subtle use of military means to extend US domination over the entire Muslim world. The US, he argued, wanted to control oil procurement themselves and to prevent the broader Muslim world from using oil revenues to extend their interests. To him, Muslim leaders acquiescing in the selling of that oil were not state leaders engaged in a business transaction but were instead willing accomplices to the committing of a global crime. Taken together, this convoluted logic justified the violent overthrow of Western-friendly Arab governments, as well as ongoing terrorist attacks against not only Western countries but also against those Muslim leaders he deemed insufficiently devout. Under this doctrine, oil-production facilities were either assets to be controlled or targets to be destroyed. In either case, oil played a central role in the war he wanted to wage against the West.

The substance of that narrative became difficult to ignore the longer the war on terror went on. The invasion and occupation of Iraq was a case in point. The initial justification to attack Iraq and overthrow Saddam Hussein was his supposed link to 9/11 and the Al-Qaeda network. When that link proved tenuous and difficult to prove – many thought it did not exist[9] – a second pretext for invasion was proffered: the need to confront and halt the advanced program of WMD Iraq supposedly had. The initial effort to defeat the Iraqi forces and oust its leader worked quickly and went largely according to plan: the subsequent search for WMD, not so much. Initial battlefield victories proved but a prelude to a lengthy, bloody, and colossally expensive occupation effort, during which the US mission to eliminate a WMD program morphed into an awkward and painful effort to stabilize and democratize Iraq. As deaths and costs mounted, the Iraqi guerilla opposition became more robust, and the WMD remained unfound, the justification for the invasion increasingly rang hollow, and the more credible Bin Laden's original claim became, particularly to those already predisposed to believing it. It became easy to portray US action in Iraq as unrelated to terrorism or stockpiled WMDs: instead it was just a naked extension of US power in order to control and reshape Iraq's oil industry.

That interpretation fit neatly into the long narrative of the geopolitics of oil, and its latest version differed little from the established pattern. US efforts in Iraq were really about asserting US control over Middle Eastern oil and US foreign policy interests with Gulf producers began and ended with that. This narrative accused the US of fostering regional instability to justify further encroachment on the region. It had chosen regional allies based on their willingness to act as surrogates for US interests, and those governments now were beholden to what the US wanted and did their bidding. US military strategy itself provided the evidence: analysis of its military capacities and policy in the Middle East included forward-based and deployed forces,[10] indicating the country was willing to do what was necessary to procure oil. It was therefore hard to swallow defense secretary Donald Rumsfeld's protestation that the Iraq War had "nothing, literally nothing, to do with oil":[11] as long as the US and its allies relied heavily on Middle Eastern oil, it remained possible to frame everything they did in the region through that lens.

September 11 had demonstrated that there were links between oil and terrorism, one that required a full diagnosis and deconstruction if it was to be managed.[12] The oil industry represented much of what the Al-Qaeda terrorist network despised: an increasingly integrated global economy, a secularized and consumerist society, and the relentless process of cultural Westernization that came with it. It also fed their preferred narrative: market economies subjugated people rather than enriching them, allowed vast sums of wealth to accrue to venal and corrupt rulers, and provided very little benefit to everyday citizens. High oil prices intensified inequality between oil-producing states and their non-oil Arab brethren, fueling resentment and anger. Impoverished young people saw the corrupt management of oil revenue and their own sometimes limited economic opportunities:[13] that combination fueled yet more resentment, and subsequently made it easier to recruit new converts into terrorist organizations.

The geopolitical and security problems generated by the struggle over oil seemed pervasive and went beyond the Iraq conflict and the problem of terrorism. As prices rose, the struggle to control the revenues they generated could tear countries apart rather than stabilize them. In Iraq, the Kurdish population occupying the North pushed for independence from Baghdad and wanted control over territorial oil resources to help fund it. In Africa, Sudan remained wracked by civil war in which control over oil revenues mattered, as did Nigeria, where terrorist groups regularly made raids on oil-production facilities in an effort to deprive the country's government of needed revenue. The 2011 Arab Spring witnessed angry citizens rebelling against corrupt leaders: in Libya, protestors overthrew Muammar Gaddafi, the brutal dictator who had used oil revenue for decades to solidify and extend his rule. Many of the world's most troublesome geopolitical hotspots seemed linked to the problems of oil and the struggle to control revenues, and they seemed to get hotter the higher prices went. In response, the US and their allies began worrying about not just state-based geopolitical threats but also on smaller military engagements designed to secure limited stabilization objectives in failed states.[14] Reconstructing and stabilizing societies torn apart by civil conflict required new kinds of forces, equipment, and doctrine.[15] Oil politics now seemed to affect virtually every aspect of US national security policy.

Domestic US Politics

These themes became increasingly relevant in presidential domestic politics. Even while engaged in the war on terrorism, president Bush could admit that the US was addicted to oil.[16] Put simply, that meant the US had become so dependent on securing supply that they tolerated things they would rather not and refrained from doing things they knew they should, all in the name of preserving oil flow. The need to procure oil played too great a role in foreign policy discussions, and the attention and resources paid to securing supply meant less of these things were available for other priorities.

There was a domestic price to be paid too. High prices put a drag on the economy: growth therefore slowed, and the economy suffered. The domestic optics of oil production proved politically problematic. As struggling consumers spent an ever-greater portion of their income to buy needed fuel, they got the added pleasure of watching oil company profits balloon. They grew angry, perhaps enough to start looking seriously for alternative energy sources or to find ways to punish oil companies.[17] Anti-oil activists found an increasingly receptive audience as it became politically palatable to challenge the "tyranny of oil."[18] The geopolitics and politics of oil began mattering at home and became increasingly relevant electorally.

People could easily see the problems reliance on imported oil created: the list seemed never-ending. It had mired US forces in the swamp of the domestic conflicts of oil-producing states. It hurt the domestic economy by hampering efforts to spur competitiveness: as companies and individuals had to pay more for energy, it left fewer funds for deployment elsewhere. Oil dependency also made US citizens "poorer" because they spent an increasing portion of their disposable income on energy, leaving less money for other things. Dependency on oil also forced the United States to go diplomatically easy on oil exporters, holding back criticism of their regimes to keep the oil flowing to them and their allies. Anything that lessened reliance on oil, and foreign oil in particular, seemed good for the economy and security of the United States.

That theme reverberated throughout the presidential campaign of 2008, where criticisms of oil dependency became standard campaign rhetoric in both the Democratic and Republican parties. Not surprisingly, each party proposed different solutions – Republicans favored increasing domestic US production, Democrats focused on the pursuit of alternative energy – but both agreed that oil dependency was a strategic weakness. The topic of renewable energy certainly peppered the speeches of Democratic contender and eventual presidential winner Barack Obama, who articulated an ambitious energy vision. Obama promised regulations designed to lower carbon usage and curb the political influence of the oil industry. He used his acceptance speech for the Democratic nomination to champion energy change, promising that within ten years the US would end its dependence on oil from the Middle East. He advocated for a windfall profits tax on oil companies' excess profits, revenues that would be transferred to consumers to help them pay energy bills.[19] He thought the US should "harness the ingenuity of farmers and scientists and entrepreneurs to free this nation from the tyranny of oil for once and for all."[20] He proposed increasing research funds for renewable fuels, promoted legislative efforts to raise fuel economy standards, and promised he would invest government funds to create the infrastructure necessary to allow motor vehicles to run on alternative energy sources.[21]

Upon assuming the presidency, Obama continued making ambitious pledges to free the United States from its dependency on fossil fuels. In his Inaugural Address, Obama's soaring rhetoric promised that his government would harness the power of the wind and seas and soils to run factories and power cars.[22] He followed that up by proposing numerous pieces of environmental legislation, including raising minimum fuel economy standards for vehicles and strengthening legislation that limited emissions. He promoted renewable and alternative energy resources at every opportunity, drawing upon popular books and political arguments in advocating for alternative energy.[23] His legislative proposals in his presidency's early years indicated every intention of following up on the environmental promises he had made.

Yet, despite these ambitions and lofty goals, progress toward those goals remained hampered. To oil companies, the public hostility toward carbon had clearly resonated at the ballot box and therefore required a proactive response. What emerged was a political strategy designed to combat what they saw as an activist president riding a rising tide of angry public sentiment, a sentiment that might enable that president to pass legislation harmful to their interests. That strategy emphasized three consistent points. First, oil companies pointed out that procuring more oil to meet escalating global demand was not some kind of nefarious ploy but was simply an economic reality that required a response. Global energy demand would rise, there was no escaping the world's current reliance on oil, and that alternative energies could at best complement, but not replace, carbon. Second, they continued advocating for increased domestic exploration and drilling, arguing that it could mitigate against overreliance on foreign oil and thereby align domestic production with national security interests. Third, they noted that oil exploration generated a lot of economic benefits that were more than welcome in the wake of the financial crisis. Much of their profits went back into exploration and development, thereby creating much-needed employment and growth.

Fourth, the political strategy also resisted the pitting of carbon interests against others. Rather than allowing a binary split of interests to develop – one pitting carbon producers against advocates for renewable and alternative energy – it made greater long-term sense, and was more reflective of reality, to frame energy procurement as a problem that included all sources of energy.

Some energy advocates promoted a regional energy integration strategy that would see the United States increase its domestic production while also importing more oil from Canada and Mexico, rather than the Middle East. Growing regional integration of oil production would lessen import dependence on these other areas. This idea made some legislative headway: in 2009, one US senator proposed a bill that would coordinate energy production and distribution between the United States and other "willing countries," which practically meant Canada and Mexico, and recommended that the US secretaries of state and energy create a working group to do just that.[24] The political strategy of linking oil production to a host of other positive political initiatives lessened the impact powerful anti-oil sentiment had.

Oil executives knew that the economic conditions occurring between 2002 and 2014 – record-high oil prices and profits, followed by a financial meltdown and a deep recession, followed by a rapid oil price recovery while the rest of the economy lingered – were particularly challenging in terms of managing what the consuming public thought of them. While this in itself was nothing new, public anger seemed particularly intense this time, the opposition to oil more widespread, and the likelihood of restrictive regulation more probable. It had become even more necessary to publicly present the sobering realities of what was driving energy demand, why it was necessary to procure more oil, and the economic benefits oil production provided. It would take time to remedy the supply crunch;

what oil companies needed was encouragement, not restraint. Reiterating those facts to a skeptical public became more than just standard oil-industry political fare: it became a tool to build more rather than less operational and strategic freedom. Such were the domestic political effects of oil politics in the United States.

The China Effect: Mercantilism, Growth, and the Contest for Oil

If the world was indeed running short of oil, then countries needed to do what was necessary to obtain it. Dependency was a vulnerability that governments had to address, and that was as true for emerging markets as it was for the developed world. In the case of a rapidly growing and emerging China, its leaders seemed to agree. As oil prices rose and fears of scarcity grew, addressing oil import vulnerability became a cornerstone not only of what the Chinese government said but also what it did. China's economy grew astonishingly quickly during the period 2000–15: its demand for imported commodities of all types had consequently skyrocketed. Economic observers credited rising Chinese demand with inducing price rises in literally everything. Commodities in general went on a price tear as investors assumed Chinese demand would gobble up all that could be produced. This certainly appeared true in the oil market: Chinese economic growth fueled expectations of limitless future demand already outlined.

The greater China's economic potential appeared, the more it captured popular imagination and attention. China's growth generated a staggering avalanche of books, articles, and public commentaries dissecting what they had done, how they had done it, and what it portended for the future. Those works ranged from the economically descriptive to the geopolitical distressing: the former simply chronicled the pace of Chinese economic growth, while the latter fretted about the geopolitical power an increasingly rich China would inevitably wield.[25] In all cases, it was clear the world was going to have to pay ever-increasing attention to what China said and what its economy was doing.

That attention – some complimentary, some not – put China's leaders in a somewhat awkward position. They maintained that China was a developing country and would remain so for the foreseeable future. It still had a lot of emerging left to do, and much of its vaunted economic potential remained theoretical rather than real. Large chunks of its population continued to toil in relative poverty, and despite its impressive growth, it was going to take decades for China's standard of living to approach Western levels. Before it could do so, its economy would have to overcome enormous challenges, ranging from capital formation to the acquisition of technological and management capacity. Its companies would have to vastly increase their experience, management expertise, and deployed technology if they were going to compete effectively against Western companies. China was starting from a position of economic weakness, not strength, and its government knew it. It consequently developed an economic strategy utilizing government resources to support and enhance its economic capabilities.

China endorsed and implemented a state capitalist model to facilitate its economic rise. That meant its national government would shepherd the direction its economy took. That model drew on the economic lineage of mercantilism outlined in the first chapter and seemed as much a geopolitical as it was an economic concept. To refresh, state capitalism considers the building of economic strength as a key component and extension of national power.[26] China was hardly the first and was certainly not the only country employing it, and there remained variations in what that model looked like and the policies enacted in its name.[27] Yet the political purpose remained constant: countries employed it because they believed they suffered from economic disadvantages and needed state help to catch up.

State capitalism often enjoys domestic political support, particularly if the perception of weakness is widespread and the population held a collective willingness to endure what was necessary to rectify it. In China's case, both those conditions seemingly held, and the country proved disciplined and motivated to pursue the economic direction its government set. Moreover, if successful, it might unleash a limitless economic potential, given China's size.

China's policy on oil procurement, and indeed its resource-acquisition strategy in general, illustrated how its version of state capitalism would work. China needed all kinds of commodities beyond what it could provide domestically and was not content to simply source them on the open market from foreign companies. It wanted its own companies to become active international players in commodity extraction and proved willing to do what was necessary to help them become so. In the case of oil, the Chinese government authorized, encouraged, and provided state support for its domestic oil companies to expand internationally, building such explicit direction directly into its state-directed five-year economic plans. That policy had garnered a simple yet accurate label the "going out" strategy: its intensity accelerated as China's growth progressed and the need to acquire resources of all types grew.[28]

In the oil industry, that strategy proved especially effective because the Chinese government retained a strong ownership stake in its domestic oil companies. Three companies dominated the Chinese oil landscape: the Chinese National Petroleum Company (CNPC), Sinopec, and the Chinese National Offshore Oil Company (CNOOC). These companies were pillars that aided Chinese industrial development, enjoyed close links with the Chinese Communist Party, and received broad and far-reaching aid from the Chinese government.[29] One measure of such aid included an increasingly assertive oil diplomacy, in which diplomatic personnel pursued relationships designed specifically to gain extraction access to commodity-rich countries. Those relationships would prove helpful in managing the conflicts with other countries a more aggressive resource nationalism would inevitably bring.[30] Secondly, China provided state-backed guaranteed loans to its companies that featured low interest rates and generous repayment terms. This helped make the financial burden of international expansion easier to bear. China also continued shielding much of its domestic oil market from foreign competition: the foreign activity that was allowed mandated technology transfers and joint ventures as a necessary precondition for investment. China's bureaucracy had built administrative capacities designed to funnel capital toward high-growth industries quickly. This combination of supports made the going out strategy financially and operationally feasible, as its companies would likely suffer initial losses as they gained experience in international activity. All of this helped aggrandize China's national power and became a key element in the country's grand strategy.[31]

State capitalism also allowed China's companies to tolerate more risk than what many Western companies were willing to absorb, allowing them to invest in places Western companies either were wary of or believed the potential investment returns were too low. China's companies learned and adapted quickly, focusing exploration efforts in specific ways and in specific areas. China conducted its assertive oil diplomacy in the Middle East, as its reliance on Middle Eastern crude grew rapidly during the period 2002–14.[32] Diplomatic outreach efforts and visits from senior Chinese leaders became a regular part of China's foreign activity in the region, and when opportunities presented themselves China's companies and diplomatic personnel did not hesitate to pursue them. They participated successfully in the auctioning of exploration rights in postwar Iraq: ultimately its companies obtained more drilling rights than did their Russian or American competitors, largely because Chinese companies offered better terms.[33] Chinese companies also became active in Central Asia, focusing on gaining access and building infrastructure to extract oil and gas resources.[34] State backing provided China's companies with a significant capacity to tolerate risk in exploration activities.

China did not confine its investment to the developing world. They also began acquiring production assets in developed markets, thereby learning to navigate the regulatory systems that monitored foreign investment in those countries. In 2005 CNOOC attempted to purchase UNOCAL, a mid-sized US-based oil producer, a bid that raised considerable surprise and some political hackles in the United States. Opponents mused publicly about the wisdom of allowing a state-owned foreign company from an emerging US economic rival to purchase US oil assets at a time when both oil prices and fears of scarcity were rising. That opposition ultimately doomed the offer, but CNOOC banked the political and investment experience, and it certainly did not daunt the company's willingness to try again.

It did so on Monday, July 23, 2012, when it publicly announced another big acquisition: it was tendering an all-cash offer to buy Canadian oil and gas company Nexen for $15.2 billion. The offer, at $26 per share, came at a $10 premium over the existing share price, attractive by any standard. Yet the bid rocked the foundations of the Canadian oil industry and public, not just because of its scale but also because of the political adroitness with which it was made. The purchase of Nexen – a mid-sized oil company with approximately 4,000 employees holding significant assets in the North Sea and in the Alberta oil sands – was the largest single foreign investment transaction in Canadian history. Not surprisingly, China took great care in "selling" the investment to the Canadian public. They agreed to maintain employment levels, to retain local decision-making authority, and reinforce the investment over a period of years. Taken together, these measures convinced the Canadian government that the investment crossed the "net benefit to Canada" threshold necessary for its approval, which it subsequently gave. CNOOC now had a substantial asset in the Canadian oil and gas sector and had proven its capacity to invest in a highly regulated economy and to win over an initially suspicious home government.

It was in Africa, however, where Chinese companies used the state capitalist model to its greatest effect. Statistically, the amount of trade and investment between China and Africa began to grow quickly, and the bulk of that economic activity was in the procurement of primary resource commodities. It became clear that Africa was going to play a significant role in China's economic plans and that Chinese investment was also going to be a key player in determining Africa's future. Chinese oil forays into Africa included significant investments into Sudan, a country beset by civil war, as well as Angola, as its companies evidently tolerating the high levels of corruption besetting the oil industry there.[35] These partnerships proved increasingly successful: by 2004 Africa was supplying approximately 30 per cent of China's required oil imports, with more set to follow.[36]

The broader statistics of China's increasingly confident going-out strategy revealed how successful it was. Between 2002 and 2012, China's oil companies inked about $95 billion worth of investment deals spaced across forty-three transactions.[37] Their companies' exploration budgets and production levels grew throughout the decade and soon began rivaling those of the supermajors. By 2012 CNPC's overall oil production (including domestic and foreign operations) measured over 2 mbd. Between 2006 and 2010, CNOOC's production rose from 372,000 barrels/day to 720,000 b/d.[38] By the end of 2012 PetroChina was producing approximately 900,000 b/d,[39] and its exploration budget measured close to $30 billion dollars, on par or slightly below what ExxonMobil and Chevron were spending.[40] By 2013 China had committed over $90 billion to acquiring additional oil assets, much of which went into acquisition efforts of existing resource companies. It was also busy constructing transport and refining facilities that could move and process the discovered oil.[41] Among their targets were leases in the Alberta oil sands, reserves in Kazakhstan, neighboring fields dotted around East Asia, Venezuela, Gabon, and a host of others. In each acquisition China's companies gained more production capacity, built relationships, and gained experience.

Clear-eyed economic realism drove the state capitalism strategy, and no apologies were made about the way it was conducted. In China's perception, its companies were coming late to the globalization and oil-production game. They had spent decades in economic isolation, and now, after deciding to break that isolation and expand abroad, they confronted the same established set of challenges other companies did and were several decades behind. Control of much of the world's oil resources remained lodged in state-owned companies and governments, and the technical, financial, and operational challenges in accessing what was left were formidable. Demand continued to grow, and fears of peak oil affected Chinese decision-making as much as it did anyone else's. Moreover, Chinese companies faced an additional challenge: entrenched and savvy foreign competitors who had already scoured, leased, and/or developed much of the world's known oil-production fields. Those companies had decades of experience operating in sometimes inhospitable terrain and had centuries of combined international operating experience. It was an intimidating set of challenges, and it is questionable whether any company, bereft of state help, could have overcome them.

That being said, their success did not go unnoticed, and the criticism still came. China's "helping hand" to its domestic companies raised more than a few political protestations. It also began ringing alarm bells to those worried about what state capitalism portended for the global economy. Critics noted that China's international expansion efforts posed a direct threat to the commercial success of its own companies because they would indirectly shut them out of new production areas. Deputy secretary of state Robert Zoellick was one such individual. As early as September 2005 he would give testimony to the National Committee on US–China relations, stating that the Chinese expansion approach represented a "mercantilist strategy" designed to "lock up" energy supplies around the world.[42] Other charges followed. One was unfairness: critics noted that success of the going-out strategy could not have happened without explicit government support that private companies did not get.

The second criticism was political non-interference: Chinese foreign investment came with no apparent political strings attached to the host governments with whom it did business. China did not appear to care what those governments did with the revenues oil production generated, unlike the Western supermajors who had to constantly worry about activist shareholders who may object to how and with whom they did business and what the associated governments might do with their share of the take. Chinese investors simply asked host governments what they wanted and gave it to them in exchange for access to their commodities. That made them attractive to local governments who wanted the investment without the moralizing.

The third charge built on the second: it argued Chinese investment undercut emerging standards in social and environmental performance conditioning what oil companies did. Competitors viewed China's granting of financial assistance and infrastructure packages to local governments to be at best an unfair subsidy and at worst an outright bribe. Chinese companies appeared willing to tolerate working conditions below those practiced by the supermajors, whose shareholders, legal strictures, and attentive public would never tolerate their doing what China's companies appeared able to. Taken together, Chinese investment practices undermined other efforts to raise operational standards across the industry.[43]

These criticisms likely puzzled Chinese state officials, who saw little difference between what they were doing now and what Western companies had done not so long ago. As we have noted, both the United States and Great Britain had in the past certainly proved willing to help their companies do international exploration and secure leases when it served their interests.[44] What was wrong with China doing the same thing now? It seemed hypocritical to criticize China for doing no more in chasing its own economic interests than what others had done for decades in chasing theirs. Moreover, successful Chinese investment in new oil markets had not shut anyone out: the supermajors had had opportunities to make similar investments and had chosen not to according to their own decision-making calculus. What China's firms did or did not do would not change that. Indeed, Chinese investment might be even doing Western companies a favor by providing the investment funds that might help economically stabilize a particular country. If that investment allowed the country to improve its regulatory environment and living standards generally, it might pave the way for later Western involvement.

Finally, China's oil companies could hardly be blamed for investing where and how they did: few alternate investment opportunities were available They were in many cases competing for access to fields that the supermajors did not want or had discarded. Seen from this light, it really was not clear who was shutting whom out. One Chinese energy official complained that "CNPCs legal and financial inexperience makes it difficult for it to compete with the major international oil and gas companies to gain oil exploration rights in promising areas." He further observed, "Western monopoly capital, with the support and assistance of their governments, has scrambled and seized the main oil and gas markets in all parts of the world."[45] If China had overpaid in its initial investments, it was to effectively gain a toehold on an international market that was already intensely competitive.[46] China argued that Western agencies also offered state aid and Official Development Assistance (ODA) through its established multilateral agencies.[47] Those agencies may have been able to place conditions on the extension of that aid, but it was unrealistic to expect a company to do the same. Over the long run, China contributed to, rather than clashed with, Western economic interests. They were bringing more oil to market from diverse and new sources, were building energy infrastructure, were contributing to a more integrated global market, and were working to raise the incomes of new oil producers. These were not the actions of a dangerous economic rival.

Yet there was no mistaking that these actions also carried geopolitical implications. Surging economic growth did embolden China's economic leaders with new confidence and assertiveness. Strictly speaking, China did not "need" to enact the going out strategy: it could have relied on the global market to supply it with what was needed. It chose instead to become an active player in its own right. It wanted its companies to be globally competitive and to have a say in the system that procured the commodities that were the building blocks of its growth. One entrepreneur in Indonesia noted that in the oil industry, "if an oil field is worth 100 to ExxonMobil, it is worth 110 to China. There is a major difference. To China, oil is a strategic interest and CNOOC represents this state strategic interest, so they are willing to pay for their interests. ExxonMobil doesn't have this dimension of strategic interest."[48] China now faced the energy security issues afflicting Western industrialized markets for decades and adopted broadly similar measures for dealing with them.

China's emergence as an economic power portended much for the future. The geopolitical landscape in the oil industry was beginning to shift: by 2010 China was importing more oil from Saudi Arabia than was the United States. Chinese oil companies had pushed the geographic frontiers of exploration and were becoming increasingly confident and competent at doing so. China had acted with focus: few other foreign policy goals diluted its purpose of enhancing economic strength. By 2014, its companies had vaulted into the front ranks of international oil competitors and its economy continued its rapid growth.

The Geopolitics of Oil Money

Not all the geopolitical issues associated with oil were confined to its extraction and sale. The politics of oil for oil importers centers around energy security, fears of scarcity, and the impact oil exploration might have on other foreign policy priorities. For those exporting a lot of oil – and whose economies produced little else – the political and geopolitical problems appear more enviable but are just as real. When oil prices are high, they begin to receive a lot of revenue, and what they do with that money matters, politically and geopolitically. The next section focuses our inquiry that could be boiled down to two simple questions. One, what did they do with all that money? Two, how did those decisions affect other actors in the global economy?

High oil prices did generate a lot of money for exporters. Saudi Arabia, for example, exported in the neighborhood of 9 mbd, and each barrel continued to fetch over $100/barrel on the international market and cost but a few dollars to produce. Consequently, the value of Saudi oil exports measured in the hundreds of billions of dollars annually; oil comprised about 50 per cent of its GDP and was responsible for over 90 per cent of its export earnings.[49] Other oil exporters experienced similar inflows of riches. For example, the United Arab Emirates (UAE), populated by 9 million people, produced over 3 mbd and exported almost all of it.

The funds provided governments with room to spend. In the case of the UAE, those funds helped complete an impressive urbanization effort in its major cities of Abu Dhabi and Dubai, featuring luxury residences, extravagant hotels, and impressive architectural feats, including the construction of the world's tallest building, the Burj Kahlifa. It also provided its citizens with generous social allowances, subsidies for domestic energy consumption,[50] and an impressive array of social benefits, all without collecting income taxes. That was just one example: the list of countries benefiting from the profits generated by high oil prices could go on. Uniting them all was the distorted economic and political incentives caused by deploying the massive amounts of cash pouring into countries producing oil. Much of that money appears to have been stolen, funding the extravagant lifestyles for those able to tap into oil money:

in some cases the degree of oil corruption spurred by rising prices grew to gargantuan proportions.[51] Given all this, the management of oil money would begin mattering to politics and geopolitics.

Specific geopolitical problems arose around the management of that money. Even with oil exporters doing an impressive amount of domestic spending, there were a lot of funds leftover. Some oil exporters saved much of that revenue in the form of SWFs, which were government-owned pools of capital that were independently managed with an eye toward generating long-term economic returns for the country. The concept of SWFs seemed simple enough: countries enjoying surpluses of incoming revenue would save and invest a portion of it outside of general revenues, protecting against the "grabbing hand"[52] of governments who might be eager to spend it immediately. Those funds generated returns for the benefit of future generations, for the proverbial "rainy day," and to ensure monetary wealth generated in times of resource plenty would last beyond a particular boom period. SWFs were designed to protect capital while generating returns needed to fund state spending far into the future.[53] The idea of SWFs was certainly not particularly new, nor were they used only by oil-producing states.[54] But, as oil prices increased, the investable assets they had at their disposal grew very quickly.

Prominent Middle Eastern SWFs included the Abu Dhabi Investment Authority (ADIA) and the Saudi Arabia Monetary Agency (SAMA). As oil prices rose, each saw their asset base grow by hundreds of billions of dollars: by the end of 2014 their investable assets in some cases measured nearly a trillion dollars.[55] They then faced the enviable but challenging problem of what to do with them.

SWFs caused political concerns that other pools of money did not. Indeed, there were other large pools of money floating around the financial system, primarily pension funds and mutual funds, having comparable or even larger totals of investable assets. However, those funds operated independently of host governments and had regulatory requirements enhancing investment transparency and demonstrating independence of decision-making. By contrast, a number of oil-exporting SWFs hardly qualified as transparent, and critics charged they also were not really independent. The fact of government ownership could easily be conflated with the assumption of government direction, stoking fears that SWF investments might be colored by a political hue.[56]

Such suspicions caused geopolitical concerns in governments whose economies received SWF investment. First was the already-noted transparency: no one outside the funds' management really knew how much money they had, what their performance targets were, or what their overall investment strategy was. Second, observers fretted that SWF investment often seemed to target industries and companies holding security implications, particularly high-tech companies. Third, SWFs also seemed to be accumulating a lot of debt instruments, particularly sovereign debt. As the United States and Western Europe increasingly ran deficits to pay for their spending commitments, they borrowed money from the "glut of global savings" held by commodity and trade exporters. Investors were eager to find safe investment products and proved willing to hold government debt even at the very low interest rates then prevailing. To summarize the geopolitical concerns, SWFs funds were large, lacked transparency, got capital from exporting commodities, held a lot of US and European government debt, and were owned by undemocratic governments whose interests were not always aligned with the countries issuing the debt.[57]

SWF investors countered these claims by making broader and more consistent efforts to improve investor transparency and to show independence. They also continued to argue that they were passive investors, and indeed were an ideal source of capital for companies looking to execute long-term strategies. Their targeting of high-tech companies was far from a nefarious plot. It was simply a testament to the growth potential those companies had and the investment potential SWFs saw in them. Indeed, it would be far more worrisome if those sectors did not attract foreign investment, which would imply that better investment opportunities lay elsewhere. SWF defenders noted that their overall investment strategies mirrored those employed by other pools of investment capital and that little real evidence of government-directed targeting existed.

The geopolitics of SWF investment came into bold relief during the financial crisis of 2008, a time when cash and confidence were suddenly both in short supply. The US began scouring the globe for the first in order to reignite the second, and the funds oil exporters held in reserve suddenly became an enormously valuable and coveted asset. Domestic US banks needed a jolt of capital, and cash needed to be injected directly into the US economic system to keep it from freezing up. Consequently, oil exporters began receiving pleas from crisis-afflicted companies and governments to provide the needed liquidity. It was a notable about, and loss of, face. The United States – which had rejected CNOOC's foreign bid for UNOCAL just a few years before and had cast the most vocal suspicion at SWFs as being government instruments – now clamored to obtain more investment from these very same governments in order to bandage the wounds its own financial system had generated. The irony was not lost on SWF managers, and they noted that investment prudence limited what they either could or would do. It took prodding to convince them to deploy more capital, and even as they did, they had to resist continued criticism even from those pleading for investment capital. SWF funds, one analyst noted, could be viewed as either a threat or a salvation.[58]

The symbolism of SWF investment power was not lost on either the providers or the recipients of that capital. The spectacle of apparently stable, well-funded, state-driven, often oil-based economies bailing out the world's largest developed economies symbolized a lot, none of it particularly attractive for Western nations. Those holding state-owned SWFs with large capital reserves could feel a measure of smug satisfaction. Many countries, not just oil producers, had built up such savings as an insurance mechanism against the dangers liberalized financial markets obviously held. Now the United States was in the throes of its own financial meltdown, for which there had been warnings and plenty of fairly obvious symptoms indicating a financial bubble was brewing.[59] Yet the US system either could not, or chose not, to recognize the bubble, did nothing to halt its growth, and seemed taken utterly by surprise when it burst. That contrasted poorly with the state capitalism model, which provided a stability that seemed better able to cope with financial shock. The US, long the most vocal critic of state capitalism, now seemed dependent on the financial goodwill of the countries practicing it, and a good number of them were oil producers.[60]

This placed oil producers at the very heart of an emerging geopolitical and financial contest, one that was deeply interrelated with both the optics and reality of oil. Invested SWF funds drew their capital from profits generated by selling commodities and manufactured exporters, usually consumed by developed markets. That generated money that had to go somewhere: usually it was simply reinvested back into the global financial system, buying the stocks, bonds, and sovereign debt of Western economies. That financial system now looked much like a simple giant recycling program. Importers paid for oil and other exports with US dollars that sovereign governments then reinvested back into US financial markets, further increasing their leverage over the US system. Buying imported oil at inflated prices generated a financial double whammy: it transferred US wealth abroad and increased the influence exporters and oil producers had over both the financial system and in the funding of government debt. This did not seem at all like a good deal to oil consumers, but how to break out of it was not clear.

Indeed, the geopolitical significance of the 2008 crisis spread beyond financial markets and spilled into the fundamental questions of leadership in the global economy. The reputation and principles underpinning the US financial system were at the very least tarnished if not outright wounded. SWFs and others had ridden to their financial rescue during the crisis, and state-driven economies looked like they had better managed and recovered faster from that crisis than had more open economies. That gave the world something to think about: developing markets now had options in choosing what types of economic system they should employ in managing their own economies.

Secondly, oil revenue helped fund an explosion of sovereign debt, owed primarily by the most advanced economies to the developing ones. To be sure, the US and others were equal-opportunity borrowers: they drew as much foreign capital from non-oil exporters as they did from oil exporters. While there was a mutual dependency in debt – developed markets may borrow a lot of money, but they are by far the safest financial bets, are most likely to pay the money back – the dependency seemed more skewed in favor of those providing the funds than those asking for them. What if oil exporters and others stopped holding US and Western European debt or demanded better interest rates before acquiring more? How dependent was the US on their ongoing financial goodwill? What price would they have to pay – monetary and otherwise – to maintain that goodwill?

The geopolitics of finance, often powered by oil revenue and the power of statism, came into full view as oil prices remained elevated and the financial crisis took its toll. High oil prices appeared to favor oil exporters, both monetarily and geopolitically, and provided them with increased options both domestically and internationally. There were three things that could happen to that oil revenue: it could be saved, spent, or stolen. The part that was stolen is discussed below: it contributed in some cases to a reemergence of the resource curse. The first two had a significant impact on the global economy. The part spent was easy to see: as prices rose, so too did displays of opulent wealth, as ambitious governments or individuals used gargantuan oil-based fortunes to fuel extravagant spending binges. Oil barons bought professional sports teams, invested in prime real estate, and paid top dollar for luxury goods in the market for bling. Oil-rich governments built enormous cosmopolitan cities that seemed to spring out of the desert.

Though perhaps inspiring envy, such opulence hardly constituted the stuff of geopolitical worry. The more important geopolitical part was the money saved and invested by governments. Much of that money was reinvested into the financial system, generating benefits for exporters and apparently weakening importers. That in turn created perceived financial vulnerabilities, as well as long-term geopolitical musings about leadership in the global economy.

Oil, the Consolidation of State Power, and the Resource Curse

Influxes of oil revenue mattered to the functioning of the states receiving it and provided options to those wielding power that helped them keep it. Oil and gas revenue certainly mattered to Russia, where oil revenue provided the government with more centralized power and geopolitical clout. Oil revenue gave the domestic economy a powerful boost. During the 1990s Russian growth rates had remained poor, and the financial crisis of 1997, with its attendant drop in oil prices, had crippled it even more. That decade reshaped the Russian oil and gas industry. Initially, the privatization of state-held companies was hoped to spread ownership throughout the Russian populace and thereby give them a stake in the success of market reforms. However, few Russian citizens understood well how markets worked, and the ones that did, particularly if they were ruthless enough, built economic power by buying back those shares on the cheap, gaining control of Russian state industries for a fraction of what they were worth.[61] The "Wild West" private scramble to purchase Russian state assets created a powerful wealthy group today collectively known as the oligarchs.[62]

The oligarchs were businessmen who employed aggressive and sometimes violent means to gain control over post-Soviet oil and gas assets.[63] They fought for control of the fields themselves as well as the export terminals linking Russia's vast natural bounty with the outside world. Russia's vast reserves of oil and gas were its primary source of export revenue. Though they generated little actual profit given the prices prevailing during the 1990s, their export revenue potential was gigantic should those prices ever rise. They remained the primary economic card Russia could play in generating foreign exchange, and the oligarchs knew that controlling those fields and terminals could generate enormous personal wealth.

The Russian government wished to increase oil production and encouraged owners to try to pump out ever more oil. Russia started cultivating foreign direct investors who could supply it the requisite technologies to develop its offshore oil and gas resources. British and American supermajor oil companies began developing resources in the Arctic and Sakhalin Island. Russia also proved adept at increasing production in its Siberian oil fields, squeezing more oil out of Soviet-era decaying infrastructure. The result was that Russian oil production increased by over 3 mbd between 1998 and 2004,[64] and more was scheduled on the horizon, as prices increased. Indeed, without such Russian increases, the fears of peak oil and the problem of inflated prices afflicting importing markets might have been worse than they were.[65] Generating more oil and gas seemed key to Russia's economic future: and the rise in global prices boded well for its revenue stream.

Those revenues were also key to its political future as well. Rising oil and gas revenues became geopolitical tools for consolidating Russian political authority in Moscow and increasing Russia's influence and power abroad. Both were key tenets of the political strategy consistently pursued by Vladimir Putin, who assumed office as Russia's president in 2000 and who has remained there, more or less, ever since.[66] Putin's vision for Russia's future included a key role for oil and gas exports. He believed the way out of his country's economic and geopolitical doldrums lay in centralizing political power in his own hands and extending that state power over natural resource development.

Political predominance over the oil and gas industry was something taken for granted in the Soviet era but had been forgotten in the post–Cold War private scramble for riches. As prices rose and state revenues increased, Putin began moving firmly to remind the oligarchs of the dominance of Moscow, moving ruthlessly against them if they waded into political waters. Those striking an independent or critical political line were censored or imprisoned. The most famous case was of Mikhail Khodorkovsky, chairman of Yukos Oil, who received a jail term for advocating too strongly for alternatives to Putin's rule.[67] Other oligarchs took the lesson well and began staying well clear of playing active role in the country's politics.

Higher oil prices further aided Putin's centralization efforts. As oil prices rose, so too did the revenue flowing into Russia. Oil export revenues measured $36 billion in 2000; by 2007 they topped $173 billion. Oil taxes increased along with those revenues: by 2007 taxes on oil accounted for nearly 37 per cent of Russia's federal budget revenue, and for every $1 per barrel increase in world prices, an additional $1.9 billion flowed into the Russian state treasury.[68] Putin used incoming state revenues to revitalize the military and security forces, neutralize the nascent independent media, and to isolate and then eliminate potential opponents.[69] He ensured the Russian state would retain majority control over Gazprom, the natural gas colossus that would become the world's largest energy company, and that it would continue to hold ownership stakes in the country's larger oil companies. Rising energy prices created the foundation for Putin's consolidation of power and provided the revenue for the state treasury.

Because oil revenue became and remained so core to Russian economic strength, the struggle for control over it never fully ceased. It became especially strained during the financial crisis, when oil prices plummeted and Russia's tax revenues crashed along with them. Yet, by then Putin's control was firmly enough established that the price fall did not threaten his position. His government weathered the price downturn by adjusting tax laws that kept a measure of money flowing into the treasury while also ensuring domestic companies could remain somewhat profitable. Those measures remained in place until prices began to recover, but there were clear limits as to how far he would go in granting further regulatory help to Russia's energy sector. When presented with arguments on why the oil industry needed more state help to cope with the downturn, he reportedly retorted, "Moscow does not believe in tears, only blood."[70] The companies themselves would still be the ones having to bear the further costs of managing the crisis.

The era of price rise saw oil and energy production reassert itself as perhaps the key factor fueling the national interests of Russia. Putin's centralization drive was hardly unprecedented, and exerting control over energy companies provided him the resources to do so, and do so rapidly.[71] However, that effort increased Russia's economic dependency on natural resource revenues, which increasingly looked like the only economic card they had to play. The more Russia ramped up production, the more their economy became subject to the vagaries of oil and gas prices, a vulnerability that would make itself readily apparent when oil and gas prices began to drop in 2014.

Russia was not the only country that used oil revenue to fuel nationalist ambitions. Other oil producers also consolidated political power and distributed resource revenue to increase their domestic support. Even as they were building an economic modernization program, Gulf Oil producers also continued increasing expenditures on military and security forces. Saudi Arabia's military expenditures measured US$54 billion in 2010: by 2014 they measured US$84 billion. In the same period, the UAE's military expenditures went from $20 billion to $25 billion, a comparatively modest figure but still substantial given the country's small size and population.[72] Between 2010 and 2014, Russia's military spending went up from US$49 billion to US$68 billion.[73] In Saudi Arabia economic reform was coupled with an increasingly assertive leadership wary of any sign of domestic turmoil. In response to the pro-democracy Arab Spring movement – which arose in Tunisia in 2010 and spread rapidly to Egypt, Libya, Yemen, and later Syria – Saudi Arabia's leaders authorized a new suite of social programs totaling some $130 billion.[74] Similar uprisings did not happen in the Saudi kingdom.

In Latin America increasing oil revenues funded the political ambitions of established leaders. In Venezuela rapidly rising oil prices motivated the country to keep production high: it hovered between 2.5 and 3 mbd between 2005 and 2014, and in 2010 the country earned about $90 billion in exports.[75] That enabled leader Hugo Chavez to spend enormous sums domestically in distributing oil revenues. It also emboldened him to conduct increasingly aggressive and antagonistic policies, particularly against the United States, that ironically made it difficult for foreign firms to operate there.[76] Oil revenues also helped Brazil's socialist parties, led first by popular Luis Inacio Lula Da Silva and then by his picked successor Dilma Rouseff, to begin increasing national control over its enormous offshore oil reserves.[77] Brazil authorized massive investments in the oil industry and hoped the ensuring revenues generated would pay for the social redistribution platforms that were the party's hallmark.

Oil revenue had profound political effects on many of the countries producing it. It allowed some to centralize power and allowed others to ride out political storms that were engulfing others and, in other circumstances, might have threatened the stability of their governments. Rising defense expenditures were symptomatic of increased oil revenue. Governments had choices, but the temptation to build political programs on a foundation of oil money proved very powerful.

Global Governance of the Global Oil Business

A final political and geopolitical trend witnessed during the era of high prices was a growing number of global governance efforts wanting to exert influence on how the oil industry worked. This was a slow development, given how state-centric the oil industry is and how national interests clearly weighed heavily in determining what both importers and exporters do.[78] Yet many nations realized that there was a set of common problems they all shared, problems that became particularly acute in times of high prices. They might all benefit from having an established set of "rules of the road" that influenced, as far as possible, what countries and companies choose to do.

These rules sets are prominent in the realms of trade, finance, and development, but they are not as well developed in energy, given state desires to continue exerting control.[79] As prices and incomes rose and the market involved more players, the institutions that did try to govern it also came under increasing strain. Their legitimacy depended on governments' willingness to endorse them and abide by their recommendations. This they would only do if they thought they served a broader national interest.

One such problem was the coordination of policy responses when prices rose and shortages appeared. As prices rose, consuming governments began trying to coordinate policy responses, reflecting recognition of the need for better governance of energy.[80] On the demand side the IEA continued garnering information and fostering relationships between the world's major consumers of oil. It faced challenges as prices rose, primarily in terms of membership and of purpose. The IEA's historical role was, in part, to coordinate policy responses among oil importers, particularly when a supply shock occurred. Indeed, it had been born out of a response to an unexpected supply shock and the weak existing mechanisms to coordinate a response. In subsequent years the IEA helped forge and coordinate agreements among its member countries during times of plenty that determined what they would collectively do in times of shortage.

In that purpose the IEA had scored successes: its members collectively agreed to build petroleum reserves and storage capacities and to develop coordination mechanisms for their potential release. Yet that role became more difficult to fulfill the more that demand shifted away from its current members and toward emerging markets. To remain relevant, the IEA would have to find a way to incorporate those countries into its organizational fold and get them to buy into established policy prescriptions.

That was going to be tricky. First, to be effective, emerging sources of demand would want to have participated in, and have say over, whatever policy directives they were signing on to. Second, a precondition for joining the IEA involved a commitment to assessment, monitoring, and information-sharing provisions, and it was far from clear that prospective new members would want to do those things. The third problem, and probably the biggest long-term one, had to do with the nature of membership. Though a legally separate entity, the IEA's membership derived from Organization of Economic Cooperation and Development (OECD). Its statutes mandated that member states show commitments to human rights, transparency in business practices, and a commitment to democratic norms. Many emerging markets would not qualify under these tests and would not likely be willing change their operational ways simply to gain IEA membership. Yet, without their participation, the IEA's capacity to coordinate effective global policy responses to oil price shocks would erode.[81] The IEA needed the support and participation of the emerging developing markets if it was to remain relevant.[82]

In response, the IEA created an "associate" status that incorporated new consumers, particularly India and China, into the fold. In terms of the oil market, Chinese investment actually complemented, rather than contradicted, many Western objectives. This status committed China to pursuing goals such as information sharing and transparency, as well as ongoing dialogues on key energy issues. They too committed to maintaining a strategic petroleum reserve and to continue engaging in talks with the IEA on the conditions under which it might be released. In this respect, China proved willing to become part of the integrated global energy system,[83] as coordinating responses to oil price shocks remained a shared interest among importers.

A second growing governance trend also began affecting the global management of the oil system, one emanating not from a country or an international organization. This one instead emerged from a combination of social trends that, taken together, began to impact significantly on how the oil industry was expected to operate. A growing number of people began paying attention to the oil business, and the more they knew about it the more they questioned and criticized how it worked. Many believed it needed more and better rules to halt its more egregious behavior. The higher oil prices went and the more of afflicted politics and geopolitics, the more attention was paid to how the industry operated and what, if anything, could be done to influence what its participants chose to do.

As the industry gained prominence, opponents of it began launching criticisms along a variety of fronts and with varying intensity. Some objected to how the industry operated, arguing that it damaged ecosystems, treated Indigenous populations poorly, and ran huge risks of oil spills and other engineering mishaps. Others disliked the gargantuan profits oil sales generated for the companies and the select individuals lucky enough to be part of it. The industry seemed to epitomize a growing global problem of wealth inequality; still others objected to the very existence of the industry itself, arguing that it had little interest other than its own self-preservation and that the continued burning of fossil fuels represented a threat to the environment that put the future of the planet at stake. While such criticisms were hardly new, their intensity seemed to grow in lockstep with the industry's profits and prominence.

For critics, evidence abounded. To begin, rising prices and profits provided massive incentive for corruption: few countries seemed to manage oil revenues well. The textbook example for doing so was perhaps Norway, a country exporting 2.5 mbd and which saved almost all the generated earnings in an SWF. This reserve of oil revenues became the backbone of a solidly funded suite of long-term social and pension programs, and the country suffers no obvious symptoms of the resource curse.[84] Yet for every Norway there seemed to be many more counterexamples of extravagant spending, pilferage, and waste. Perhaps the most extreme lay in Equatorial Guinea, ruled by the Obiang family, who seemed to treat the country's growing oil revenues largely as a family bank account. Reports of their opulent lifestyles contrasted poorly with the dire squalor most of the country's citizens continued to dwell in.[85] In between these extremes ranged a variety of country responses in the handling of oil wealth.[86] But on balance examples of poor or incompetent management of oil money – if not outright thievery – seemed too easy to find and more the norm than not.

A second source of oil opposition arose from general critics of economic globalization, of which the oil industry was a key player. As the quest for more profit and streamlined supply chains drove companies to expand into more countries, it eroded a government's capacity to regulate its own economy. Globalization gave companies too much power, power they could then use to force countries to lower their regulatory standards in a competitive "race to the bottom." Wages, operating and safety conditions, and workers' rights would all be sacrificed in the name of attracting investment. Because it was labor-intensive, often operated in developing countries in remote geographic locales, and generated such massive profits, the oil industry was particularly susceptible to such charges. Oil companies often retorted that host countries did indeed have bargaining power – they after all had the oil the companies needed – but the charge of potential exploitation remained.

A third source of criticism came from those opposed to the industry because of its contribution to climate change. The oil industry, according to its critics, spelled doom for the environment because of what it did and what it reinforced. The extraction of oil caused untold environmental damage, the burning of oil polluted the atmosphere, and the race to acquire more resources corrupted governments and made them unwilling to pursue alternate energy sources. Pictures of in-situ mining operations in the Alberta oil sands – which appeared roughly akin to the Land of Mordor portrayed in the *Lord of the Rings* novels – featured prominently in this argument. So too did visions of engineering mishaps, the most prominent of which occurred in the Gulf of Mexico, where a BP offshore rig suffered a catastrophic well rupture, which generated one of the largest oil spills in history. These images and problems convinced onlookers that enabling more oil extraction and reinforcing a carbon-based economy needed to be halted, or at least slowed down.

Such criticisms spurred responses, including a growing network of institutional efforts designed to combat the more egregious effects of globalization. The United Nations established its "Global Compact" initiative, which established a list of principles of sustainable globalization that companies who joined pledged to respect.[87] Other organizations emerged from private efforts, often focusing on individual aspects of global business. The "Publish What You Pay" initiative encouraged companies to reveal whatever payments they had made to foreign nationals in securing business, with the idea that greater transparency might reduce the incentive and the capacity for bribery.[88] The Extractive Industries Transparency Index (EITI) followed a similar purpose, focusing on increasing transparency in the specific contractual terms that governed resource extraction.[89] Other organizations, ranging from Greenpeace International to the Sierra Club, focused on environmental concerns. These were just some examples of NGOs dedicating ever more effort to monitoring and critiquing what was going on in the oil industry.

There were limitations on what these organizations could accomplish without the full backing of governments and how much they could directly influence what companies did. Endorsement of their standards usually remained voluntary. Their primary targets were large private-sector companies, whose investments were easily monitored and whose stock meetings could be disrupted by shareholder resolution. That actually left most of the oil industry unscathed: state-owned companies would not be susceptible to such shareholder pressure, and their strategies and operations often did not go beyond their borders and therefore they were unlikely to be concerned about the social welfare implications of someone else's foreign direct investment. Yet the trend toward increased external monitoring and demands for social performance grew and gained momentum. It marked an increasingly powerful competitive reality in the industry that was not going to go away.

High Prices, Politics, and the Geopolitics of Oil

By 2014 several political and geopolitical challenges had emerged that seemed linked to oil and were accentuated by the high prices oil then commanded. Oil procurement certainly impacted the foreign policy interests of the world's biggest economies. It mattered to the United States, where procuring energy and ensuring its safe transport remained a core principle of national security policy. September 11, 2001, turned US security attention to issues surrounding terrorism and failed states: oil and oil money appeared intrinsically linked to both. The ensuing war on terror mired the US in some very key geopolitical hotspots, including an invasion of Iraq and a further reinforcement of the positioning of US forces in the Persian Gulf. Those efforts provided evidence for those looking for oil-based explanations of US foreign policy.

Second, oil geopolitics changed with the rise of powerful emerging market importers, particularly China. China's rapid economic growth meant that its energy consumption would grow: its economic model demanded that it become a bigger player in that market. Its foreign policy cultivated economic strength and appeared concerned with little else. Moreover, its companies did not seem to play by the same set of rules: state capitalism allowed them to tread where others dared not and do what others could not. Criticism for the "unfairness" of Chinese competitive practices engendered little more than a shrug and a pointed reference to the history of Western companies and governments who had done much the same thing. China was now a formidable international oil player and was not going to change course simply because others did not like how they did things.

For oil exporters, higher oil revenues helped reinforce and centralize political power and allowed them to initiate extravagant spending plans and pursue ambitious domestic political agendas. Russia used incoming oil revenues to do both, and Putin's political fortunes benefited from the higher take its state treasury received. However, relying too much on oil revenue for political support generated a precarious existence: such support could erode if prices went down. A period of high oil prices therefore creates a mixed bag of political opportunities and dangers for oil exporters. They may enjoy the money oil revenues generate but face a strong consequent temptation to reinforce, rather than diversify, the country's economic reliance on oil.

Fourth, the geopolitics of finance demonstrated how oil profits could be recycled into the global financial system in a way that generated geopolitical as well as monetary effects. Oil imports at elevated prices worsened trade balances, depressed an importer's currency, and damaged its terms of trade. Excessive oil prices inflated financial bubbles and made the financial system more unstable. After the financial crisis, the apparent steadiness of the state-driven model, one employed by many oil exporters, seemed attractive and worthy of emulation.

Fifth, as the industry expanded and gained popular notoriety, calls for better governance of it emerged. The IEA widened its membership base and tried to strengthen its coordination capacity. The UN and other agencies crafted voluntary standards conditioning how companies were supposed to operate. NGOs directed their focus at oil and tried to create similar sorts of expectations. Oil companies became subject to ever-greater social scrutiny and demand for better environmental and operational performance. Efforts to wean off oil, both domestically and internationally, gained momentum. All this mandated more rather than less of a coordinated global response.

Admittedly, none of these trends were directly, still less solely, "caused" by the high price of oil. Lots of things had contributed to them, and many had been percolating for some time. But the prolonged period of high prices accelerated them, acting as a kind of steroid that threw the problems of an oil-based economy into ever-bolder relief. When prices were high, it became difficult to ignore problems associated with oil. It generated a flood of revenue, strengthened the geopolitical hand of exporters, hurt oil-dependent economies, helped intensify terrorism, damaged the environment, and forced governments to pay more attention to oil than they wanted to.

But they also carried with them the seeds of their own destruction. When prices are high, investment capital floods new exploration sites, improves recovery technologies, and brings more oil to the market, first at a trickle, then a flow, and then often a flood.[90] This eventually generates an inevitable price drop: the question then is how fast, how far, and how much pain it will cause. That reality can be forgotten, or conveniently ignored, when in the midst of an oil boom, and in 2014, few observers seemed willing to countenance that this was about to happen. Yet it did, in a rather dramatic fashion. The next chapter chronicles the genesis and effect of the price drop of 2014, one that has continued through the onset of the global pandemic in the spring of 2020. That chapter features both old and new dynamics, built on the trends noted in this chapter, trends that may indeed have permanently changed the nature of the oil industry.

chapter six

The Politics and Markets of a Price Fall: 2014–2019

In the fall of 2017, Mohammed Bin Salman (MBS) – one of the youngest, and certainly the most ambitious, of Saudi Arabia's crown princes – confined members of the Saudi financial elite to the rooms and lobbies of the Ritz Carlton hotel in Riyadh. Their alleged transgression: the pilfering of the Saudi state treasury through rigged business dealings, embezzlement of state funds earmarked for development projects, using family and tribal connections to steer public money into private pockets, and other acts of monetary corruption. MBS argued that it was only logical that the Saudi elite pay back a portion of their wealth to the state to compensate it for what they had stolen. While imprisoning them in an upscale hotel hardly classifies as the epitome of hardship, those afflicted felt pained enough to surrender a significant portion of their wealth and thereby give MBS the public victory he wanted. The shakedown netted a windfall of US$13 billion for the Saudi state treasury and allowed MBS to portray himself as a defender of the people's money to boot.[1]

To be sure, his subsequent purchase of a $400 million dollar yacht would tarnish any man-of-the-people public persona he had hoped to cultivate. Moreover, his later apparent sanctioning of the murder of a Saudi journalist who had been living in the United States proved how ruthlessly he would move against domestic critics. Yet those events would occur later. The 2017 act of imprisoning the Saudi elite sent at least a couple of messages, some at the time mildly hopeful, yet still ominous. One was that the Saudi government, and increasingly him personally, was running the show. Whatever gains corruption and connections might garner in Saudi Arabia could be taken away if those enjoying them did not support what the Al-Saud family wanted to do. A second, more muddled message was what this might portend for the Saudi state's future. Few believed that this one act heralded in a new era of transparency, openness, and accountability that would now characterize the dealings of the Saudi state. But it did look at least like a tentative forward step in a long road of reform, one in which successive Saudi rulers nudged their culturally conservative country along a liberalizing path. Perhaps a crackdown on a corrupt financial elite was part of a wider effort that the youthful prince was planning to sustain. Maybe more was on the horizon, and the world closely watched the ongoing Saudi drama playing out in the hotel lobby with a measure of curiosity, if not hope.

Others offered a more pedestrian explanation. Maybe the Saudi government simply needed the money. After all, it was hurting fiscally: the previous three years had witnessed a massive drop in the revenue that had been flowing into the Saudi state treasury, 90 per cent of which came from the nationally controlled production and sale of almost 10 mbd of crude oil. One in every ten barrels of oil the world consumed came from Saudi fields. Each cost but a few dollars to produce and had for almost a decade routinely fetched more than $100 on global markets, thereby creating a gusher of inflowing cash for the Saudi state. Yet that cash tsunami had slowed to a comparative trickle after prices fell by half in the fall of 2014, where they had remained for three subsequent years. Maybe recouping some extra cash might be necessary.

It was difficult to summon much sympathy for the Saudi fiscal plight. After all, the price drop was no accident: the Saudi government had done everything in its power to engineer it. Saudi Arabia had hoped that a massive price drop would drive other, more expensive producers out of the global oil game, and the monetary pain they were now enduring was a price willingly paid if it preserved their long-term market share of the world's oil revenue. Saudi Arabia was, after all, in a bind. High oil prices funded economic modernization and diversification, yet those efforts were far from complete. Its reliance on oil remained almost absolute. When oil prices declined, it had few other industries that could generate alternate sources of revenue, and none are nearly big enough to fill the fiscal gap low oil prices create.

Meanwhile, the ruling Al-Saud family continued to live with a political bargain fashioned with the Saudi people decades ago, one in which ongoing support for the monarchy's rule is exchanged for the provision of generous social programs funded by oil revenue. Yet elaborate social programs – sometimes resembling more a mattress rather than a net – were set to become more expensive, particularly as the Saudi population grew. The generous promises made to a country of 30 million people were going to be prohibitively expensive for a population that by 2040 might measure twice that. The Saudi economy also needed to generate millions of new jobs to keep the exploding population of young people occupied and productive: not all of them could work for Saudi Aramco.

Finally, lurking in the background was a growing, and for Saudi Arabia ominous, reality. The age of oil seemed poised to end, or at least slow down dramatically, if the world was going to cut carbon emissions and thereby meet its collective stated goals of preventing climate change. Basing your economy on selling oil to a world looking to use progressively less of it is a risky long-term bet. Indeed it might be as sure a route as there is to economic oblivion. The stakes could not be higher for the Saudi kingdom: if oil revenue fell permanently with nothing to replace it, it might generate political tremors powerful enough to shake the country apart.

The Price Fall of 2014

The only reason to go to all the effort and expense necessary to extract oil is to sell it into a market that needs it and will pay a profitable price for it. For most of the past fourteen years, that had seemed almost a given. Producers did not have to worry much about demand: a willing buyer for all the crude produced seemed assured. Yet a precipitous drop in oil prices in the fall of 2014 indicated just how fast things could change. Price levels topping $100/barrel suddenly fell by half, and stayed there for the ensuing six years. Assumptions of perceived scarcity and permanently inflated prices evaporated in the face of a supply glut that somehow caught supposedly wary market players by surprise. Not only was the price fall shocking in itself, so too was the seeming unpreparedness of those who might have guessed it was coming. What happened to make the market overshoot as it did? Why was the price fall not anticipated better? How would importers and exporters react, economically, politically, and geopolitically? What would it mean for the future? This chapter devotes itself to answering those questions.

The Price Drop

In the fall of 2014, the extended era of high prices came to an end. The cause seemed innocent enough: a regularly scheduled quarterly meeting of the OPEC oil cartel reached a decision generating consequences for the oil market and the price a barrel of oil would fetch. Perhaps it was more of a non-decision: Saudi Arabia, the cartel's most prolific producer, chose to maintain its production output despite calls for a cut emanating from its OPEC partners. Those countries wanted Saudi Arabia to lower their production as a way to address the increasingly obvious supply overhang looming in the market. As the single OPEC country with enough production volume to make a real difference in the amount of oil reaching that market, only a significant Saudi Arabian supply cut could address that overhang. The Saudis said no, and in doing so they all but guaranteed that excess supply would start flooding the marketplace with oil it did not need and could not use. That would clearly affect price, yet few anticipated how rapidly price would fall or how long it would stay there.

Faced with a looming tidal wave of excess supply, oil prices did not simply deflate, they collapsed. Crude oil prices that had averaged close to $100/barrel for much of the preceding three years rapidly fell to less than half of that. In June 2014, prices of Brent Crude averaged $110 a barrel: by January 2015 those prices had fallen to $51 a barrel. The plunge did not stop there: in the space of fourteen months, between the November 2014 OPEC meeting and the end of 2015, the price for a barrel of oil fell by almost two-thirds.[2] The following year brought no relief to oil producers: prices continued dropping, reaching a low of US$28.35 by January 2016.

Cumulatively, between the late fall of 2014 and the beginning of 2016, the price for a barrel of oil lost over $80.[3] Moreover, unlike the aftermath of the 2008 financial crisis, oil prices showed no sign that they would rebound. They remained low for over three years and only began rising again in the spring of 2018, only to subsequently fall again. They only recently come anywhere close to the $100/barrel previously thought routine. Figure 7 shows the prices of a barrel of WTI oil over the six-year period between 2013 and 2019.

Not surprisingly, that price plunge changed the conversations people had about oil. Fears of tight supply and of "running out" vanished in the wake of a supply onslaught. Reputable observers of the oil market now began warning that low, not high, oil prices are going to be a more-or-less permanent fixture of the oil market, a marked reversal of what had been argued but a few years before.[4] Suppliers began scrambling for market share. Government budgets previously flush with oil revenue now required extensive trimming to erase the red ink, given that they were now receiving less than half as much money for their oil exports. Private oil companies had to cut costs and staff and consolidate operations: many

Figure 7. Oil Prices, West Texas Intermediate, US$/Barrel, August 2013–August 2019

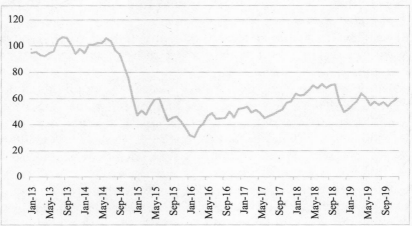

Source: US Energy Information Administration, various years.

newer or highly leveraged firms went out of business entirely. Gloom replaced boom in the towns located on the frontier of oil production, where it was difficult to imagine a more rapid and complete reversal in economic fortune.

Saudi Arabia's oil officials were not surprised that this might happen. Indeed, assuring that it would had been the prime reason why they kept their taps open. They were also prepared for the onslaught of criticism their decision inevitably received, as they had clear and, to their minds, defensible reasons for doing what they did. The country had, over the past decade, watched with trepidation the massive amounts of money flowing into oil exploration and development projects around the world. They noted that such investments targeted increasingly expensive fields and had successfully brought millions of new barrels to the market.[5] They had witnessed China's oil companies enter the market and become formidable players, and even had hosted Chinese diplomats anxious to curry Saudi favor. They noted how dependent Russia had become on oil exports to fuel its economy and fund political centralization, which meant they too would likely continue to dump ever more crude into a high-priced market. They had become exasperated with their OPEC colleagues, who pointedly refused to endure production cuts themselves while simultaneously advocating for Saudi restraint. Finally, like everyone else, they had paid close attention to the fracking revolution going on in the United States, whose productivity amazed and worried Saudi observers as it turned what had been the world's biggest oil importer into a production rival and perhaps even an export competitor.

All of that created the conditions for oversupply, and in response Saudi officials issued warnings – publicly, privately, and repeatedly – that it could not go on. All those collective efforts would surely bring more oil to the market than it could absorb, and that would deflate price. Some collective restraint was necessary if high prices – which every producer said they wanted – were to be preserved. Few listened: getting collective commitment to slow down production volumes proved fruitless as long as price remained as high as it was. There was no way to induce the US to slow its fracking efforts: thousands of drillers now chased their fortunes in the Permian and other shale rock basins, much as they had in Edwin Drake's day. There was no

Standard Oil or John D. Rockefeller to curb their excess. Shale drilling efforts now dotted the US landscape much as traditional derricks did then; and the US's regulatory and mineral ownership systems encouraged yet more production. Russia needed oil revenue and would sell all it could, China wanted energy security and a growing say in the oil market. Both were consequently unlikely to halt their expansion efforts. Even Saudi Arabia's injunctions and cajoling among its OPEC colleagues did not work. Their dependency on oil revenue was too high, and they were loath to endure the pain of breaking domestic spending promises that would necessarily follow a production cut, particularly after the tumult of the Arab Spring. By default, the world seemed to look to Saudi Arabia to take the lead in production cuts, somehow expecting that they would.

They were mistaken. Saudi Arabia would not play the role of swing producer people thought they had played in the past. Indeed, the country had never particularly liked that label and had wanted to shed it for some time.[6] Saudi Arabia did have the most flexible production and the largest reserve capacity and an impressive enough volume to influence market prices. Yet the assumption they would cut production to maintain price – and then tolerate others producing full tilt while sheltering under the price banner Saudi cuts provided – was an expectation of commercial altruism bordering on the laughable. Pain had to be shared equally. Saudi Arabia would go along, but not alone, with a general production cut, the only strategy having a shot at keeping the market in balance and prices elevated. Their warnings went unheeded: established oil producers continued to spend, explore, and produce, motivated by the riches $100/barrel oil provided. If production cuts could not be induced by scalpel, they would be compelled by scimitar. Saudi taps would remain open, and the whirlwind reaped.

Saudi oil officials knew their decision would cause pain and that they would suffer some of it themselves. Yet they also knew they were better positioned to endure that pain than were either their OPEC brethren or those operating in the more expensive production sites springing up around the globe. Saudi Arabian oil remained cheap to produce and would still generate significant profit even if prices fell by half: few others could say that. The country had prepared for the day when prices would fall, salting away hundreds of billions of dollars in SWF and other savings vehicles that would give them substantial financial cushion to withstand the brutal market reckoning. It could wait and endure until achieving its broader objectives, which was to drive high-cost producers out of the market and retain Saudi Arabia's market share of the consuming that did go on.

The decision was not well received. Some OPEC members were angry at the necessary fiscal adjustments they were going to have to make. They needed higher rather than lower prices to generate a fiscal break even. Clawing back domestic expenditures and taking on unexpected debt was not only going to hurt, it might engender severe political consequences if broken fiscal promises angered too many supporters. The Saudis countered by noting that a price fall would over time advantage all of OPEC, who had lower production costs, against the threat posed by non-OPEC suppliers. Better to salvage OPEC's collective market influence than watch it be eroded by outside production, even if it meant short-term pain. This would eventually give them all an opportunity to court international customers, thereby protecting their hard-won market share.[7]

It would be the non-OPEC suppliers who were going to suffer the most, particularly those new sources of expensive oil that the previous decade of exploration had brought onstream. Explorers in the Bakken shale or in the Alberta oil sands were going to have to cut costs massively to remain profitable. If they could not do that, then they would have to exit the industry. Either way, they would likely end up producing less oil. Others would also be affected: Russia's fiscal woes might well return, and China's oil companies might have less revenue flowing in to fuel its ambitious international strategy. But these were hardly Saudi Arabia's problems.

Saudi officials were reasonably honest about their motives. Never one to pull punches, Saudi Arabia's oil minister Ali al-Naimi outlined his country's logic in a speech delivered on February 23, 2016, in Houston two years into the price cut. Facing a packed house of anxious and rattled oil producers from around the globe who might have been looking for some relief, al-Naimi refused to give them any. He defended his country's 2014 decision by reiterating and reinforcing Saudi frustration at watching countries and companies indiscriminately ramp up production to cash in on the $100/barrel bonanza, with no apparent thought given to the long-term consequences. To summarize matters, al-Naimi stated simply, "inefficient, uneconomic oil producers will have to get out. That is tough to say, but it is a fact."[8]

At first blush, Saudi admonitions of others telling them to "improve your operational efficiency or die" – emanating from a country whose oil-production costs are so low – seemed a little rich. With such low costs, Saudi Aramco could tolerate a good deal of internal inefficiency itself, while still being the world's top producer and most valuable company.[9] Moreover, there was residual strategic anger at Saudi Arabia that went beyond such public blandishments. The inflicted price drop initiated by the Saudis seemed to target US fracking producers in particular: it looked much like a focused economic assault on a booming US industry. Saudi oil officials of course denied this, making a repeated public case of welcoming that increased US production as an additional source of resiliency to a sometimes-strained market.[10] Yet few bought this assertion, at least not entirely. A price fall of that magnitude certainly seemed designed to slow or stall the fracking revolution and protect market share.

Perceived hypocrisy aside, Saudi Arabia was playing a much deeper, and perhaps desperate, game. The entire country was, and is, in the oil business for the long haul. It had built the financial and political wherewithal to withstand short- and medium-term financial pain, even the self-inflicted kind, if it generated long-term gain. However, they could not have anticipated all of what followed. The price fall helped trigger events in the 2014–19 period that would call into question not only the effect of prices but also the future viability of the oil industry itself.

Adjusting to the New Reality: Market Reactions to the Price Drop

The fall in oil prices certainly hit private oil companies hard, particularly those who had global operations in expensive fields. The pain was real. Faced with a massive, sudden, and unexpected revenue drop, companies suddenly found their financial positions tenuous. Cash flow, profits, stock prices, and all the other financial measures used to evaluate commercial success took a pounding. Oil producers that had been generating healthy margins at $100/barrel suddenly began losing money as prices dipped to $50, then $40, and then lower. The hemorrhage of operating losses turned into a fatal gusher. Many shuttered operations, sold operations at a loss, or became acquisition targets of larger competitors with deeper pockets and more stable financial streams. Income from oil sales dropped: projects dependent on high oil income flow halted, capital expenditure plummeted. All these things got worse the longer the price fall went on.

Warren Buffett, perhaps the world's most famous and successful investor, probably was not surprised. He has long noted that "when the tide goes out, it is easy to see who has been swimming naked." Though directing that comment at financial markets and the irrational decisions financial bubbles sometimes generate, his insight is also applicable to oil companies and oil markets. Few people appeared to have seen the oil price fall coming, still less to have prepared well before it happened. Perhaps they had convinced themselves that this time really was different, that oil prices would remain elevated forever, and that the lessons of the past no longer applied.[11] Maybe they had banished warnings of supply overhang from the hallowed halls of executive suites, where forecasts of rain on the high oil price parade were not welcome. In any event, the few voices and warnings about the potential for oil gluts and price drops went unheard. Those uttering them may have garnered satisfaction at having been right but could offer little aid once the price drop actually happened.

Yet, in hindsight, overextension is perhaps not surprising. It is difficult for private companies to avoid overextending their investments in times of oil price booms. Oil company executives, investors, government fiscal agencies, and financial markets all feel the gravitational pull of profit, which mandates ever-increasing investment and production when prices are high. Even if a private-sector oil executive believes that a price fall is likely, it is not clear what they can do about it, in the sense of managing their companies any differently than they did. Operationally, one cannot shutter operations, lay off staff, cut salaries, and slash exploration expenditures in preparation for an oil price fall that may not happen for months or years, if it does at all. Any CEO doing that would have a short tenure, and boards of directors would likely replace them with more optimistic and aggressive types.[12]

It was also easy to forget that at least some of those executives, particularly those running the supermajors, had proven careful in their
expansion decisions in the mid-2000s, given how unpredictable they
knew prices could be. They had faced market pressures to increase production even faster than they did, and as chapter four showed, either
could not or would not do it. It was new producers that had brought
new production to market. Given the heights oil prices attained, the
length of time they stayed there, and the consensus that they would
likely continue, overextension and overproduction was probably inevitable. It took time for the new reality to set in, and a period of shock
and denial was perhaps understandable. Producers may have hoped
that any price decline was an aberration from an expected norm that
might return shortly.[13] The longer and more boisterous a party is, the
harder it may be to convince attendees that it is indeed over.

When reality did sink in, predictable responses followed. The fall
in prices necessarily implied cutbacks, particularly in exploration
expenditure, which dropped precipitously and quickly. Upstream
investments in oil and gas exploration that had measured $780 billion
in 2014 dropped by over $200 billion in 2015.[14] An expected next step
was the exit of financially weak companies, particularly the smaller
fracking companies for whom the shock of the price fall proved fatal.
Many found their cash flow constrained, and they proved unable to
meet debt obligations. Bankruptcies began piling up: between the
fall of 2014 and the spring of 2020, over 250 oil companies filed for
bankruptcy in the United States and a further 18 in Canada,[15] and
their collective unsecured debt totaled about $100 billion.[16] Third
was the parsing of investment targets, as well as budgets. Investments in high-price oil locations slowed to a trickle. Money directed
toward the Alberta oil sands fell by more than half between 2014 and
2018: in the fourth quarter of 2014 that investment had totaled over
$20 billion Canadian dollars: by 2016 it had dropped to $9.2 billion,
and by the fourth quarter of 2019 it measured $8.2 billion.[17] Invest-
ment slowed if not stopped, taking with it not only the hundreds
of thousands[18] of direct oil jobs but also decimating the supporting
services growing up around the booming exploration towns.

The supermajors seemed generally better-positioned than others
to be able to ride it out. They reigned in their exploration expenditures

as the price fall continued. In 2016 ExxonMobil spent US$19 billion in upstream exploration; Royal Dutch Shell targeted $25 billion as their preferred expenditure target; Chevron's exploration budget measured $26 billion, all of which were down significantly from what they had been in 2014.[19] The supermajors also began divesting from unprofitable production sites: Royal Dutch Shell even made divestment a key strategic theme, rather than just a reaction to a price decline.[20] Maintaining cost control also became more important: the supermajors reduced costs through the regular means of employee attrition, rigorous management of operational costs, and improving efficiencies. They remained ever vigilant in looking for technological solutions that might lower drilling and extraction costs.[21]

Yet, even when prices fell, large companies did not lose sight for a potential acquisition opportunity, particularly from the rapidly depreciating assets of smaller, more financially strained companies. Larger companies often have larger cash reserves than do smaller ones, reserves that not only help them weather price storms but also allow the acquisition of new assets on the cheap. They began acquiring fracking operations, whose initial stages had been driven largely by the efforts of smaller producers. Indeed, some had criticized the supermajors for being too slow to embrace fracking, allowing smaller producers to dominate initial production while the supermajors preoccupied themselves with expensive foreign exploration. As oil prices fell and smaller producers became strained, the supermajors began enhancing their position in fracking.[22]

Yet, in the midst of all this drama, the oil market was capable of some surprises. To begin, if the Saudis had hoped that all this corporate bloodletting would decrease North American production, they were in for disappointment. Production in both US and Canadian fields actually continued increasing, and at a surprisingly rapid pace, even as prices remained low. As noted earlier, North America dominated the rise of global oil production witnessed in the decade between 2009 and 2019. Over that time, Canadian oil production went up by 2.3 mbd, from 3.3 mbd to 5.6 mbd. More astounding still of course was the rise in the US that continued right through 2019. Over the course of the entire decade, and even with all the consolidation and cost cutting the price fall engendered, US production still went from 6 mbd to over 12 mbd, a gain of almost 6 mbd, with potentially more to follow.[23] They outperformed all other oil producers in increasing production capacity. During the same decade, Russian production went up a little over 1 mbd, Saudi production went up 2 mbd, Iraq 2 mbd, and the UAE's production increased by 1.2 mbd. Other major oil producers witnessed minimal increases, or even saw drops, in oil production. By 2019 the US had become the world's largest oil producer, and the trend continued upward. There may have been fewer, less profitable companies doing it, but their output did not slow.

It seemed shocking that the US could continue increasing production quickly, even as companies were shedding costs and investment at such a rapid rate. There are several explanations why they could do that. First, the companies themselves proved more resilient to the price drop than many had assumed they could be: they cut costs and expenditures and made difficult employee decisions. They were aided by a domestic financial system adept and flexible enough to manage the monetary fallout. Companies consolidated, restructured debt, merged, found bridge financing, or employed other financially creative ways to survive. Secondly, surviving companies continuously improved their technologies to lower production costs per barrel. Third, since the startup costs of fracking wells were comparatively low, they could be idled quickly without enormous loss. Fourth, even though a company may have technically "gone under" financially, their productive assets did not simply disappear: they often were simply acquired by someone else able to run them more efficiently and then quickly brought back onstream. New fracking companies became efficient at producing the assets they had and eventually became financially viable even when prices remained low. The oil economy may have received a shock, but the US system had dealt with shocks before.

The fall in prices did not compel the reduction in North American production the Saudis had hoped for. It continued to go up. Moreover, the effects of the price fall spilled beyond the borders of the oil marketplace, generating economic effects that many people outside the industry actually liked. Lower oil prices provided an economic stimulus that helped spur a broad US economic surge. The politics and geopolitics of oil became less immediately problematic as surplus oil began flooding the system. Talk of peak oil receded, and people stopped worrying about supply shortage or the actions countries might need to take to rectify it. Taken together, the political and geopolitical effects of the price fall were as profound as the economic ones, shifting the calculations states and governments made.

The United States: The Politics and Geopolitics of the Price Fall

The twin effects of a fall in price and continued US production increases engendered a massive, and perhaps unanticipated, geopolitical shift in the oil industry. Those exporting oil not only took a financial hit, they also continued to suffer an unanticipated export blow. US production remained high, meaning their imports would remain low. Consequently, US import dependence did not reemerge: in fact it took pains to ease restrictions on oil exports, making the county an export competitor rather than a target market. US production was not going down. The following chart indicates that the fall in oil prices seemed nothing more than a speedbump on the road of increasing US production:

Figure 8. US Domestic Oil Production and Oil Prices

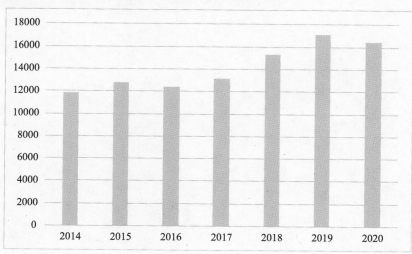

Figure 9. Oil Prices (US Dollars), 2014–2021

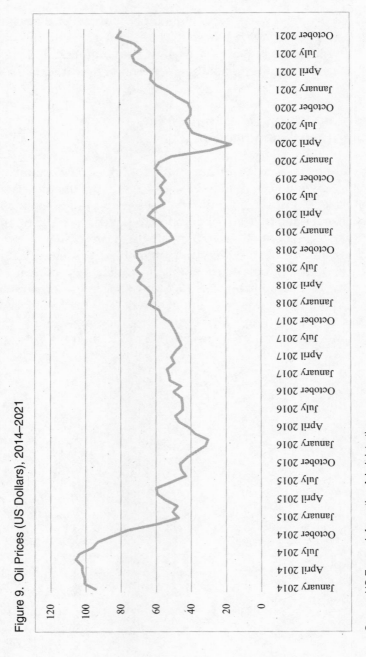

Source: US Energy Information Administration.

So strong was US production growth that the fabled phrase "energy independence" began to enter the economic and geopolitical lexicon. It was an idea with which the US had thought a lot about but had little direct experience with, and was a more complicated idea than it initially sounded. Even as US production grew, it still imported (and started to export) millions of barrels of oil a day and certainly gave no indication that it wanted to pursue an autarkic energy policy. Instead, the increase in US oil production became a production supplement to the global system, one that reinforced the robust and integrated global energy market the US had always professed to want.[24] The US would continue to buy, sell, and transport oil all over the world and hoped others would do the same. Their ships and container ports remained as busy as ever, offloading and onboarding oil and gas from transport tankers. US fracking reinforced, rather than weakened, the idea of a global energy market.

There may have been long-term questions about how long the fracking boom would last or how much oil it would generate. But there was no mistaking the direction US energy production was taking, a direction that generated plenty of short-term impacts to keep analysts and government leaders busy. Opinions on what to do varied by analyst and by governing ideology. The initial stages of the fracking boom presented president Obama with an array of choices to make, particularly as his second term drew to a close. The US remained divided on what to do with its energy bounty, and Obama's choices reflected that divergence. He had entered office promising to wean the US off fossil fuels and reduce dependence on foreign oil. He ended up presiding over the most rapid increase in oil and gas production in recent US history. While he clearly did support alternative energy, he could not ignore the obvious strategic advantages increased domestic oil production provided, nor the contribution that production had made in restoring US economic health after the financial crisis.[25]

Obama's domestic and international oil and gas record now looks mixed. He pushed environmental policies when he could but compromised on them when he felt he had to. He strengthened regulations around fracking but did not ban it. He placed a moratorium on drilling in the Gulf of Mexico after the horrendous BP oil spill,[26] but production rebounded once the moratorium ended. He had resisted the construction of more oil transport infrastructure by nixing construction of the Keystone XL pipeline, designed to transport Alberta heavy crude from its oil sands deposits to refineries along the Gulf Coast in Texas. But he also allowed new drilling to commence in the Arctic. His efforts to curb coal use in electricity production did achieve a marked increase in the use of renewables for electricity generation. But electricity plants also often began using increasing volumes of cheap natural gas, rather than wind and solar. The growth in domestic oil and gas production motivated the US to rescind its decades-old prohibition against exporting domestic oil and gas. That reinforced a global market but would not lower global reliance on carbon. Obvious or easy choices were few.

Choices were also complicated on the foreign policy front. To begin, fracking complicated Obama's general support of efforts to curb global carbon emissions. The apparent global will to do something about climate change noted in the previous chapter continued growing. It proved powerful enough to forge an international consensus that crystallized in 2015, when representatives from governments the world over convened in Paris to discuss and eventually ratify a global agreement to halt the rise in temperatures the attendees claimed was occurring. The Paris Climate Accords heralded what many hoped would be a new era in climate change negotiations, and more importantly action. The accords pledged all signatories to binding commitments to lower their carbon emissions: the overall goal was to limit overall global temperature rise, ensuring that it would remain below 2 degrees Celsius. This was the threshold scientists believed would keep the effects of global warming more-or-less manageable. The agreement came into effect in November 2016: its signatories included 155 nations whose collective economies represented the vast majority of the world's greenhouse gas emitters.[27] The agreement depended on US support if it was to have any teeth. It also meant eventual curbs on global oil and gas use, and eventual production, would have to come if the emissions targets were to be met.

Yet increased domestic oil and gas production also generated foreign policy benefits that could not be ignored. For example, the US relationship with Saudi Arabia was going to be affected. The US now needed Saudi imports less, if at all. Theoretically, that would lessen the impact oil considerations had on US foreign policy in the Middle East, allowing US diplomats to concentrate on other things. Lower oil prices also inflicted pain on some US adversaries, most notably Russia. Russia's dependence on oil and gas revenue made them vulnerable to a price fall: and US sanctions on Russia, particularly for its invasion of Crimea, inflicted a significant bite on Russia's ability to raise oil production and generate additional cash. The price fall combined with increased US production strengthened US geopolitical leverage. It weakened any ability oil exporters may have had to play the "oil card" in their negotiations with the US.[28]

US foreign and economic policy began reaping numerous other practical and theoretical benefits from having both lower oil prices and high production. Oil import reductions lowered the US trade deficit in goods, much of which came from the import of oil. Lower oil prices also provided a boost to domestic and international economies by lowering energy input prices. The chance of energy-driven financial bubbles augmented by inflated oil revenue receded, thereby making the US financial system a bit more stable. The US dollar rose in value against its competitors, and electorally it was easy to point out the benefits of lower oil prices to the US economy generally.[29] The list of economic benefits from having more oil production was long.

On both domestic and foreign policy fronts, Obama's oil and energy legacy seems best summarized as incrementally progressive and mixed, tinged with a bit of irony. His was not the revolutionary presidency in alternative and renewable energy he had sometimes promised on the campaign trail. It was a study in contrasts: US participation and leadership on climate change initiatives would be paired with its growing place as an oil and gas production powerhouse. A president who had promoted renewable energy so strongly and had signed the US onto the ambitious goals of the Paris Accords also became the leader of what was becoming the world's largest supplier of oil and gas. He began his presidency watching oil prices rise and US foreign oil dependency grow; he ended it with oil prices having fallen by two-thirds and US production levels breaking production records. This would by most measures seem to be a tremendous domestic accomplishment, but one difficult for Obama to trumpet, given how much political capital he had invested in the idea of renewable energy. His policies reflected the divided republic he governed and the divergent views of what to do with the oil and gas bounty it was reaping.

It was an impressively powerful energy legacy to bequeath to his successor, incoming president Donald Trump. Trump, to understate things, was not Obama. He would show little in the way of balance or nuance in the ways he chose to manage US energy during his presidency. After garnering a surprise victory in 2016, he entered office in January 2017 having made a very different set of promises about energy than had Obama. On the campaign trail Trump had not only ignored or avoided any commitment to promoting renewable energy, he had in fact gone in the other direction, promising to reinvigorate coal production in the United States. He generally promoted the virtues of burning carbon and often questioned if not insulted the science on global warming. When it came to oil, he showed no qualms about reinforcing increased US oil production, claiming that it generated great benefits for the United States and fit well into his "America First" agenda.

On the campaign trail he had pledged to undo many of the energy regulatory initiatives Obama had put in place, and upon entering office in January 2017 he began doing exactly that. Almost immediately he issued an executive order overturning Obama's ban on the Keystone XL pipeline, while also beginning a systematic rollback of regulations that had been designed to limit the scope of energy exploration. Consequently, his administration witnessed a steady increase in oil and gas production, as the fracking boom continued. Trump's cabinet picks reflected a preference for oil-friendly personnel. He chose as energy secretary Rick Perry, who had previously served as governor of Texas and had long supported increased US oil production. He also chose Rex Tillerson, former chief executive officer of ExxonMobil, as his incoming secretary of state. He instructed these and other cabinet officials to begin working to roll back regulations on business activity in general and in the oil business in particular. He withdrew the United States from the Paris Climate Accords within a month of taking office, claiming that it disadvantaged the US economy and inflicted needless hardship on US workers while leaving other countries free to pollute. His administration worked to lower, if not eliminate, the mileage requirements for American-made vehicles. His approach to oil and carbon use generally, while admittedly being consistent, showed little in the way of policy balance or energy transition. It could not have differed more from what Obama had pledged and done.

Trump also seemed to think that increased energy production would help US diplomacy. Early in his tenure he coined a phrase that would resonate throughout the energy world – "energy dominance." Trump did not define precisely what that meant, but it certainly conjured up a powerful enough imagery that his supporters could endorse. The term seemed to imply that surging US domestic oil and gas production was somehow going to provide the US an overwhelmingly powerful political and economic tool, one that could extract concessions from countries that ran afoul of Trump's preferences. Left open to interpretation was what those policies were, what countries were breaking them, and how exactly it was that surging US oil production would induce countries to do what they otherwise would not.

It was never made clear what nations in particular Trump thought it might be useful to "dominate." If anything Trump seemed to think it should apply equally if not more to allies than it did to potential adversaries.[30] As Trump's presidency progressed, the theory of "energy dominance" was not going to translate easily into the practice of US foreign policy. For example, one foreign policy area where increased domestic oil production might have helped was the use of sanctions against oil-producing countries whose behavior Trump wanted to change or who he simply wanted to punish. Sanctions are a tricky thing, both to define and to execute properly.[31] They involve the use of economic instruments that inflict enough economic pain on the targeted state to induce some desired change in their behavior. They require careful calibration and consistent execution to be effective. It is also helpful if specific policy objectives are defined in advance so that expected policy change is clear and the inflicted pain is in proportion to the desired outcome.[32]

Trump certainly used sanctions liberally, but rarely showed evidence of such careful calibration or disciplined application. They were applied indiscriminately, and rarely were accompanied by a clear statement of what the objectives were and when observers would know that they had been met. His favorite economic tool was the imposition of tariffs on imports, which functioned as a kind of economic sanction. In short order Trump imposed tariffs on Canadian and Mexican imports to compel negotiation of a new continental-wide trade agreement and did this despite the protestation of the US business community that such tariffs inflicted as much harm on US interests as they did on foreigners. He also imposed tariffs on specific exports from the European Union, and in March 2018 Trump launched the first step in a trade war with China that escalated rapidly. That trade war eventually cost US customers billions of extra dollars, knocked $1.7 trillion off the market value of US publicly traded companies,[33] and ended up closing China's market to US soybean farmers, which was by far their largest (sometime sole) customer. These sanctions applied to the US's largest trading partners, allies and potential adversaries alike. At the end of his presidency, it was not clear what tangible gains they produced for US interests, still less whether those gains were worth the associated costs.

Yet, as Trump's presidency progressed and all these tariffs attempted to slap allies around, it became difficult to find concrete examples of how Trump had used the surging US energy position to wring concessions from countries who appeared most vulnerable to it. Presumably, US energy production would allow him to drive harder bargains with energy exporters whose policies he presumably wanted to change. Yet his foreign policy took the opposite track. He routinely saved his most lavish praise for those very same oil producers, often idolizing what he saw as their leadership abilities, and refused to criticize their domestic actions in the way previous US presidents had. Trump's policies toward Russia showed, at the very least, inconsistency and awkwardness. To be fair, his government did maintain and increase the economic sanctions the Obama administration had leveled in response to Russia's conduct abroad.[34] Yet Trump himself continued to lavish praise on Vladimir Putin that bordered on the deferential: their ensuing bromance appeared more cozy than confrontational. He proved willing to accept Putin's denial over the word of his own intelligence agencies when allegations of Russian interference in US and other democratic elections arose. He said little over accusations that Putin certainly persecuted and perhaps even authorized the murder of political opponents, and even implied that the US was capable of equally dastardly things.

In the case of Saudi Arabia, Trump did not even feign attempts to wield the US oil production stick. He cultivated a strong personal relationship with the king of Saudi Arabia as well as his heir apparent, the already mentioned Mohammed Bin Salman. He pushed for continued sales of high US military hardware to the Saudi kingdom, despite entrenched congressional opposition to those sales.[35] He did little to confront Saudi Arabia over the murder of Saudi journalist Jamal Khashoggi, which independent reports confirmed was state-sponsored and done at the behest of Bin Salman himself. This was hardly the stuff of dominance.

His policies toward other oil producers also reflected inconsistency. In the case of Iran, he again aggressively pursued sanctions but then permitted them to relax. He withdrew the United States from the Joint Comprehensive Plan of Action,[36] the deal brokered between Iran and the US, the European Union, the UK, and China designed to slow Iran's nuclear enrichment program in exchange for progressive economic relief. He did increase US sanctions against Venezuela, thereby certainly accentuating the domestic crises there and inflicting yet more pain upon the Venezuelan people. But his political ends in doing so seemed obscure and certainly had little to do with alleviating a burgeoning humanitarian disaster. Again, it is hard to see what clear objectives or plan animated such policies, and how "energy dominance" made them work.

In hindsight, it is not clear how US energy production could ever have had the decisive geopolitical heft Trump thought it would. The US was not about to shut off flows of imports and exports, which would hurt its own economy and would certainly be odd, considering how much time and foreign policy effort the country had historically spent promoting open markets to govern energy flow. US production was impressive but was certainly not enough to satiate all the demands of emerging markets who would continue buying the foreign oil the US no longer did. Most of the benefits of increased oil production accrued domestically and came in the form of low oil prices and reduced import dependency. There may indeed be foreign policy benefits from increased energy output, but they seem difficult to realize in day-to-day diplomacy, as increased US energy output cannot by itself compel another country to take an action different from what it preferred or stop it doing what it otherwise would. It can only make the costs of these strategies worse, thereby perhaps raising the attractiveness of doing something else. But, like other economic tools, the energy card must be applied in a consistent way over an extended period of time to clearly defined political outcomes. None of that fit in well with Trump's style of governing.

In some ways the tool of "energy dominance" seemed much like the "oil embargo" record played in reverse. To refresh memories, oil embargoes were placed on the United States in the 1970s by exporters anxious to show displeasure at US policy. They too caused momentary pain but did not achieve the wider political goals those exporters had hoped for. The oil system proved resilient and adjusted rapidly to shock, and people also proved resilient in the face of the shortages oil embargoes created. Similarly it was not clear that having excess domestic production generates tangible foreign policy power. The structural changes occurring in the oil market do matter over the long term – something we will address in the last chapter – but its policy impacts are systemic rather than specific to one country. It is hard today to use energy production to dominate anyone: the game is too wide for that.

China: Restrained State Capitalism?

The fall in oil prices generated plenty of other effects in both importers and exporters. To begin, it took the edge off the worry that state capitalism, and the countries practicing it, were going to lock up the world's oil supplies. Suddenly China's investments in developing markets to procure commodities caused less angst: instead, Western powers shifted critical attention to China's efforts to build commercial strength in the high-tech sector.[37] As oil supply became plentiful, worries about being able to procure more of it or running out faded, and it became less believable to frame the struggle for resources as some kind of gladiatorial death match. The closer one looked, the less threatening Chinese oil investment appeared, at least in terms of its geopolitical impact. China could only react to, or shape marginally, oil market developments: it could not dictate them, and its companies' actions looked very similar to what was being done by the supermajors.[38] The fall in oil prices certainly gave the same boost to the Chinese economy that it gave to others, but it also hurt the bottom line of its oil companies, also as it did others. China entered the period of falling prices with a legacy of an ongoing ambitious international expansion plan: that plan now seemed dictated more by market realities than geopolitics.

Some realities were not going to change. First, China was still going to need a lot more imported oil and would become increasingly dependent on the international market to procure it. China's domestic oil production had stagnated. In the period 2014–19, it consistently extracted between 3.6 and 4.4 mbd from domestic fields,[39] and in that same period China watched its import levels rise. In 2014 imports measured 6 mbd; by 2019 they had grown to over 10 mbd.[40] By 2017 China had surpassed the United States in its dependency on foreign oil, importing 8.4 mbd to the US's 7.9 mbd.[41] Given the fracking revolution, it looked like China's import needs would go up while American needs would fall. Saudi Arabia was China's top oil import partner: by 2019 China consumed close to 2 mbd of Saudi crude. China also drew on numerous other suppliers, both within and outside of OPEC: these included Russia, Iran, Brazil, Angola, Venezuela, Gabon, and even a bit from the United States.[42] Such diversity indicated that China depended on an integrated market and looked to a diversity of suppliers to ensure its oil security, much like other oil-dependent economies had practiced in the past.

Other indicators helped slack the worry about China's oil diplomacy and state development strategies. In coping with the price fall, it became difficult to distinguish what China's NOCs did from what the West's supermajors were doing. Its companies also focused on cost containment, consolidation of current investments, and maintaining profitable extraction,[43] much as the US and European companies did. They also initially cut their production significantly to cope with the supply overhang and boost prices.[44] Foreign investment and exploration deals slowed down: and focus returned on ingesting what had been acquired rather than getting more. All of this would be familiar to oil executives from other countries.

Moreover, detailed analysis of China's acquisition and foreign operational activity revealed little evidence of it "locking up" resources. China's NOC oil production remained traded on global markets and became part of the broad international oil "pool": they were not diverted back to the Chinese market.[45] In coping with the price decline, China's companies pressed for ever-greater independence to make market-based decisions separate from the political interests of Beijing, particularly in international operations.[46] State sanction was not always sought before decisions were made,[47] and a drive for independence also typified the companies' internationalization efforts.[48] The period 2014–19 marked the next step in the evolution of China's NOCs, one marked by greater managerial independence in decision-making, which hardly looked like the stuff of aggressive mercantilism.[49]

Moderation returned to external interpretations of China's oil investment behavior. To be sure, the country retained an ambitious international economic plan. One focus remained the Silk Road initiative, a trillion-dollar investment plan that involved constructing a network of infrastructure and trading hubs that connected dozens of countries to a Chinese-dominated regional trading network. China's 2016 economic five-year plan reinforced that expansion, calling for ongoing state focus on building the economy and enhancing state economic strength.[50] Yet cracks in the Chinese investment juggernaut, at least in the oil business, began to show. Its oil investments in developing markets became plagued with the same problems other oil companies have always faced,[51] ranging from cost overruns to labor issues to recalcitrant governments pressing for an ever-better deal. China's overall totals of foreign direct investment still targeted primarily the developed world: in 2019 the United States and Europe combined received over 50 per cent of China's annual investment, and held 65 per cent of its accumulated investment stock.[52] By contrast China's total accumulated investment stock in the continent of Africa measured $46 billion, which totaled fifth, ranking behind the totals held by the US, the United Kingdom, France, and the Netherlands.[53] China has signaled that investment into Africa's energy and commodity sectors will remain a state priority, but the glut of oil and gas now on the market made its energy investments less of a strategic worry. That worry now shifted to the nefarious high-tech plots of Huawei rather than the investments of CNOOC.

China's state direction was much more in evidence in the domestic market, where the difference between state capitalism and more market-based capitalism became clear. Where the US was willing to let the market work and endure the painful restructuring market realties would demand, China was not, or at least not as much. While its companies moved to slow expansion and to cut operational costs on the international front, they responded clearly to government directive when it came to domestic oil policy. One of those directives was to boost domestic oil production even if prices were low. After enduring a three-year period of consolidation, Chinese companies in 2018 began spending once again to raise domestic production, raising domestic oil investment rose 25 per cent and continuing to expand its upward trend.[54] It even sought deals with the Trump administration that would ship more US gas and oil to China's shores, and began allowing a measure of US capital to invest in its industry.[55] The state goal of raising domestic oil production remained clear.

China remains vulnerable in the sense that it needs imports. Despite its investments and strategies, China's domestic production continued to hover around 4 mbd a day throughout the 2014–19 period. That required it to import an additional 10 mbd. Its collective international exploration efforts have added hundreds of thousands of barrels of new daily supply to global markets. But the country will need millions of new barrels and is going to need more and more every year. That has motivated domestic invest-ment: China has announced massive increases in domestic capital expenditure in its energy sector, to the tune of US$77 billion.[56] Yet, even with those efforts to meet their production targets, they are projected to at best garner an additional 2 mbd of extra domes-tic production. China's needs for imports will still grow and, as it does, China's strategic interest in the international market will grow as well. But, as of this writing, the oil market appears well supplied and will be able to meet this need.

China coped with the price fall much as one would expect. Its companies initially enacted strategies to contain costs. As it became progressively more dependent on imports, it emphasized state-led efforts to raise domestic oil expenditures and production. Domes-tic production rose but certainly did not keep pace with projected increases in demand. Over the long term, this import dependency might change: China too possesses considerable shale rock reserves that they can theoretically access, and it has sent engineering teams to the United States to fully decipher how the fracking process works. However, current technological and investment barriers limit their production potential. Between 2014 and 2019, China's reliance on the international oil market grew: it will continue grappling with that dependency for the foreseeable future. Geopolitical worries about its economic conduct have now shifted to other arenas.

Maintaining Power in the Time of Economic Strain: Russia and Saudi Arabia

If the world's largest importers had to adapt to the fall in prices, so too did the world's largest exporters. Some were better prepared for the price fall than were others, and they adapted in various ways. Saudi Arabia clearly appeared ready: it had determined prices were too high and that it was in their interest to see them fall. They had prepared financially and politically for the price drop. Yet it was not clear how well they could manage the geopolitical effects, which were just as real. The US, which had previously absorbed huge quantities of Saudi oil production and upon whose strategic partnership Saudi Arabia relied, had become a production rival and potential export competitor.[57] New oil brought to market eroded Saudi market share and made them worry about demand security.[58] There were therefore many sides to consider in any price scenario.

The price fall affected Saudi domestic plans, in particular whether the country could continue its policy of modernization and economic development while taking in far less oil revenue. The country had been caught by the problem of fiscal overextension and misspent money during a price boom in the 1980s and were now clearly worried about making the same mistake. Certainly that possibility had worried king Abdullah bin Abdulaziz Al Saud, who had upon assuming power in 2005 inaugurated an ambitious economic modernization program, one that he championed until his death in 2015. That program promoted diversification, attempted to improve the country's overall education system, and sponsored an ambitious international educational exchange program. It was expensive and required consistent long-term state investment if it was to succeed. His successors would have to endorse and continue that economic reform trajectory, even as prices fell. To date, they have appeared willing to do so, announcing an economic vision confidently titled Vision 2030 designed to eventually create a robust and diversified economy far less reliant on oil.[59] Unveiled in 2016 and presenting itself as a blueprint for transforming the Saudi economy, it emphasized economic change, governance transparency, and improving the general competitiveness in the Saudi Arabian business climate.

That plan was going to have to be paid for, and even Saudi Arabia has found the pain of the price drop daunting. It began to dip into its SWF to fund social benefits and even began considering the partial privatization of state-owned Saudi Aramco to help fund domestic state expenditures. In October 2019 the country finalized a deal to float 3 per cent of the company on the domestic market, with an additional foreign listing to come later.[60] Investors, they believed, would flock to a public listing of an oil company that had the largest reserves and lowest production costs of any on earth. Money invested in Saudi Aramco would generate cash that could then be used to shore up its SWF and would help further the process of diversification and transition that it desperately needed if it was to wean its economy off oil.

Other Middle Eastern and smaller oil-producing countries also felt the sting of falling oil prices. In some cases it made their countries more difficult to manage. Iraq continued its reconstruction efforts under the ongoing threat of ISIS militants, who continued to target its petroleum facilities, either to destroy their revenue-producing potential or to take that revenue for themselves. Yet, even with this, Iraq was able to increase its oil production such that it routinely totaled between 4.5 and 4.8 mbd between 2014 and 2019. Iran also took a severe budgetary hit by oil price declines, one that augmented the pain of the economic sanctions it was already suffering. Its budgetary dependence on oil was almost complete, and by some accounts Iran needed a price of $200/barrel to meet the spending promises it had made. Saudi Arabia, by contrast, needed a break-even price of approximately $60/barrel.[61] The kingdoms of the UAE and Qatar remained stable, but their relatively small populations and immense oil reserves provided ample fiscal cushion and kept the countries on a more or less stable track. The price fall damaged the domestic finances of Gulf exporters but has not caused political upheaval.

The fall in oil prices did hurt the world's other major oil exporter, Russia. In 2013 Russia was one of the world's dominant oil producers, producing 10.9 mbd. Not surprisingly the oil price drop engendered difficulties in Russia and hurt government finances badly, pushing the government into deficit. When oil prices collapsed in 2014, Russia's state budget, and overall economy, took a severe hit: in 2015 Russia's economy shrank by 1.9 per cent, and it remained mired in persistently low growth rates for the entire period.[62] The economic shock motivated some drastic domestic economic policy decisions designed to reignite the economy and the energy sector. For example, in December 2014 the Russian government chose to let the ruble float on international markets, resulting in it losing almost half of its value against the US dollar.[63]

While this helped keep companies modestly profitable, it eroded the net purchasing power and wealth of Russia's citizens and by extension the Russian government itself. Russia continued to alter domestic tax and regulatory requirements to ease company financial obligations to help the companies get through the price drop.[64] In a sense the country was caught. It depended heavily on oil and gas revenues and had invested much effort in increasing production. Yet the more oil they dumped into the global system, the less chance there would be that oil prices would ever resume an upward climb. Even as oil prices tanked, Russian oil production appeared set to climb: at the end of 2017 the investment bank Goldman Sachs predicted that Russia was on track to produce an average 11.7 mbd.[65] The trend of pumping ever more oil into a saturated market had to stop if prices were to recover: but it was a problem only collective action could solve.

After a couple years of dealing with the price drop, most of the major oil producers had felt enough pain from decreased oil revenues to want to do something about it. The one thing they could do to help reignite oil prices was agree to a collective production cut. OPEC countries decided to do so in November 2016, agreeing to an equitably shared production cut that included improved quota allotments for Iran and Iraq but that also balanced cuts among the other members.[66] Moreover, it would not be just OPEC doing the cutting. After two years of discussion, Russia also agreed to a collective production cut designed to remove surplus inventories from the global oil market.[67] Deemed the OPEC-plus one agreement, these mutual cuts in production levels were designed to help engender a moderate price rebound[68] by removing 1.5 mbd from their collective output. Russia shouldered 300,000 b/d of that total, the rest apportioned proportionately across the OPEC members. That helped push prices up throughout 2017, and they reached the targeted $60–$70/barrel initially hoped for.[69] Encouraged by this price rebound, both OPEC and Russia agreed to extend the production cut until the end of 2018, at which point oil had reached $80/barrel.

However, their financial reprieve proved short lived. When they eased back on production cuts in the fall of 2018 – hoping that the previous effort would have rebalanced the market – it proved to have not done so. US shale and other sources kept increasing production and continued to pour ever more oil into the market, and prices once again fell below $60. This prompted yet another extension of the collective agreement to cut production that was expected to last until the first quarter of 2020. Not surprisingly, some countries were proving impatient and increasingly desperate for prices to regain an upward trend: one report noted that Libya required a price of $207/barrel to fund current expenditures and argued that many other countries also required inflated oil revenues to meet even basic social service spending commitments.[70] Pressure on their finances continued to build as prices remained subdued.

The price fall caused pain throughout the OPEC countries by lowering their government revenue. Even the more robust OPEC producers had limited capacity to absorb that pain: as the barrels they produced generated less than half the revenue they had just a few years before. The cartel has held together, and its collective production output remained relatively consistent over the 2014–19 time period: they collectively were producing around 35 mbd, approximately one-third of the global production total.[71] They had even informally added members, using the collective interest of boosting price to forge agreements. Yet whether those agreements would hold, and whether they collectively could do much to influence price over the long term given the new sources of oil entering the market, remained an open question.

Other Oil Producers: The Resource Curse Hits Home

Other oil producers suffered from the price fall even more than did the OPEC-plus producers. For these other producers, the abrupt end to a period of high oil prices revealed the degree to which they had gotten used to, and built a dependency on, high oil prices. Moreover, their suffering was not just economic: it could be measured in increased political instability as well. Take the case of Brazil, which over the 2010–14 period enjoyed annual growth averaging over 3 per cent and had gained entry into the BRIC club of quickly growing developing nations.[72] Yet much of its growth remained tied to the buoyant price of oil, of which Brazil produced over 2 mbd. The fall in oil prices halted this impressive economic growth story in its tracks: in 2015 Brazil's economic output actually shrank by −3.5 per cent, and subsequent growth in succeeding years remained anemic.[73] It too began delaying additional oil-exploration expenditures, cutting back on production, and felt its domestic budget contract severely.

That was only going to be the beginning of the country's oil-related problems. Low oil prices generated political challenges as well. Brazil's state-owned oil company Petrobras had been leading the charge in the rapid increase in investment and production levels Brazil achieved during the price run up. Yet, as the company had allocated more money to developing resources, some of that money seemed to have been "diverted" into non-productive purposes, which is a polite way to say that a lot of that money had found its way back into the pockets of government officials. Subsequent investigations into Petrobras's activities during the price run up demonstrated that the company's relationship with senior political leadership had proven incestuous and corrupt. The company had attempted to curry favor with Brazil's senior political establishment by paying out massive sums of money in bribes and payoffs. State legislators had also gotten in on the act: they too had received illicit payments from Brazilian construction firms to secure the massive project contracts designed to increase the country's overall oil output. As the investigation dug deeper, it found that literally mountains of cash were involved: the amount of bribes and kickbacks apparently totaled in the hundreds of billions of dollars.[74]

That corruption spread right to the top. In May 2016 the Brazilian legislature voted to impeach incumbent president Dilma Rouseff, whose government contained members widely implicated in the bribery scandal. They also implicated Rouseff herself, as she had served on the board of Petrobras during the period in which the bribery scandal occurred. Also implicated was her popular predecessor Luis Inacio Lula da Silva, who in 2018 received a twelve-year sentence for corruption related once again to the distribution of oil investment money.[75] The corruption scandal helped eventually topple the socialist government, and in 2018 the Labour Party lost power to the Conservatives headed by Jair Bolsonaro, a conservative politician and former military officer whose policies would reflect a nationalistic and populist bent. The fortunes of oil clearly affected the trajectory of Brazil's domestic politics.

There were other even more extreme examples where the price fall proved not just painful but ultimately threatened the stability of the country itself. The obvious case is Venezuela, where the price fall revealed the peril Venezuela's habitual mismanagement of its vast oil revenues had created. Successors to populist leader Hugo Chavez had continued his socialist leanings, moderating his revolutionary impulses in favor of using oil revenues to buttress domestic social stability.[76] Yet that became expensive, and as oil revenues dropped, so too did Venezuela's overall economic prospects. Politically the situation deteriorated rapidly as leaders scrambled to consolidate power amidst widespread and growing opposition to domestic economic distress. Venezuelan president Nicolas Maduro won a snap reelection in May 2018 that many outside observers criticized as being illegitimate.[77]

International criticism followed, as did ongoing challenges to Maduro's rule. The criticism prompted US president Trump to install economic sanctions against Venezuela's already teetering economy. Those sanctions forbade US companies from doing business with PDSVA, Venezuela's state-owned oil giant, limiting its export capacity and causing its domestic tankers to overflow.[78] The combined economic and political crises in Venezuela created conditions bordering on chaos. Over a million Venezuelan refugees subsequently left the increasingly desperate country: food remained scarce and stability difficult to maintain.

In other places the political consequences of the price fall also appeared severe. Many smaller oil producers continued to struggle economically: some analysts predicted that ongoing low oil prices would necessitate monetary bailouts of small oil-dependent countries, such as Azerbaijan, Nigeria, and Ecuador, in addition to Venezuela.[79] Other significant oil suppliers remain mired in domestic political conflict, made potentially more desperate as rival factions struggle to control what oil production power their country had. Ongoing political strife in Nigeria and Equatorial Guinea has made their production levels volatile and generally lessening.[80] South Sudan continued to engage in brutal hostilities during a civil war, much of it driven by a desire to control oil production and thereby garner whatever revenue it generated.[81] The struggle to control dwindling oil revenues continued to afflict developing oil-dependent countries.

The fall in oil prices also caused political turmoil even in the developed markets that produced it. Oil sands production had vaulted Canada into fifth place of the world's largest producers, with an estimated total of almost 5 mbd.[82] In Canada, a country legendary for its moderation and somewhat boring predictability, the fall in prices hit established economic and political dynamics hard. Canadian oil sands production remained among the most expensive in the world, and price falls of 50 per cent suddenly made that production unprofitable. Consequently, oil sands producers began laying off staff and slowing investment almost immediately. The country's political class began debating whether additional transport infrastructure should be built to support what looked to be an increasingly uneconomic source of oil. Oil sands production suffered from habitual transport bottlenecks that resulted in a deep price discount for Canadian oil on world markets: by some measures that discount measured close to 50 per cent. It was so extreme that Alberta premier Rachel Notley imposed a moratorium on further oil sands export in December 2018.[83]

The political results the oil price generated were also significant. In 2015 Alberta elected its first provincial New Democratic Party (NDP) government: the left-leaning NDP was the first party in decades to break the Conservative Party's dominance of Alberta's provincial politics. The NDP continued to struggle with economic aftershocks of the price fall, much as any party likely would have. Alberta's economy languished during her tenure, by some measures losing over 100,000 jobs since the price downturn.[84] Gaining approval to building requisite pipelines to move Alberta's oil – either south to US refineries or east or west to access global shipping routes – went beyond being mere economic investment projects. They engendered heated political controversy and became an outright national saga about the economic future of the country and whether it should include oil and gas production at all.[85] Opposition from environmental and Indigenous groups to further pipeline development remained strong enough to defeat the economic arguments for them. Yet without sufficient transport networks, investment in Alberta's oil sands made progressively less sense, and companies began abandoning their oil sands investments.[86] All of this was too much for Notley's government: by 2019 she had been replaced by Conservative premier Jason Kenney, who promised to revive the Alberta oil industry, though being unclear as to how.

2014–2019: Looking to the Future?

In all these case low prices did not end the politics and geopolitics of oil: they simply shifted them. Oil exporters needed to sell oil almost as much as oil importers need to buy it: that became increasingly obvious when oil prices dropped and stayed low. Exporters scrambled to protect their economies and meet the spending promises they made to their own people. Importers gained from low oil prices, which acted as an artificial stimulant to their economies, while boosting global economic growth generally. The reality of plenty shifted the bargaining power between importers and exporters. Importers appeared able to pursue foreign policy objectives that might in other environments have clashed with the imperatives of oil security. The power oil suppliers had when prices were high ebbed, and the fear that reliance on oil imports generated dissipated. Low oil prices engendered domestic instability and strained the governments of countries dependent on oil exports, generating a variety of effects from mere economic pain to near revolution.[87] Some countries imploded, some reformed, and a significant number simply carried on more or less as before. The oil price fall generated a variety of political effects that depended very much on local circumstances, the degree to which the country depended on oil revenues, and how wisely the country had allocated the revenues from the previous boom.

Even as the era of low prices continued, the oil market would nevertheless confront both old and new challenges. One of those was output and whether enough new oil would enter the system to meet rising need. By 2019 clouds were once again forming on the global production horizon. Projected economic growth continued building demand for new oil, but few additional supplies were being brought to market, as investment had been slashed. The United States, Canada, and Iraq had managed to increase their production output, but few others could say similar things. Even those countries enduring voluntary production cuts could not easily produce more than their previous maximum without a lot of new invested capital.

Many producers have continued to struggle with maintaining current production levels, while some have even started to decline. Even increased domestic investment did not bring China's production up significantly. Steep production declines were also projected for Indonesia, Malaysia, Vietnam, and Thailand.[88] Additional oil extracted from the North Sea might at best add another 500,000 b/d to global supply by 2023. OPEC's collective production largely held steady: its membership was expected to add 750,000 b/d of new additional supply between 2017 and 2023.[89] Russian production remained stable, yet ongoing sanctions made it difficult for Russia to obtain the technology and investment necessary to develop new fields. Globally, upstream expenditure for oil and gas in 2019 finally rebounded a bit and was expected to increase by 4 per cent, much of it directed at the Middle East.[90] But that was not going to be enough to offset projected increases in demand. Put simply, significant sources of new production growth were not easy to see.

Any alternative sources of supply appearing to have their own issues with which to contend. Most related to above-ground or political risk. UAE, Nigeria, and Saudi Arabia were expected to hold production more or less steady in an ongoing effort to manage prices. Dire political conditions hindered oil production in Venezuela. The imposition of US sanctions continued to severely inhibit Iranian production, which measured 2.5 mbd, down from the 3.7 mbd it had achieved in 2005.[91] One OPEC production bright spot was Iraq: it has increased production from 2 mbd in 2005 to an average of 4.5 mbd in 2019, with ambitious plans to bring that total to 6 mbd.[92] Yet even that increase has built into it an assumption of continued political stability, which was hardly a given. Moreover, even if Iraq's lofty production targets were reached, it might not change global totals, given production declines in other places.

Many OPEC states also projected that their domestic consumption of oil and gas would grow, as their young, enlarging, and increasingly affluent populations consume an increasing share of their domestically produced energy.[93] This will leave less for export: predicted collective overall OPEC supply growth measures 800,000 b/d between now and 2024,[94] a hardly impressive figure. The largest sources of production growth – US fracking and increased production from the Canadian oil sands – face constraints in well productivity, investment, social opposition, and potentially growing regulatory burdens, motivated by the significant portion of the electorate that wants to limit both oil sands and fracking production.[95] Increasing global oil supply has a lot of hurdles to overcome.

Climate Change, Activism, and the Investment Community

Even as producers struggled with defending market share, oil-dependent governments coped with budgetary falls, and companies pondered how much to invest, another storm cloud loomed on the oil market horizon that they had to contend with. This one not only impeded further production but was working to end that production entirely. Put simply, the politics of climate change and the perceived monumental and necessary efforts to stop it, began taking up seemingly ever-greater political bandwidth almost everywhere in the world (except perhaps in the Republican Party in the United States). Certainly environmental criticism of the oil industry and the burning of carbon was by itself nothing new. Oil companies have vied with environmental groups for decades, each contesting the veracity of the science of global warming, differing heavily on whether it was occurring or how much the burning of fossil fuels contributed to it.[96] However, by 2019 the idea that global warming, even for oil companies, was a "contested" position became harder to maintain as scientific evidence of its reality continued to mount.

The crowd of people joining the chorus over concerns about climate change grew. It was no longer just scientists, activists, or politicians leading eco-friendly parties. Warning about the perils of climate change had now entered the very heart of the financial world as well. In 2015 the increasing "mainstreaming" of financial concern over climate change seemed evident when Mark Carney, then governor of the Bank of England, highlighted these risks.[97] In a speech targeted to an assembled crowd of insurance executives, he noted how deeply at risk their actuarial computations might be if climate change projections proved true. He warned that future claims and losses associated with catastrophic weather events could be gargantuan and that insurers extending climate-related policies would find themselves in an increasingly expensive and risky business. He warned oil companies in particularly that they faced the possibility of having hundreds of billions of dollars of assets "stranded" – rendered unusable if regulatory constraints on oil extraction continued to pile up. Carney's warning certainly got the attention of people at the very heart of the global financial and economic system: after all he was one of them. Now oil companies had to worry about not only current production but also about whether it would even be possible to develop the fields they had already spent billions of dollars finding.

Other factors accelerated overall concern about climate change. The previously mentioned Paris Climate Accords was clearly one. It indicated that the consensus on "doing something" about climate change should top government agendas. Governments began enacting a series of provisions to do just that, provisions usually targeted at using less carbon. Another one happened in September 2019, when the United Nations held a follow-up convention to discuss ongoing efforts to ameliorate climate change. The most impassioned voice at the meeting belonged to Greta Thunberg, a sixteen-year-old Swedish climate-change activist who castigated and shamed government leaders for their ongoing focus on economic growth and the inadequate attention she thought they paid to combating climate change. Her advocacy efforts garnered her a Nobel Peace Prize nomination, eventually earned her a *Time* magazine "Person of the Year Award," and inspired millions of followers to engage in "climate strikes" designed to raise awareness and motivate action. Her recommendations may have lacked immediate practicality, but they had certainly proven the power to inspire. They even earned her a couple of condescending tweets from Donald Trump, as sure a sign of achieving attention as one could hope for. Hers was but the most visible voice of an increasingly vocal group wanting to halt the burning of carbon, period.

Capital markets also demanded that energy companies do more in the renewable "space," and calls that they do so became more stringent. Investors put increasing priority on the attention companies paid to environmental, social, and governance (ESG) issues,[98] and of course in the oil business the E mattered an awful lot. Some of the world's largest investment funds began leading the way. Larry Fink, chief executive office of Blackwater, one of the world's largest investment groups, posted a letter to shareholders indicating that sustainability would be a guiding principle in all the company's future investment.[99] Other large investors also made very public statements about divesting from fossil fuels and in demanding greater environmental performance from the companies they did invest in. These included the Church of England, numerous pension funds, and even ironically enough the investment arm of the Rockefeller Foundation.[100] Their motivations to do so are symbolic but also practical. They have made efforts to shun fossil fuel investment increasingly commonplace, made those refusing to do so increasingly investment pariahs, and wielded the power of investment capital to compel change. The moves they made did seem to make a difference in the capital markets: the share of oil and gas companies in stock market indexes continued to broadly decline.[101]

Oil companies had to take note. Some began at least some tentative steps to build their capacities in renewable energy. They had to balance the preservation of the cash cow of oil and gas extraction and sale with the longer-term monetary potential renewables held. The large private supermajors consequently initiated a series of acquisitions in renewable energy. Some investments totaled in the hundreds of millions of dollars, particularly in wind and solar technologies.[102] They also invested significantly in carbon capture and renewable technologies designed to make the extraction of oil and gas less carbon intensive. Critics continued to charge that these efforts were far too little and perhaps too late: the collective investment pledges of the major private oil companies on renewables amounted to less than 5 per cent of their investment budgets, hardly heralding a stunning course change in their business strategy. But something was clearly happening.

It was a delicate balance to walk; clearly not everyone bought what Carney and others were selling. Even while investing in renewables, many oil and gas producers kept increasing their long-term oil output projections, indicating that they thought the oil and gas economy had some legs yet. In February 2019 the *Economist* ran a cover story on ExxonMobil, noting that the oil and gas giant planned to double its output of oil and gas in the coming years. Moreover, the IEA did not agree that present carbon assets would necessarily be stranded[103] noting that the world's need for oil was too great for demand to fall off that quickly. As noted in earlier chapters, demand for oil was high and was set to rise for a while. What to do about it, in terms of how much to double down on oil and gas production versus accelerating development of alternate energy sources, was the biggest strategic question oil companies faced.

There was, however, a trend that seemed unmistakable. The oil industry had repeatedly faced investor activism, impassioned climate activists, governments bent on promoting renewable energy, and periods of depressed stock price before. But they had rarely faced the coalescing of such collective opposition at more or less the same time. Governments around the world had pledged to lower carbon emissions at the Paris Climate Accords. Large chunks of the world's population proved willing to rally around the impassioned message of one teenager. Capital markets were doing what they did, giving a clear indication of what way the wind was blowing (to use a renewable energy metaphor). It seemed like an ominous combination, one that was unlikely to go away and was going to change the future contours, maybe even the existence, of the industry.

Looking Forward

The Saudi-engineered price drop did many things, some predicted, some not. It certainly was a warning shot within OPEC, stating that production reduction burdens had to be shared. It also was a call to return rationality in evaluating prices, to remove excess supply from the market, and calm the waters of what looked like an inflated investment community. Yet, if the goal in engineering the price drop was to halt the revolution in hydrocarbon production going on in the United States, it failed. The US ascendency in oil (and natural gas) production did not stop; if anything it increased in pace. The US financial and oil-production system had proven resilient and was able to clean up the mess the low oil price environment had inflicted. The fall in oil prices did ease geopolitical concerns among importers: the system provided sufficient oil at lower prices, which provided an economic boost and allowed governments to worry about other things.

It was not clear, however, that the Saudis expected oil prices to remain low for as long as they did. Low prices persisted over the 2014–19 period, despite exporters' efforts to revive them by production cuts, and by the end of 2019 the patience of the OPEC-plus group of oil producers appeared to be wearing thin. Long-term global demand would continue to increase, worrying those who pay attention to potential shortfalls in the future. Cuts and delays in investment expenditure now could engender an oil shortage just a few years into the future, which would drive prices up and revive fears of scarcity. Taken together, the regulatory burden on exploring for, developing, and delivering new oil was becoming increasingly difficult, and societal monitoring and opposition appears to be growing. The impact environmental concerns had on investor choices became real: investors now pressured oil companies to demonstrate better environmental performance and often refused to fund oil companies at all.

The start of 2020 posed as many questions as it answered. Would oil plenty remain a permanent fixture of the oil market? If so, would it finally break the incestuous and often painful relationship between oil, politics, and geopolitics? What would those who produced oil, and relied on the money it generated, do? There was plenty to ponder and, by the early spring of 2020, plenty of time to do the pondering. After all, that was when oil analysts (like everyone else) learned how to do their work in Zoom meetings with their pajama bottoms still on because they, like the rest of the world, were operating in lockdown mode caused by the outbreak of the COVID-19 pandemic. What the pandemic – and other industry and political trends – will do to the future of the oil industry is the subject of our last chapter.

chapter seven

2020 and Beyond: Oil in the Post-pandemic World

Oil retains its special place among commodities for anyone interested in the political and geopolitical consequences of economic activity. It still holds a powerful combination of being both economically indispensable and politically problematic. Previous chapters have documented the why and the how of oil market dynamics, and familiar geopolitical currents continue eddying through the workings of the industry. Governments care very much about its present state and future prospects with an intensity that varies according to oil's perceived scarcity or plenty. As 2020 began, that intensity was not very high: most oil observers probably assumed that what had gone on during the previous five years would likely continue. Prices remained low, supply plentiful and predictable, and consumption was rising slowly but at a predictable rate. Consuming and producing governments, individuals, and businesses continued to grapple with oil market challenges much as they always had.

Yet 2020 would prove profoundly different and shocking, and not just for oil. A virus outbreak in China's Wuhan province migrated and marched its way across the world, generating a global pandemic on a scale not seen since the 1918 Spanish Flu. Subsequently labeled COVID-19, the virus causing the pandemic proved much more problematic and contagious than had previous pandemic diseases. Though proving less deadly than other recent pandemic experiences, such as swine flu or Ebola – it caused far fewer deaths per number of infected patients – COVID-19 was highly contagious, and as the sheer number of infected people rose, so too did the number of deaths. As of this writing, over 3 million people the world over have died from COVID-19, some estimates put the death toll much higher,[1] and the pandemic remains far from over.[2]

The drastic measures taken to slow the virus's spread in the pandemic's early stages inflicted a huge shock on the global economy and by extension on the oil system powering it. Hastily instated bans on international travel slowed air traffic to a comparative trickle, and rows of idled commercial aircraft began crowding vacant storage runways in the Arizona desert. Jobs in the service and restaurant business evaporated as customers stopped traveling, eating out, going to movies, staying at hotels, or doing any kind of social gathering. Mandated stay-at-home public safety orders, combined with online grocery shopping sites and the rapidly exploding colossus of Amazon delivery, allowed winter cocooning to rise to a whole new level. People drove less, if at all, and once-crowded urban freeways became the abandoned .ghost zones featured in apocalyptic zombie movies. Industrial production slowed, ship transport traffic lessened, and gasoline prices plunged, in some cases falling by more than half. Unfortunately that did consumers little good because few people could go anywhere.

All of that caused oil demand to plummet rapidly throughout most of 2020 and into 2021. A global economy habitually consuming 100 mbd saw, in the space of a couple of months, demand drop by over 30 per cent. Oil markets became saturated with supply, tankers and storage vessels overflowed, and the price of oil plummeted. Indeed, at one point early in the pandemic oil prices plunged into negative territory: oil traders were literally paying people to take the oil they had bought in forward contracts off their hands. While prices did eventually rebound and somewhat stabilized throughout the course of the pandemic, industrial, commercial, and transport use of oil all remained far below their pre-pandemic levels.

One bright side, if there was one, of the pandemic was that it gave people time to think while they were in lockdown. Citizens could take time to observe the world around them, to reexamine how they lived their lives, and to question whether their collective choices were generating desirable results. Some occupants of cities built around heavy manufacturing facilities began seeing blue skies once again, as industrial pollution abated. Those fortunate enough to be able to work remotely found a new freedom in doing so that many liked: though socially isolating, few missed the daily commute and office grind. Bereft of the opportunity for foreign travel, residents of cities and towns rediscovered local charms and the value of close family and friends. All of this heralded a potentially new way of living and working, some of which is likely to persist into the post-pandemic world.

Meanwhile, the political world continued along its unpredictable and sometimes unsettling way. A tumultuous US presidency careened along its disjointed path and toward a painful conclusion. Governments varied in the approaches they took to dealing with the pandemic and generated different outcomes in the prevention of death and the eventual resumption of even basic economic activity. Even while the pandemic raged, other issues did not take a holiday. Some became more intense than ever and compelled increasing measures of public attention. Global movements protesting racial inequality grew and gained strength the world over. A fairly contested US election came under assault from the very person charged with protecting it, culminating in an armed mob's convergence on the US Capitol Building. While these realities – some pandemic inspired, others not – appear to have little immediately to do with oil, they do indicate that much of what was happening in the world generated unwanted results and that maybe it was time to seriously rethink how we did some things.

One of the more obvious of those things is how we power our economies, and our overall reliance on carbon-based energy sources in the living of our lives. Much of what went on during the pandemic did directly affect the oil market and might continue into the post-pandemic world. People questioned how and how much they really needed to consume, how often they needed to travel, and whether Zoom video calls really were an effective substitute for face-to-face business meetings. Economists and businesspeople began to ponder the future and what the post-pandemic oil world would look like.

Would people rapidly resume similar schedules of travel and workplace commuting that they practiced before COVID-19 hit? Or would they continue the pattern of working from home that seemed to suit many? Would they more carefully consider the impact their lifestyle choices were making on the world around them, and would that motivate them to keep using less and less oil? Or would consumers, in a post-pandemic binge of consumerism, travel, and hedonism, rapidly drive up carbon usage once again? If they did, what would the future of oil production, consumption, and oil politics look like? Would things be better, worse, or more or less the same?

This chapter investigates these puzzles and offers provisional observations (it is too soon for answers) that oil market students might ponder. There are challenges in identifying and protecting the good things about the oil economy – and yes, there are a few – while also mitigating its more harmful effects. There is necessarily more speculation and observation here rather than direct evidence – we often have to guess about what people, companies, and governments might do, rather than examining what they actually did – but most of it is built on a basis of fact. We have to think about the future somehow and in some way, and this is a (likely highly flawed) attempt at doing so. So here goes.

States vs. Markets: Who Will Run Things in the Oil Market?

Power will continue shifting in the oil industry. It always has. Power migrates between producers and consumers, oil companies and host governments, importers and exporters. Because of this fluidity, it is sometimes difficult to say with confidence where the locus of control in the oil industry is. This is nothing particularly new; Louis Turner identified it more than half a century ago. Writing about the era of the Seven Sisters, he summed up that reality as follows: "There is, then, no simple relationship between (oil) majors and their parent governments ... to find a pattern, one must look at the ebbs and flows of the underlying power relationships of the various governments concerned."[3] Something similar could be said today. Power is an elusive and transitory concept in the oil business: it is difficult to pinpoint where it resides, anticipate where it might flow, or know which lever to pull to achieve some preferred outcome, even if everyone could agree on what that was.

For the last fifty years, states in the oil business have generally held the upper hand. They reclaimed control in the oil-production business, established powerful NOCs who dominated oil production, and began exerting direction over most of the world's known oil reserves and its largest, most productive fields. Yet today, state-directed oil producers look increasingly worried, as their control seems to be weakening, their power ebbing, their influence receding. Over the past decade, and perhaps longer, the oil business has increasingly looked like a real market, and a robustly competitive one at that. An extended period of high prices, technological advances in extraction, and more sophisticated trading capacities has made it easier to look for, drill for, find, extract, refine, buy, sell, trade, and reroute oil to meet whatever demand might be emerging and wherever price might be highest. The fracking revolution has added a new, powerful source of supply that can rapidly adjust output according to market demand, a technique that can be deployed quickly in other countries, should they choose to do so. Companies explore new geographies, own leases scattered across the globe, and continue discovering new fields and enhancing production technologies. To those bent on controlling supply, this is not good news.

Even the established NOCs are themselves looking increasingly like their IOC competitors. Many continue pushing for greater decision-making independence from their state owners and operate according to a more market-centric logic. NOC company executives sometimes appear to crave the emphasis on efficiency and cost containment evinced by international oil companies[4] and want the decision-making freedom that would allow them to do similar things. Taken together, as more sources of oil enter the global production "bathtub" – and if demand, and price, start to go up, an important caveat discussed later – it will become difficult for even a strongly coordinated set of state producers to manage supply and to continue exerting anything remotely resembling control. Ironically, just at a time when a lot of developed markets are spouting protectionist economic rhetoric and are questioning globalization generally,[5] pressure is building in the oil market to move in the other direction.

The conflict between markets and state management of the oil system will therefore likely remain. States that still depend on oil revenues to fuel their economies and fund budgets will continue resisting letting markets dominate completely. Who wins, or at least gains the upper hand, in that ongoing contest will depend on a number of other factors. The dominant ones are price, overall supply, and long-term demand. We look at each in turn.

The Future of Price

If you had to pick one word to describe the future of oil prices, that word likely would be "volatile." Achieving a "Goldilocks" price – one that is high enough to ensure profitability, fund state treasuries, and provide sufficient supply but not so high as to induce an avalanche of new exploration and a flood of excess supply that drives down price – remains perhaps *the* quandary the oil market has always had to solve. We have seen throughout this book how various eras and combinations have tried to solve it, and in the end they have always come back to some kind of supply management system to get the job done. Today OPEC, sometimes in combination with Russia, still tries this tactic because the benefits of supply control are clearly real to those able to wield it. The question is whether they still can, whether their alliance will hold, and what long-term difference it will make to the oil market.

Controlling output will depend on OPEC's internal discipline in limiting members' output. Its ability to do that, even at the best of times, remains questionable.[6] Saudi Arabia often carried the de facto burden of swing producer whether it wanted to or not. Its recent efforts to shed that label may have inadvertently reinforced it, as it became clear that it alone among OPEC countries possesses the output and reserve capacity to make a material supply difference. OPEC's unity has frayed but not broken during the extended period of low prices chronicled in chapter six. If oil prices remain low, its members will continue to enjoy a steady stream of income and their profitability will remain solid because they retain the ace-in-the-hole of low production costs. An extended period of low prices might also give OPEC its best chance to recapture an ability to manage supply, as oil investment leaves other, more expensive fields. But there always remains the incentive for each member to cheat, to produce more barrels in order to generate more income, and therefore dump too much oil on the marketplace.

Ongoing low prices have compelled predictable responses in IOCs. Over the period of low prices, private companies have been successful in cutting costs and delaying investment expenditures, all in order to add cash to their bottom lines. Among the supermajors, there even has been a resurgent debate about doing now what they did in the latter half of the 1990s when low oil prices also seemed to be a permanent fixture: merge. Business news in the winter of 2020 speculated that Chevron and ExxonMobil were considering merging to create a colossus of a domestic company that could then enact the efficiency measures merged companies are assumed to do. The same kinds of arguments – cost control, economies of scale, more streamlined operations (code word for administrative job losses) – made then are being made today. Clearly private companies have considered the possibility that prices might remain low for a while. Current supply dynamics lends credence to that view. Supply seems currently robust and ongoing production capacity strong: talk of "peak oil" is nowhere to be found. The world now has plenty of oil to meet what is needed.

That does not mean that the supply system can be ignored entirely. Prices might jump, and jump considerably. They certainly did in the spring of 2022, when Russia's invasion of Ukraine caused already jittery oil prices to jump quickly. Most estimates indicate that the world's demand for oil is set to grow. Meanwhile, regulatory constraints on production – particularly on the high-growth production areas found in North America – continue to increase, making new projects harder to get approvals for and more expensive to do. Companies generally have invested less over the past few years and have withdrawn from many of the producing areas that made up for the production shortfall and rising prices occurring a decade ago.

Much of that needed new growth in output came from US fracking wells and the Canadian oil sands. Today both these sources are suffering in terms of investment. Some companies have judged that, in an era of persistently low oil prices, powerful activist movements, perceived hostile federal governments and interminable regulatory delays, making new investments in these regions is just not worth it. In the case of the Alberta oil sands, transporting output poses an additional problem, as it is becoming increasingly difficult to move product due to a lack of current pipeline capacity and the apparent unwillingness to build more.[7] Without new transport facilities, and with ongoing dropping of investment, that output might level off or even shrink. There are also additional constraints being placed in the United States on the expansion of fracking. Though output from fracking wells has remained elevated and high, investment in it has slowed, and regulatory burdens are increasing. The Biden administration has staked out a general opposition to it and has given every indication that its intent is to make the regulatory framework around fracking more stringent. In short, some of the primary sources of additional new supply are today subject to strong forces inhibiting increased production in the future.

If economic activity grows quickly in the post-pandemic world, that might cause a recurrence of rapidly increasing prices. If that world sees a strong uptick in consumer behavior – in buying new clothes to fit post-COVID-19 (often larger) bodies, traveling to see relatives, or driving to see just about anything anywhere – carbon consumption is going to rise quickly, and so too will oil prices. That has long engendered worry within the IEA that the global supply system is set for another crunch[8] because investment is not keeping up with projected need. A supply crunch, and a pretty severe one, may be looming on the horizon (indeed may already have happened by the time this book gets to print). If it occurs, prices will rise, and rise significantly. However, this time, if a supply crunch happens, it will be a self-inflicted one; it will not be because the oil is not there.

If prices rise, how will suppliers react? OPEC has an incentive to limit production and thereby keep prices high, particularly if the regulatory burdens on production elsewhere keep additional new supply off the market. Those burdens would in effect solve OPEC's supply management problem for them. For most OPEC members, oil revenue continues to provide the vast majority of state revenue, which might explode if demand spikes and alternate supply is not there to meet it. That might create vast increases in their revenue. Meanwhile, consumer and political pressure to encourage and allow more oil production will grow if prices for oil products start rapidly going up.

OPEC and other oil producers might enjoy a subsequent financial bonanza. However, the giddiness such success engenders may make it more affordable to delay addressing their major long-term vulnerability. What if global demand drops, significantly and more or less permanently? This is the trillion-dollar question afflicting all participants in the oil market: whether ongoing momentum to transition to non-carbon energy sources occurs faster than anticipated and before the countries and companies producing oil are fully ready. So, what is going to happen to demand?

The Future of the Oil Market: Demand

Some might think it silly to even be discussing the future of the oil industry. In their eyes, it does not and cannot have one. They argue that the climate effects of depending on carbon-based energy sources are large, uniformly negative, impossible to ignore or deny, and increasingly immediate. Far from being the "horizon" problem once characterizing the topic of climate change – where the costs born to avert climate change are incurred now.but the benefits will not accrue for decades – the evidence of dangerous climate anomalies seems to be all around us right now. The scientific evidence and consensus around the reality of a warming climate continues to accumulate. The persistent evidence of "wacky" weather, once-in-a-century storms that now occur several times in a decade, and seemingly relentless fires and floods now give additional weight to the musings from farmers and rural folk that something is indeed "now different 'round here." The growing awareness of, and desire to do something about, climate change seems widespread. This time might really be different, and if one wants to stop climate change, a good place to start is to put oil companies out of business, or at least make them draw energy from some other source.

The United States seems now to be on board with that goal. Incoming president Joseph Biden worked quickly and early in his administration to differentiate his climate approach from that of his predecessor. To be sure, that was not hard to do, as Trump's presidency appeared devoid of any concern for the environment at all. Not only did Trump himself appear environmentally illiterate, his presidency also seemed downright dangerous and hostile toward efforts to stop climate change, and a good many other things as well. His talent for stoking and inflaming domestic division seemed unmatched, his disdain for global agreements of any kind for anything absolute. Perhaps most alarmingly for those wanting more American leadership on climate-change issues was that his approach enjoyed consistent and unwavering support by a large chunk of the American electorate. They liked what he was doing and, if anything, wanted to see more of it.

Upon taking the reins of power after such a divisive presidency, one of Biden's seemingly self-appointed tasks was healer-in-chief. Not only did he need to calm domestic tension, he also moved to reassure foreign allies of what US intentions were and whether its word on climate change, or indeed anything else, could really be trusted long term. Quickly rejoining the Paris Climate Accords was one way of doing that. So too was the appointment of senator and previous presidential candidate John Kerry as his climate ambassador. But Biden has not stopped there; he continues to press for greater US leadership on climate change. For example, on April 22, 2021, "Earth Day," Biden pledged that the United States would halve its carbon emissions by the year 2030,[9] and he convened a climate summit that invited dozens of country leaders to renew and reaffirm their collective pledge to lower carbon emissions and thereby move forward on meeting their climate-change targets.[10]

He was not alone. The Earth Day politicians were also joined by the financiers. On the very same day (technically the night before), the Glasgow Financial Alliance for Net Zero made similar announcements. Chaired by Mark Carney, former governor of the Bank of England and the Bank of Canada, this alliance united over 160 leading firms in the financial, insurance, and banking businesses whose collective assets measured US$70 trillion. Its members committed themselves to "align operational and attributable emissions from their portfolios with pathways to net-zero by 2050 or sooner." The goal of the alliance was to "work to mobilise the trillions of dollars necessary to build a global emissions economy and deliver on the goals of the Paris agreement."[11] Taken together, it appears that many of the world's top bankers and most important politicians now seem aligned on the common goal of taking strong environmental action quickly and making it stick. Encouraging signs indeed that the transition toward non-carbon-based energy sources is fully underway.

So what could possibly go wrong? Not to be deliberately dour, but Biden's pledges echo in tone and content those made by another Democratic president fifty years earlier. The incoming administration of Jimmy Carter ascended to the US presidency in 1976 under remarkably similar circumstances as did Biden. He too carried with him an ambitious domestic agenda that would hopefully help heal the country after the painful Watergate period that had just destroyed the presidency of Richard Nixon. A key element of that agenda was also the pursuit of renewable energy resources to wean the country off carbon. Carter certainly looked and acted the part. He installed solar panels on the roof of the White House. He pushed for ever-higher mileage requirements for domestically produced cars. He empowered and strengthened environmental restrictions generally. He, much like Biden, began his term with optimism and widespread public support and seemed to think that making the world greener would not only generate economic and political benefits but would somehow restore America's moral standing as well.

That is not the way Carter's term ended. He would find achieving his environmental goals tough slogging, the entrenched opposition formidable, the victories few. Congressional opponents from oil-producing states questioned the science of climate change. They argued against heavy regulation of the oil and gas sector, opposed the intrusive government that Carter's administration seemed to epitomize, and repeatedly pointed to the guaranteed jobs and economic benefits oil production brought to their state. Oil companies waged relentless public relations campaigns on the benefits of oil and gas and exercised their formidable influence in the corridors of power. Achieving breakthroughs in alternative energy technologies proved expensive, slow, and unpredictable: scaling those breakthroughs up to service a broad spectrum of the US economy proved to be a decades-long, not a years-long, task. All the while, time spent on promoting alternative energy policies and convincing, arguing with, and cajoling against this entrenched opposition sucked up presidential time and effort that was then not available to pursue other things. His efforts did not wean the US off oil, and his presidency became doomed largely by a faltering oil-dependent economy that suffered from the price rises inflicted by the Iranian Revolution.

At the end of his term, Carter lamented his efforts to break the US dependence on foreign oil, doing so in a lengthy and a somewhat dispiriting way: "In looking back on the 'moral equivalent of war' against energy waste and excessive vulnerability from oil imports, I see nothing exhilarating or pleasant. It was a bruising fight, and no final clear-cut victory could be photographed and hung on the wall for our grandchildren to admire."[12]

One could argue that Biden's efforts might suffer a similar fate. The post-pandemic economy may grow strongly and prove impatient in waiting for renewables to take the place of carbon sources. Politicians get busy and distracted: other more immediate issues might emerge that divert presidential attention away from the critically important but longer-term goal of managing the energy transition. Taxpayers may be progressively less willing to fund investments in non-carbon technologies. Elections may return to power a Republican Party that either prevents Biden from doing what he wants or eventually undoes everything he did. Those benefiting from carbon dependency will work to preserve their interests in the corridors of power, much as they always have and as entrenched political interests of all types usually do. What are now promising environmentally friendly technologies may not pan out, may be commercially too expensive, or may be unable to compete with established carbon-based alternatives. Long-promised jobs in the environmental sector may not materialize. Price increases in gasoline may demand that governments loosen regulation. All these factors still exist and could doom Biden's administration to a Carter-esque fate.

Yet that seems unlikely. After fifty years a lot of things have changed, and one would think they ought to be enough to cause the proverbial "tipping point"[13] in which momentum toward an increasingly carbon-free, or at least carbon-neutral, future is becoming unstoppable. Certainly a number of big, important entities – mainly national governments and large companies – think that it has, and have pledged themselves to hurry it along. That includes the car companies. General Motors has committed to eliminating gasoline and diesel light-duty cars and SUVs by 2035.[14] Other major car companies, including BMW, Ford, Mercedes Benz, Volkswagen, and Volvo, have made similar pledges.[15] Numerous countries and regions – too numerous to list here –are joining them, at least publicly stating, if not outright committing, that they will ban the sale of gasoline-powered automobiles by certain dates (2035 seems to be the most popular one).[16]

The financial community is following right behind, or perhaps they might be the ones pulling the car companies and countries along. The already-mentioned Earth Day alliance of financiers are not alone. Larry Fink continues issuing his letters advocating for ever-greater climate considerations to be included in how Blackrock makes investment decisions and what it demands of the companies it invests in. No greater growth industry exists in business schools today than in developing centers and capacities dedicated to studying sustainable finance. The market for renewable resource products continues to grow, those able to make a commercially viable, environmentally friendly product seem to be rewarded more than handsomely by public stock markets, while those sticking to oil are being financially pummeled. In the fall of 2020 the oil giant

ExxonMobil dropped out of the Dow Jones group of companies used to monitor overall stock market performance, after being one of the index's staples for decades.

The financial and activist community appear increasingly empowered in pressuring companies to increase their overall capacities in what is now referred to as environmental, social, and governance (ESG) performance. For oil companies the E is a particularly troublesome thing for some investors. No matter how well those companies might do on the S and G scores, their environmental footprint is too large to ignore. Large numbers of capital providers, pension and investment funds, and banks are pledging themselves to either avoid investing in oil companies at all or do so only if companies continue to exhibit ever-greater performance in lowering the carbon emissions of what they do and provide a clear roadmap to carbon neutrality. All these developments can be taken as pretty telling indicators that the times indeed are a-changing and that the world is in a different place now than it was in Carter's time.

Other criticisms are now leveled at oil companies that were rarely leveled then. Critics also contend that oil companies should be the ones doing more to develop alternate sources of energy. After all, they have the money and the engineering expertise to develop these alternate sources, and it seemingly makes good sense for them to do so, as renewable sources will increasingly be their future income base. Critics find it puzzling that oil companies continue doing the financially wrong thing: spending tens of billions of dollars annually on oil and gas exploration, finding new reserves that can never be burned if the world is to avoid catastrophic climate change. They also do not do enough of the right thing. By one source, oil companies spend less than 1 per cent of their budgets on developing renewable energy resources.[17] Even more galling to oil critics is how dedicated such companies appear to be in perpetuating oil use while simultaneously trumpeting their paltry renewable energy efforts on corporate websites. The avenues for attack on oil companies today seem rather wide.

They are having an effect: companies do recognize that some change is necessary. The large and largely familiar oil companies – ExxonMobil, Chevron, BP, Total, and Royal Dutch Shell, to name the most prominent ones – certainly fall into this category, as do the smaller but still sizable private-sector oil companies in North America and Europe. They are all grappling with the strategic problem of how to maintain their core businesses in oil and gas extraction while figuring out how to rebrand and retool themselves as "energy" rather than "oil and gas" companies. Some are taking more aggressive stances in building their capacity in non-carbon energy sectors than are others, and it is an open question how successful they will ultimately be. But at the very least they appear aware of the need to try, or at least appear to try, to significantly change their energy production mix from carbon to non-carbon.

In doing so, oil companies will rely on the inherent strengths they have demonstrated and built up over their decades of operation. It is never wise to count out the ingenuity and resourcefulness of the engineers operating in the oil patch or the executives running oil companies. The last several years of low prices and constrained costs have spawned strong technical improvements in how oil is extracted: put simply, it now costs less to do so, and the process emits less carbon. Meanwhile, oil companies continue grappling with the strategic problem of whether, how, and how much to invest in non-carbon-based forms of extraction. The competitive demands of activist shareholders and ESG investment funds are forcing operational changes in private-sector companies. Whether they are moving far enough and fast enough remains contested, but the fact that they are moving is generally not.

A couple of further notes about ESG investing are worth stating here. First is to remember that consumers and investors are sometimes inconsistent and fickle beasts. Investment funds today are demanding all kinds of ESG performance from private-sector oil companies, and often seem dissatisfied no matter what those companies do. Yet investors are, in some sense, a filter of consumer preferences. They are but one step removed from those doing the actual oil consuming. Consumers cannot, except through their investment dollars, reward or punish oil companies directly for their good or bad ESG performance. They cannot, as yet, choose to buy "ethically" produced oil the way one can purchase fair trade coffee, organic vegetables, or hormone-free meat, and it remains an open question whether consumers would pay more for oil sourced from one jurisdiction versus one sourced from another. It is difficult to believe they would, or that enough of them would to materially change what big oil producers did. ESG may reflect investor preference, but it also has to take into account what consumers of oil are experiencing.

ESG over the past few years has benefitted because, during that time frame, oil and gas products have been relatively cheap. During the pandemic it has been an easier matter to minimize their use, demand has not yet picked up, and prices remained low. Fund managers could easily avoid investing in oil companies simply because the returns were not there, whether they really cared about ESG or not. But what if these conditions do not hold? Prices might increase dramatically if the global economy rebounds quickly from the global pandemic; if so there will be lots of money to be made in oil. Commitment to ESG by fund managers will be sorely tested then if their investors see them passing up very profitable oil and gas investments. It is an open question whether the collective commitment glue of such fund managers will be strong enough to prevent other capital providers from jumping at those opportunities. Investing funds seeking returns may need to start looking at oil again if the returns go up significantly.

A third point to make about ESG is that it sometimes seems inconsistently applied. Oil companies get heavy attention, while other companies seem to get away scot-free on ESG issues if their product seems to advance the climate's interest. Investors and critics continue to throw all kinds of shade at oil companies: meanwhile they have no problem sinking mountains of cash into Tesla no matter how much weed Elon Musk smokes on the Joe Rogan podcast. Such actions seem hardly in tune with cutting-edge governance mechanisms that are supposed to monitor and constrain CEO behavior, and any oil company executive pulling the same stunt would likely have a very short job tenure. Yet enthusiasm for electric cars seems so strong that it in effect made Musk millions of dollars richer at the end of the podcast then he was at the beginning.

A final, and more serious, thing to consider about ESG and environmental activism over the future of oil is honesty. Are ESG investors approaching oil and gas investing by acknowledging that oil and gas production will go on for a while yet and that it is in everyone's collective interest that it be done to the highest standards, with a clear roadmap laid for the energy transition? Or is the goal one of extinction by regulation, to make it so hard for private oil and gas companies to operate and source capital that they simply give up? If the goal is the latter, we should be careful what we wish for. Admittedly, for those holding that view, targeting publicly traded companies makes sense. But such efforts only work in countries that take environmental activism seriously and have companies reliant on outside capital investment, and those conditions apply only to a small sector of the oil-production universe. The largest sectors of that universe, the NOCs, rarely rely significantly on outside investors and may not particularly care what those investors want. Nor are they vulnerable to environmental activism: their home countries are rarely well known for tolerating protest movements of any sort. Those companies are often critical to their country's fiscal position, do not need external capital, and rarely have public relations vulnerabilities. They are unlikely to abandon their mainstream business of oil production.

That leaves the private-sector IOCs. Activist efforts might succeed in pushing out the very companies that are the most likely to evince a real rather than rhetorical commitment to improved social performance. Would it be a good thing if oil producers domiciled in democratic, highly regulated, ESG-attentive, shareholder-responsive, and increasingly environmentally conscious regions like Canada, Norway, continental Europe, and the United States to be driven out of the oil-production game because they cannot compete against companies who do not bear these associated costs? Well, if one believes the goal is for no oil to be produced at all, then eliminating companies most vulnerable to activist pressure is probably a good first step. But those taking that position should not kid themselves. You cannot influence the rules of a game that you no longer play, and whatever production is taken off the market from these places will be rapidly and gleefully snapped up by others.

What will those others look like? Well, they are likely not going to be democratic. The state will once again have taken over the act of oil and gas production. Their oil companies are likely to be less regulated, and their executives may not care at all about ESG. Such companies may be owned by governments who may not worry much about individual rights, do not take seriously the idea of protecting members of the LGBTQ community, are less concerned about promoting gender equity, and where a narrow band of kleptocrats often pockets almost all the profits. Supply removed from the market from Canada, the United States, Norway, and Great Britain will happily be absorbed by Saudi Arabia, Iran, Iraq, the UAE, Libya, Russia, Nigeria, Mexico, Brazil, and maybe even Venezuelan production. Even if these countries do not fill in the supply gaps, they might simply sit back and enjoy the benefits of a rapidly increasing price brought on by sudden supply decrease. Either way, these seem like bad long-term outcomes.

The impact of ever-greater consumer expectations of social performance by oil companies is real, and its impact is cumulative. However, to maximize that impact, it needs to spread to encompass an ever-greater component of the oil-producing world. The impact of company instruments – such as operational practices or emerging-industry global governance standards[18] – do matter. If IOCs continue pushing for general diffusion of such standards – primarily to ensure that their competitors bear the same ESG burdens they do – then they might become expected table stakes for international oil operations and create a level playing field in the ESG world. Such would be a welcome development. In the meantime, it seems unwise to unduly punish those who are working in good faith on improving their ESG initiatives while letting those who are not get away unscathed.

The Oil-Producing Countries: The Politics and Geopolitics of Transition

One might think that a fall in oil prices, and a long-term decline in use, would make the world a safer place. If security of supply seems assured, there is no need to worry about it or compete for it. The geopolitics of energy should calm down, and conflict over energy access seems less plausible or worrisome. Low oil prices can help boost global economic growth, contributing to lower supply costs in global economic activity and improved overall economic stability. Low oil prices also mentally equate to plentiful supply, which provides little incentive to take actions designed to procure more. Consequently, the potential for geopolitical rivalry in securing energy looks like it is more of an imagined rather than a real problem.

· That rosy scenario evaporated in the early spring of 2022 with Russia's invasion of Ukraine. That invasion showed how much the geopolitics of energy still matter. Geopolitical tensions are endemic in many oil-producing areas, some of it is oil inspired, some of it is not. Saudi Arabia continues its buildup of military and security forces and remains embroiled in a regional strategic rivalry with Iran. Both countries fund contending factions in the ongoing civil war in Yemen, which has resulted in a massive humanitarian crisis. Low oil prices continue to inflict significant damage on the Iranian economy. Israelis and Palestinians engaged in a ten-day conflict in May 2021, indicating that that dispute is far from settled, and continues to bubble away in the Middle East. A precarious tension-filled calm with the seeming potential for a sudden crisis continues to permeate many of the nations that produce a lot of the world's oil.[19]

Low oil prices can engender domestic instability and strain for governments of countries that export oil and rely on its revenues. How they react to that instability varies:[20] some implode, some reform, some choose to engage in foreign adventures to distract domestic attention, and a significant number simply try to carry on more or less as before. The geopolitical effects of low oil prices and plentiful supply remain a mixed bag for exporters. Yet now it is compounded by the global trend toward energy transition, which is not just an economic process but is clearly a geopolitically delicate problem. As problematic and corrosive as oil revenue can be to governments that are too reliant on it, that revenue does at least provide some income stability allowing those states to take steps now to avert economic disaster in the future. What exactly is going to happen to those countries if oil revenue suddenly ceases to flow, or at the very least is cut back significantly and more or less permanently?

Adjustments will have to be made in economic structure and perhaps even political process. In times of high oil prices there is a temptation for government officials to increase, rather than decrease, their fiscal reliance on oil. The money generated by high prices creates clamor for redistribution: lots of entities come to the trough wanting their share. In a period of low prices, declining demand, and energy transition, revenue from oil will not by itself generate enough income to satisfy all those outstretched palms, still less create the economic opportunity required by the rapidly growing youthful populations that populate many oil-producing states. Social spending largesse may become increasingly unaffordable and will have to be cut back, and the need to economically diversify even more readily apparent. Some clearly know this and have already advertised expansive economic diversification plans; in some cases that process is now decades old.[21] But it will take time, consistent political will, and ongoing domestic political support to do it, things that are always in short supply.

The third component of ongoing domestic political support is perhaps the most difficult to manage. One of the problems posed by having excess resource revenue is that domestic populations get used to their governments having money and not having to ask them to provide more. In Saudi Arabia personal tax rates are effectively zero, as they are in the UAE, and generous social safety nets remain in place.[22] Intellectually, it is easy to understand the necessity of economic diversification, but building the institutions capable of doing it is hard. It certainly helps to have alternate revenue-collection mechanisms, even as the percentage of that revenue attributed to oil ebbs and flows.[23] Meanwhile, if oil revenues drop, domestic political stability may erode, and serious questions start to get asked about who gets to do the governing. Consequently, the movement away from oil will start testing the stability of countries producing it.

Oil price falls affect all oil producers,[24] and each becomes preoccupied with shoring up its domestic position and ensuring its own stability. Some do a better job of that than others. It is not simply the act of producing oil that creates a dysfunctional or problematic state, nor is it automatic that a fall in oil prices will result in political revolution or chaos.[25] The resource curse does not promote revolution and authoritarianism at all times and in all places,[26] and it remains difficult to separate out the effects due to oil and the effects that may have happened anyway, as causality may run in either direction.[27] But to assume that falling oil revenues and demand will instill geopolitical calm is a dangerous assumption. It might do the opposite.

If there is a wildcard worth worrying about in the geopolitics of oil production, it is Russia. Russia's economy and state treasury remain as dependent as ever on oil and gas revenues. Complicating the Russian energy story are the hard geographic, demographic, and geopolitical realities faced by the Russian state. Russia has for decades relied on its geographic location and vast reserves of oil and gas to build supply relationships with Western Europe and more recently with East Asia, particularly in natural gas.[28] Its invasion of Ukraine revealed Western Europe's continued dependence on Russian gas, and engendered calls to do what was necessary to break that dependence. Yet the country's prominence in the gas supply system has been eroded by the construction of numerous liquefied natural gas plants around the world, and its previously strong position is coming under increasing threat from strong global supply and the availability of alternate sources. It is also suffering from the declines in oil revenue caused by low prices, declines that further weaken the country's budget and wider economy.

The Russian economy suffers structural problems that resource revenue may be able to paper over but will not cure. The corruption that has plagued resource revenue management in particular is staggering: by one estimate, the resource revenues deliberately siphoned away by Russia's oligarchic class have totaled tens if not hundreds of billions of dollars.[29] The ongoing presence of generally sclerotic state-run companies continues to drag down economic performance. Its economy is now more centralized, has lower regulatory quality, and pays less attention to the rule of law than it did even five years ago.[30] Russia's domestic companies are unable to compete on world markets, non-resource exports are almost negligible, and the country habitually scores poorly on competitiveness rankings.[31] It is also facing a demographic time bomb with an aging population, comparatively low life expectancy, low fertility rates, and virtually no immigration.

Rather than using low energy prices as a motivator to restructure and diversify its domestic economy, Russia has, if anything, doubled down on its natural resource plenty as its primary source of economic power. It has been resilient, weathering the decline in oil prices, and has managed to maintain and even increase oil production despite ongoing sanctions leveled against it by the United States. The potential for additional Russian production remains vast: yet its ability to tap that potential is questionable. Much depends on such variables as brownfield recovery rates; the exchange rate of the ruble; the availability of investment capital; Russia's willingness to tap its own shale reserves, which remain considerable, and a host of other things.[32] Sanctions have slowed investment in developing new oil-producing fields to replace current ones, which may hurt future Russian oil production if they are not eventually lifted. Economic sanctions imposed on Russia after its invasion of Ukraine will be even more crippling, and will do significant damage to the infrastructure of the Russian economy. The free-floating ruble and generous tax allowances may have allowed companies to remain profitable, yet the fiscal pressure on the country continues.

The deteriorating economy has if anything worked to increase Putin's centralized hold on power.[33] Russia's foreign policy has included attempts to disrupt democratic elections, particularly in those states on its Western border,[34] and it appears certain that it made deliberate attempts to meddle in the United States election of 2016 and perhaps even 2020, a fact now believed by virtually all observers.[35] Finally, it has militarily invaded a sovereign neighboring state in an attempt to re-establish Russian control over its Western border. These actions hardly constitute moderation, they resemble more a wounded and weakened Russian bear whose source of geopolitical influence is waning. Wounded animals are dangerous and unpredictable.

The Future of Oil Geopolitics: The United States and China

Strategically the most important factor impacting how the world is going to work in the future is the relationship between the United States and China. As the world's two largest economies, what they say, do, and are trying to achieve matters a lot, particularly if those things are in conflict. That reality is as true in the oil market as it is anywhere else. The United States remains simultaneously the world's biggest consumer and (often) biggest producer of oil, and consequently is in a powerful position to shape the future of the oil market. It retains a national interest in ensuring its own oil and broader energy security, and in protecting continued access to a reliable supply of oil at stable, predictable, and preferably low prices for itself and its allies. It also, ideologically speaking, is and has been a strong advocate for a market-based system to govern the production and distribution of oil. These goals are general and are of long-standing.

They remain, but now the US has more options for pursuing them. The United States does not now need to worry nearly as much about its own oil security as it once did, having proven the fertility of its fracking fields. This should theoretically allow its approach to the oil market to evolve while enhancing its capacity to pursue other interests and care about other things. The list of strategic and foreign policy advantages strong domestic production capacity should give the United States is impressive. It should allow the US diplomacy to be freed from the worry about procuring oil, and lower oil prices should weaken some of its perpetual adversaries who are now more dependent on selling oil than the US is on buying it. Lower oil prices might also disrupt, or at least lessen, some of the revenues that might be funneled into terrorist hands. Its adversaries and critics cannot now realistically portray its foreign policy actions through the prism of oil procurement, though they undoubtedly will continue to try. There can now be a realistic debate about the place of oil security in national security debates, and how high that place should be.

This freedom of choice, however, carries multiple edges. The US must also choose whether it will continue to bear the costs of providing "public economic goods" that have allowed the global economy, and by extension the oil market, to function. In the energy system, the question can be even more pointedly phrased. Will the US, increasingly able to draw on its own supplies of energy and having neighbors also possessing a lot of oil, leave the rest of the world to more or less fend for itself in terms of procuring oil? Will it bear the costs of ensuring the stability of oil flow, given the fact that one of the biggest beneficiaries of that stability is its emerging strategic rival? Given the current protectionist economic bent the country still largely shows, such questions remain realistic rather than theoretical, and the answers are not preordained. If the US retreats behind an energy wall that relies on its own resources and those of its neighbors, it would pose a significant challenge to the global energy system, to say the least.

The US commitment to ensuring the free flow of trade – including oil – on international waterways has been a pillar of US foreign policy. Today, the undercurrent of populism and protectionism in the United States indicates that not everyone shares that view or believes that the benefits justify the costs. Some think doing so has been too costly and that it has benefited allies and adversaries alike far more than it has the United States. If that is indeed the case, why keep doing it? It certainly would be cheaper not to. For example, observers have tried to provide a thorough accounting of the associated costs of protecting Persian Gulf oil with US military assets.[36] Joseph Stiglitz tagged the price of the US invasion of Iraq at US$3 trillion,[37] and a recent analysis from the RAND think tank indicates that the "most likely outcome of the removal of the mission to defend oil supplies and sea lines of communication from the Persian Gulf would be a reduction over time of between 12 and 15 percent of the current U.S. defense budget."[38] That is a lot of money, and saving it would be an attractive option in a country beset by post-pandemic budget deficits and that has multiple military commitments. Why not lower, if not eliminate, that commitment? Does it still warrant that level of expenditure and effort?

The US attitude toward oil politics will be one key barometer of the commitment the country holds to both underpinning an integrated global economy and its willingness to reinforce the security bond it holds with its allies. Fracking lowers the need for the US to import oil: and while other countries have their own shale resources, their production potential may take decades to develop.[39] A number of long-standing US allies still remain dependent on oil imports and the broader protection of the US security umbrella. The US has historically been willing to provide and foot the bill for that security. If concern over oil security might recede in the

United States, it might intensify in other developed and developing economies whose need for imported oil is rising. If the US does not provide the security foundation for that system, who will step up to that particular plate? (The only one that potentially could is China, more on that later.) That might result, if the US generally withdraws, in a regional power vacuum becoming increasingly large in the Persian Gulf region, or the vacuum might be filled by a more ominous geopolitical rival pursuing its own geostrategic interests. Neither option enhances US interests.

Taken in its entirety, the United States benefits from having increased domestic oil production. It benefits economically from the added boost cheaper and more plentiful energy provides, and it benefits geopolitically from being less dependent on foreign oil and in having more options in its foreign policy toolkit. While cheaper domestic energy may reinforce rather than redirect overall use of carbon energy resources, there remains plenty of signals for private companies to move toward investment in renewables. The vibrancy and resiliency of the US market remains its key advantage in adapting to an increasingly unpredictable and volatile economic future.

Turning to China, it is important to remember a point Alan Greenspan wryly noted in his autobiography: people are entitled to their own opinions, but they are not entitled to their own facts.[40] Contemporary interpretations of China's economic and foreign policy features plenty of both. Some facts are clear. China's rapid and sustained economic growth over the past two decades vastly increased the country's demand for energy and made it an important new player – perhaps even *the* key player – in global energy markets. In terms of oil, China's demand now far exceeds its domestic production capacity, and it will have to import an increasing amount of oil for the foreseeable future. China is now rivaling if not exceeding the United States as the single biggest national market for imported oil. Meanwhile, its companies are formidable international players. As China's economy grows, how it defines and pursues its national interest in the oil market is going to matter, a lot.

China faces challenges in procuring oil that look very similar to those faced historically by others, and the strategies it has adopted in managing those challenges look familiar too. Like

other countries, it has encouraged and aided its domestic companies to expand internationally. It continues to cultivate a diversity
of new oil suppliers to complement and supplement established
ones. It continues a robust domestic exploration program. It too
frets about its immediate and long-term dependency on imports,
for the same reasons that have worried American, Japanese, and
European governments for decades. It has created an oil policy
designed to increase its overall presence in the international oil
market, and forged diplomatic relationships with those that can
supply it required resources.[41] Nothing in any of this is particularly
novel or strange: the history of oil is replete with other countries
doing similar things. China is a big new player, but it is playing
the same game.

How will it continue playing? Will it attempt to change the system, or will the system change it? Maybe a bit of both. To begin, one
contested area is whether China will continue pursuing its current
policy of state capitalism, a policy that builds geopolitical strength
and influence through economic means.[42] Its economic statecraft
certainly looks like it will: it remains ambitious and builds economic
links that are designed to cement firmly the recipient countries' economic interest in aiding China's prosperity.[43] Oil dependency will
compound and complicate the strategic dilemmas China faces as it
ramps up its diplomatic and economic power and assumes more
diverse foreign policy interests. There are three major areas where
the politics of oil will intrude into China's overall grand strategy.

The first major strategic dilemma is whether and how much
the country will choose to flex its increasing geopolitical muscle
in the South China Sea. Most of China's imported oil arrives by
ship, and not surprisingly the country takes sovereignty over its
sea borders increasingly seriously. Most of its recent disputes with
the United States hinge in some way over who will control those
seaborne waterways, and many of the potential flashpoints of
conflict between the United States and China occur here. The two
countries differ in legal interpretations about how far out to sea
China's sovereignty extends: the US says 12 miles, China claims
200. The United States maintains its close strategic relationship
with Japan and Korea, longstanding US allies wary of China's

growing military might. There are disputes about control over the Spratly Islands and potential resources that might lie underneath those islands. There are clear "differences of opinion" about the current and future political independence of Taiwan. Controlling the waterways in the South China Sea, where much of China's needed imports must sail, will make management of these questions ever more important, not to say delicate.

Oil also complicates the other arms of China's economic strategy. A second arm involves developing the necessary infrastructure necessary to spread Chinese economic influence overland and eastward via reconstruction of the now infamous Silk Road. A massive, multi-trillion-dollar investment program designed to tie the economic prosperity of participating countries ever more tightly to China, the scale of the project is enormous. It was and continues to be billed as an economic project that works to the partners' mutual advantage. Yet, as is perhaps inevitable in an economic project of this ambition, political competition and worries have crept in. Even now, recipients of Silk Road investment initiatives are beginning to push back against what is perceived to be Chinese domination.[44] Its economic expansion abroad often carries with it additional burdens and increasing suspicion of the country's ultimate intention.

The third arm of China's economic strategy has been to construct a global economic institutional network that is more to its liking, leadership, and design. China has been instrumental in creating the Asian Infrastructure Investment Bank, a financial institution designed to fund regional infrastructure efforts to spur economic development. It has also participated in the launch of the New Development Bank, an organization created by the BRIC (Brazil, Russia, India, and China) economies designed to provide investment funds to emerging markets. In doing this, China and its colleagues are offering an alternative institutional set to recipient nations to the already established International Monetary Fund (IMF) and the World Bank, the Western-dominated institutions that currently perform such functions and have been doing so for decades. In the areas of trade, finance, and investment, China appears willing to create institutions that compete directly with the established Western-dominated ones. As China becomes more dependent on imported oil flow, it will increasingly care about the security of the sea-lanes, the land infrastructure, and the security of the countries providing it that oil. They are doing this already by rapidly increasing their military expenditures, in particular naval capacities that can extend Chinese interests far beyond its own shores. That buildup may accelerate, and as the country gains power, it will likely continue to broaden its political and military interests and its independent capability to pursue them.[45]

Taking these trends together, there are a couple of important geopolitical questions that will impact the oil market. If the United States chooses to relinquish a measure of its economic leadership void, will China step into the breach and fill it? Will China assert that control unilaterally, banking that a distracted and nativist US will let it have its way in places far away from the United States? If that happens, will leadership in the oil market quickly follow suit, and what will that leadership look like? Will China now take over the mantle of protecting the outflow of Persian Gulf oil? If it did, could others trust that it would view this as a collective, rather than an individual, interest? The geopolitics of great power competition are still, as always, going to play out in the oil arena.

Where Will the Oil Market Go?

There clearly are a lot of unknowns about the future of oil. Economically, over the period 2014–20, the oil and gas sector was one of the poorest-performing sectors in any stock-market index one chooses to look at. But it is hard to use the stock market as an accurate prediction of where things will go: after all, stock markets have predicted nine of the last five recessions.[46] We need to look elsewhere for guidance in the post-pandemic world. Economic growth will come back, and perhaps very strongly. Increased demand may cause a spike in oil and gas prices, as it will take some time for additional supply to be brought to market. Meanwhile those currently producing oil may find it profitable, perhaps extremely profitable, to be in the oil business. Just as recent events may make it appear that the oil business is on its last legs, a future period of high prices and profitability may make it look like the oil business has never been stronger.

The world of oil and the progress of energy transition remains full of contradictions. To take one recent example, on May 5, 2021, the *Financial Times* ran a story on the latest report from the International Energy Administration. That report argued that, if the goals of the Paris Climate Accords were going to be reached, drastic and immediate action has to be taken. One required measure would be for governments, everywhere and all at once, to mandate the immediate halting of all new oil and gas developments in the world, full stop. They also would have to throw in a similar halt on all new gas fields, coal mines, and coal-fired electricity plants for good measure. Moreover, to achieve stated climate-change goals, governments would also have to abandon all other policy initiatives and immediately work in collective solidarity to further this one objective.[47] The chances of those things actually happening are infinitesimally small: perhaps pointing out the political impracticalities of achieving stated emissions targets was the report's purpose. But at least it provided a roadmap.

Meanwhile, in that very same *Financial Times* issue, another story reported on the glee financial traders felt in what they anticipated would be a rapid rise in oil prices fueled by surging demand. Both Brent Crude and West Texas Intermediate prices had risen by a third between January and May 2021 and hovered in the US$70 range. The "euphoria" in oil prices was being driven by an expectation that post-pandemic economic revival would be coupled with massive oil-demand recovery.[48] Clearly, even the best-informed of outlets can take contrary positions on the future of the oil market and seem to be able to do it on the very same day.

That has been true for a while now. In August 2017 the *Economist* ran a cover story predicting that the end of the internal combustion engine era was in sight and was indeed much closer than many assumed. It argued that contemporary developments in technology and driving habits signaled the demise of the use of oil as a transportation fuel. As improvements in battery technology gave electric cars better performance and more range, it would allow them to better compete with a broader spectrum of gas-fueled automobiles along the performance metrics customers care about. There was even question whether the appeal of owning and driving a personal vehicle at all might eventually evaporate, as self-driving on-demand might obviate that need for city-dwellers at least. The article noted that large oil companies and car manufacturers increasingly saw the writing on the wall: they were backing away from large investment projects because they did not want to front the cost of discovering new oil deposits that would never be allowed to be extracted.[49]

Two years later, that same magazine ran the story noted earlier, that over the coming decade, ExxonMobil planned to pursue an aggressive exploration and production plan that would see its oil output roughly double. ExxonMobil's reading of the oil demand tea leaves led it to conclude that all the countertrends noted in previous paragraphs would not matter a whit. The world will still need oil, and it was going to be a very profitable business to be in. Moreover, it was making that call three years into the price-fall era noted in chapter six, which meant it was a particularly gutsy move for the time. Clearly both cover stories cannot be true at the same time. If the *Economist*'s 2017 prediction is right, then most of this books' main points are moot. However, as the 2019 cover illustrates, it is not likely to be: the age of oil has room to run yet. Such is the divided oil world we live in now: studying and understanding it remains as relevant as ever.

Conclusion: Profits, Power, and the Future of the Global Oil Industry

What would I say today if confronted once again by a student not wanting to study oil and haranguing me for making them do it anyway? After writing this book, I probably would first request that they buy it and read it. But, if offering a verbal rejoinder was on the docket, I would offer a bit more now than I did then, moving beyond facts, hopefully imparting knowledge, and perhaps even knocking on the hallowed halls of wisdom. Maybe that would be asking too much, such things are often in the eye of the beholder. In any event, what I would say would go something like this.

I would admit that the oil market retains mixed characteristics and sometimes generates strange and confusing results. Some of it is market-driven, a lot of it is state-driven, and the remainder lies somewhere in between. That system seems inefficient and unpredictable to those not steeped in its ways, and even those who are would rarely argue it is the optimal way for the world to produce and distribute the required oil. The system's utility and resilience lie in its ability to serve and balance the variety of political and economic interests of investors, producers, and consumers. Those actors and interests change and evolve, and sometimes they are not even sure what they want. So if the oil market generates puzzling, bizarre, unintended, and sometimes distasteful outcomes, we really should not be surprised.

Next, I would outline oil's positive contributions to world economy and the life we live. They are not inconsiderable. Oil still fuels national economies and allows them to provide a better and rapidly improving standard of living for their people that helps generate economic opportunities they otherwise would not have had. Combustion engines still power machines that move people around quickly and affordably. That allows them to work, see, and do new things; regularly see distant relatives who may be thousands of miles away; and see other parts of the world at an incredibly low cost. In terms of adding to overall human happiness, these are not inconsiderable benefits that many missed sorely while being deprived of them during the pandemic.

Oil also provides the feedstock for many everyday products ranging from asphalt to plastics to fertilizers that make our lives much easier and generally more interesting. It generates revenues for governments that, if spent wisely, can improve the lives of tens of millions of their citizens. It provides employment and industrial growth to hundreds of thousands of people directly, and for millions of people in related and supporting industries. The industry itself invests billions of dollars in research on technologies designed to make oil extraction more efficient and less environmentally damaging and is generating significant successes at doing so. Its investments in remote regions can generate livelihoods and economic development for the people who live there: often these individuals belong to Indigenous groups where alternate economic opportunities may be few. Oil provides enormous amounts of energy per unit of weight, is easily and conveniently moved around, and powers a global economy that has over the past several decades lifted billions of people out of abject poverty. All told, that is not a bad record.

But, like most things in life, there is ink on both sides of the ledger. Oil money is not always spent wisely and well. Rather than saved or invested in cleaner technologies, it may instead simply fuel the ambitions of tyrants or the appetites of hedonists. Oil revenue can hinder alternate economic development or diversification: people become reliant on the revenues it generates and feel less inclined to pursue other economic strategies. Those producing a lot of oil often seem to suffer for it in a lot of ways. While it is not necessarily true that states fight wars for oil,[50] contests for its control can make civil conflict more likely, make leaders more confident they will win it, and consequently may fuel an aggressive foreign policy. Oil revenue can suppress movements toward democracy and seems to hinder progress in the quest for gender equality both in terms of educational attainment and in the workplace.[51] Oil can entice governments to shower their citizens with benefits that may rob them of the entrepreneurial drive necessary to create a robust and diverse economy. The country may suffer politically should those benefits be taken away.

Criticisms continue. The influx of oil revenue when prices are high can contribute to an unstable global financial system that becomes more prone to imprudent lending and booms and busts in equity markets. The industry's hold on politics in both developing and developed countries seems very real and is difficult to break. Oil lobbyists walk the corridors of power, oil revenue fuels campaign finances, and promises of sudden riches continue to infect business dealings in the far corners of the oil world. The need to procure oil continues to at least influence foreign policy agendas and may constrain other foreign policy goals. Oil investment in remote communities may dry up suddenly if prices fall or the resource runs out, leaving those communities with half-built facilities that makes them worse rather than better off for the investment. When fields run dry, oil facilities are sometimes abandoned or not disposed of properly, seemingly leaving the problem for the next generation to manage and to pay for.[52] Oh, we should also probably mention that the burning of oil and its refined fuels emits a lot of carbon dioxide. That carbon binds itself to particles in the atmosphere, thereby making that atmosphere denser and trapping the heated air underneath, which makes the world progressively warmer. The collective minuses on the balance sheet are also real.

I would also say that nothing lasts forever in the oil business. That system is capable of transforming itself and is doing so constantly. Apparently stable oil-producing systems existing in the past all eventually eroded and evolved into something different, as the system had to adapt to changing industrial needs and evolving consumer expectations. The present system of procuring and using oil likely will be no different: the question is how, how fast, in what direction, and what are the political consequences of that evolution? There are of course polarized views on all that. There remain some whose interests are to sell and burn as much of the stuff as possible. Their income stream and/or power depends on it, and the "negative externalities" generated by that burning – measured primarily in the additional carbon dioxide it will dump into the atmosphere – either do not matter to them or are deemed to be somebody else's problem. There are others at the other end of the spectrum who would stop the burning of oil entirely and immediately if they could. They think the threat of climate change serious and significant enough to warrant whatever painful measures are necessary to stop it. All other public concerns and problems in the world can effectively be put on hold until climate justice is achieved. Oil workers losing their livelihoods, producing countries that go broke, and hundreds of billions of dollars of foregone economic growth (particularly in developing markets that are most in need of that growth) are just unfortunate but necessary roadkill on the way to a cleaner and more glorious future.

In between these extremes lies the mass of consumers and citizens who usually have the same basic set of needs and desires. Most are probably somewhat aware of climate change and want to help stop it. But they are also beset by the problems of real life, which include getting to work, the kids to practice, staying warm, and always keeping an eye on how much things cost. They want to live in a better, cleaner, safer, and more just world but do not want to suffer too much to make that happen and will certainly not like massive tax increases or draconian government directives to achieve it. Some seem content to continue doing more or less what they have always done, getting what they have always gotten, and worrying little about a system that is too big for them to impact. But an increasing number are seemingly aware of, and want to do something about, climate change, and the momentum is clear, unmistakable, and I would think unstoppable.

I would also point out how far we have indeed come on the environmental front, something often lost in the glare of daily headlines that regularly write scary stories on extreme weather or worrisome temperature trends. The world is dependent on oil and will remain so for a good while yet. But we get far more economic output out of a barrel of oil than we once did, many companies are lowering the carbon costs of producing oil, and progress toward alternate sources is clearly happening. The world did finally sign on to a global climate change accord after numerous previous attempts had failed. The US withdrawal from the Paris Agreement was short lived, was opposed by large numbers of US states and cities, and the Biden administration reentered the accord just as quickly as the Trump administration left it. Major economic and financial entities are onboard.

These tangible realities can be complemented by even a cursory look at history. One benefit of being a fifty-something is that I can either remember or have outright experienced four full generations and can see how their attitudes on things have changed. I vaguely recall how my grandparents thought about environmental issues (they didn't, putting food on the table took everything they had), how my parents thought about them (serious and growing awareness, my father spent his career as a member of a separate university faculty titled Environmental Design), the proclivities of my generation (who are in leadership positions now and are charged with making their organizations more sustainable and are doing so at a rapid clip), and how those darned kids today are thinking and acting about climate change (they seem concerned with little else). Granted, this hardly constitutes evidence, remains squarely in the realm of anecdote, and memory often is tinted by both rose-colored and thorn-covered glasses. Yet, if my perceptions are even a quarter correct, there has been enormous progress on both awareness of and willingness to do something about climate change. There is every reason to expect that will continue.

An additional point I would make is that there is a choice to be made about the approach to climate change and the weaning away from oil. Should one confront climate change as a problem to be solved (one of many), or a hill to die upon, where nothing else matters? Does it really warrant the overwhelming amount of attention and monetary resources from governments, companies, and people that it seems to be getting, as an end-of-civilization catastrophe is looming? Or should it be placed prominently, but not predominantly, in the overall mix of problems governments face, which also include concerns over equity, maintaining a functioning democracy in the face of forces conspiring to undermine it, ensuring the sustainability of public finances over the long term, curbing potential nuclear weapons proliferation (yes, those weapons are still out there) and seeing to the needs of an aging population, to name but a few?

Given what we have examined in this book, the latter would seem to be a more effective approach. Governments' day-to-day tasks are usually more about the solving of problems rather than the storming of ramparts. Voters (at least in democracies) hold them to account for the promises they have made and the results they have generated along a variety of issues. A single-minded focus on climate change may be satisfying emotionally and provides a welcome measure of focus and clarity. But this hardly reflects the reality of the day-to-day governance of diverse populations with differing views and priorities, where every individual has a voters' voice. Democratic governments by definition cannot, and probably should not, be that focused in their directives. Maybe more autocratic ones can, but exchanging more immediate attention on climate change for an increasingly domineering government is not a trade I would make. If sustainable action on climate change is the goal, the messy process of day-to-day marginal improvements seems to offer the better long-term outcome.

Another point I would make is that it would be wise to induce moderation in those advocating for a rapid transition away from oil. That transition is going to have to maintain a delicate balance between speed and pain. The faster it is pushed, the more resistance it will likely generate from those having an interest in keeping things the way they are or who have to absorb the costs. They will push back. Done improperly, that transition might even cause as many political problems as it solves. Oil production remains a key, often sole, source of government revenue for many producers, and they will not like, and will likely resist, efforts to lessen oil's importance in the energy mix. Consuming countries have built a vast infrastructure network designed to support the use of oil, particularly in transport, that will be hard, expensive, and time-consuming to replace. It is one thing to buy an electric car and then claim have done the environment a real solid (though even that is debatable). It is another thing to convince thousands of trucking companies – who collectively field hundreds of thousands of transport trucks – to quickly convert their fleets from gasoline- and diesel-powered engines to natural gas or electric engines. It is an even bigger ask of the developing world to forego the more rapid economic growth fueled by cheap and abundant carbon-based energy they might have achieved in the name of lowering global emissions. The scale of the problem should not be underestimated.

The final thing I would say to the student (and indeed is the broader purpose of this book), is that understanding the oil industry's political history gives context, balance, and some measure of reassurance. Problems portrayed as "unprecedented" in today's world are usually not. Others have faced similar concerns, found workable if imperfect solutions, and the world moved onward and upward. Despite today's fear-inducing headlines, the story of human history over the past two centuries, and in particular the last five decades, has been one of unbelievable progress. Miraculous, rapid, and undeniable improvements in the general alleviation of human misery, the opportunities ever-greater portions of the human community now have, and the increasing spreading of wealth and prosperity around the world are evidence of that progress.[53] Oil played a significant role in making that happen. The ride has not always been smooth, and the future will undoubtedly hold challenges, but that is an expected rather than exceptional thing. You now know how to identify and understand those challenges and make better, more-reasoned decisions about managing them, even as the energy transition occurs. If I can say that, it will have made the book well worth writing.

Notes

1. Introduction

1 On the notion of economic statecraft, see William J. Norris, *Chinese Economic Statecraft: Commercial Actors, Grand Strategy, and State Control* (Ithaca, NY: Cornell University Press, 2016), chapter 3. Also see Robert D. Blackwill and Jennifer M. Harris, *War by Other Means: Geoeconomics and Statecraft* (Cambridge MA: Harvard University Press, 2016).

2 A description of the conflict can be found at http://www.bbc.com /news/world-middle-east-29319423.

3 A federal judge subsequently ruled against the pipelines's construction, arguing that it continued to violate existing state and federal statutes.

4 One source gives an indicative figure: stating that cumulative investment in the oil sector is likely to reach $6 trillion by 2030. Llewelyn Hughes, *Globalizing Oil: Firms and Oil Market Governance in France, Japan, and the United States* (Cambridge: Cambridge University Press, 2014), 448 (Kindle edition).

5 John Hofmeister, *Why We Hate the Oil Companies: Straight Talk from an Energy Insider* (New York: Palgrave Macmillan, 2010).

6 Analytic concerns and treatment of the concept of "peak oil" can be found in Mathew R. Simmons, *Twilight in the Desert: The Coming Saudi Oil Shock and the World Economy* (Hoboken: John Wiley & Sons, 2005); Kenneth S. Deffeyes, *Beyond Oil: The View from Hubbert's Peak* (New York: Hill & Wang, 2005); Thomas Homer-Dixon, *The Upside of Down: Catastrophe, Creativity, and the Renewal of Civilization* (Canada: Alfred A. Knopf, 2006), chapter 4.

7 Leonardo Maugeri, "Oil: The Next Revolution. The Unprecedented Upsurge in Global Production Capacity and What It Means for the

World." Belfer Center for International Affairs, Kennedy School of Government, Harvard University, June 2012.

8 International Energy Agency, *World Energy Outlook 2018* (Paris: OECD Publishing, 2018), Executive Summary and Introduction.

9 Alan Greenspan's famous phrase indicating the presence of a potential financial bubble could easily be applied to the giddy predictions of oil prices present at the oil price peak. Alan Greenspan, *The Age of Turbulence: Adventures in a New World* (New York: Penguin Press, 2007), 176–7.

10 Greenspan, *The Age of Turbulence*, chapter 24.

11 Brooke Clayton, *Market Madness: A Century of Oil Panics, Crises, and Crashes* (New York: Council of Foreign Relations/Oxford University Press, 2015). See chapter 5 for a description of the 1998–2013 cycle.

12 Nate Silver, *The Signal and the Noise: Why so Many Predictions Fail, but Some Don't* (New York: Penguin Press, 2012).

13 Ibid., chapter 6.

14 For explanations on why humans use such "stories" to explain economic and other events – and why such stories are often profoundly wrong or at least overly optimistic – see Daniel Kahneman, *Thinking Fast and Slow* (Toronto: Doubleday Canada, 2011), 255–9.

15 Daniel Yergin, *The Prize: The Epic Quest for Oil, Money, and Power* (New York: Touchstone Press, 1991).

16 Hedley Bull, *The Anarchical Society: A Study of Order in World Politics* (New York: Columbia University Press, 1977), 71. See also G. John Ikenberry, *After Victory: Institutions, Strategic Restraint, and the Re-building of Order after Major Wars* (Princeton, NJ: Princeton University Press, 2001).

17 Hans J. Morgenthau and Kenneth W. Thompson, *Politics among Nations: The Struggle for Power and Peace* (New York: Alfred A. Knopf, 6th edition, 1985); Bull, *The Anarchical Society*; Kenneth Waltz, *Theory of International Politics* (Reading, PA: Addison-Wesley, 1979).

18 Barry Posen, *Sources of Military Doctrine* (Ithaca, NY: Cornell University Press, 1983), 3.

19 Morgenthau and Thompson, *Politics among Nations: The Struggle for Power and Peace* (New York: Alfred A. Knopf, 6th edition, 1985), chapter 9. See also Joseph S. Nye Jr., *Soft Power: The Means to Success in World Politics* (New York: Public Affairs Books, 2004).

20 Moises Naim, *The End of Power: From Boardrooms to Battlefields to States, Why Being in Charge Isn't What It Used to Be* (New York: Basic Books, 2014).

21 Carl von Clausewitz's "war is an instrument of politics by other means" is the most famous dictum of this assertion. See Peter Paret,

"Clausewitz," in *Makers of Modern Strategy: From Machiavelli to the Nuclear Age*, ed. Peter Paret (Princeton, NJ: Princeton University Press, 1986), 200–2; Carl von Clausewitz, *On War*, Michael Howard and Peter Paret, eds. (Princeton, NJ: Princeton University Press, 1984), 87; B.H. Liddell Hart, *Strategy* (London: Faber and Faber Ltd., 1954).

22 Paul Kennedy, *The Rise and Fall of the Great Powers: Economic Change and Military Conflict 1500–2000* (New York: Vintage Press, 1989).

23 Joseph Greico, *Cooperation among Nations: Europe, North America, and Non-Tariffs Barriers to Trade* (Ithaca, NY: Cornell University Press, 1990).

24 Rosemary Kelanic, *Black Gold and Blackmail: Oil and Great Power Politics* (Ithaca, NY: Cornell University Press, 2020).

25 Robert J. Art, *A Grand Strategy for America* (New York: The Century Foundation, 2003), 58–64.

26 See Michael T. Klare, *Blood and Oil: The Dangers and Consequences of America's Growing Dependency on Imported Petroleum* (New York: Metropolitan Books, 2004). A balanced account of the costs of oil dependency for US foreign policy can be found in John S. Duffield, *Over a Barrel: The Costs of U.S. Foreign Oil Dependence* (Stanford, CA: Stanford University Press, 2008).

27 On the ideas of interrelated "systems" of security, see Thomas Homer-Dixon, *Environment, Scarcity, and Violence* (Princeton, NJ: Princeton University Press, 1999); *The Ingenuity Gap*, (Toronto: Random House, 2000); and *The Upside of Down* (Toronto: Random House, 2006).

28 Thomas P. Barnett, *The Pentagon's New Map* (New York: G.P Putnam's Sons, 2005).

29 Steve Yetiv, *The Petroleum Triangle* (Ithaca, NY: Cornell University Press, 2011).

30 Barry R. Posen and Andrew L. Ross, "Competing Visions for U.S. Grand Strategy," *International Security* 21, no. 3 (Winter 1996–70; footnote 2, p. 8.

31 Raghram G. Rajan, *Fault Lines: How Hidden Fractures Still Threaten the World Economy* (Princeton, NJ: Princeton University Press, 2010).

32 There are a number of authors that have used geographic metaphors to illustrate the evolution of the global economy and the accompanying societal change it will mandate. These include Thomas Friedman's bestselling effort *The World Is Flat* (New York: Farrar, Straus, and Giroux, 2005) outlines ten such drivers that are reshaping how human society works. Other authors also offer visions of the future that differ markedly from current patterns of human activity: see Homer-Dixon, *The Upside of Down*.

33 Adam Smith's magisterial *The Wealth of Nations*, first published in 1776, indicated the benefits to be had by having countries produce products for which they held a comparative advantage and lowering of trade barriers

to allow the free exchange of goods with countries doing the same thing. Ricardo built upon and expanded the doctrine of comparative advantage. Both argued that doing so would lower and equalize prices across national borders, would result in the most efficient allocation of labor within national markets and would maximize consumer welfare.

34 Ikenberry, *After Victory*. See also G. John Ikenberry, *Liberal Leviathan: The Origins, Crises, and Transformation of American World Order* (Princeton, NJ: Princeton University Press, 2012).

35 Daniel Yergin and Joseph Stanislaw, *The Commanding Heights: The Battle for the World Economy* (New York: Simon & Schuster 2002).

36 Francis Fukuyama, *The End of History and the Last Man* (New York: The Free Press, 1992).

37 Llewelyn Hughes, *Globalizing Oil: Firms and Oil Market Governance in France, Japan, and the United States* (Cambridge: Cambridge University Press, 2014).

38 Ibid.

39 Louis Turner, *Oil Companies in the International System* (London: Royal Institute of International Affairs, 1978).

40 Joshua Kurtlantzick, *State Capitalism: How the Return of Statism Is Transforming the World* (Oxford: Oxford University Press, 2016).

41 Mikael Wigell, Sören Scholvin, and Mika Aaltola, editors, *Geo-economics and Power Politics in the 21st Century: The Revival of Economic Statecraft* (London: Routledge 2019).

42 Robert Gilpin, *The Political Economy of International Relations* (Princeton, NJ: Princeton University Press, 1987), 31.

43 Friedrich List, *Outlines of American Political Economy*, in *Schriften, Reen, Briefe* (Berlin, Bottiger Press, 1927–35), 2: 105–6. Quoted in Edward Mead Earle, "Adam Smith, Alexander Hamilton, Friedrich List: The Economic Foundations of Military Power," in *Makers of Modern Strategy: from Machiavelli to the Nuclear Age*, ed. Peter Paret (Princeton, NJ: Princeton University Press, 1986), 247.

44 The interrelationship between the use of armed force and the pursuit of commercial objective is long standing. Some accounts of the Roman Empire argue that its expansion had less to do with political philosophy and/or machinations and more to do with the need to provide food and fuel for a rapidly expanding population. Thomas Homer-Dixon, *The Upside of Down*, chapter 2.

45 The concept of interdependence has recently been included in a thorough overview of American grand strategy. Robert J. Art outlines the specific security, as well as economic, benefits the United States receives from an interdependent global economy. See Robert J. Art,

A Grand Strategy for America (Ithaca, NY: Cornell University Press, 2003), 64–9. On the relationship between interdependence and peace, see Edward D. Mansfield and Jon C. Pevehouse, "Trade Blocs, Trade Flows, and International Conflict," *International Organization* 54, no. 4 (2004): 775–809; and Eric Gartzke, Quan Li, and Charles Boehmer, "Investing in Peace: Economic Interdependence and International Conflict," *International Organization* 55, no. 2 (2001): 391–438; and Dale C. Copeland, "Economic Interdependence and War: A Theory of Trade Expectations," *International Security* 20, no. 4 (1997): 5–42.

46 Kevin Narizny, *The Political Economy of Grand Strategy* (Ithaca, NY: Cornell University Press, 2007); Lars S. Skålnes, *Politics, Markets, and Grand Strategy* (Ann Arbor: University of Michigan Press, 2000); Michael P. Gerace, *Military Power, Conflict, and Trade* (London: Frank Cass Publishers, 2004).

47 Adam Posen and Daniel K. Tarullo, co-chairs, *Report on the Working Group on Economics and National Security* (Princeton, NJ: Princeton Project on National Security, 2007), 3. Their view found echoes in the military establishment. General Charles Wald, former deputy commander of US European Command and member of the Energy Security Leadership Council, in prepared testimony delivered to the House Committee on Energy, argued that the US needed to reorganize its bureaucracy such that it could "better address the needs of a comprehensive international energy strategy, and I recommend the Department of Defense … designate an individual as their energy security policy expert and director." General Charles Wald, testimony hearing before the Committee on Energy and Natural Resources, United States Congress, 110 Congress, First Session, *Geopolitics of Oil*, January 10, 2007, 34.

48 Nate Silver, *The Signal and the Noise.*

49 Nicholas Taleb, *The Black Swan: The Impact of the Highly Improbable* (New York: Random House, 2010). See also Richard Neustadt and Ernest R. May, *Thinking in Time: The Uses of History for Decision Makers* (New York: Free Press, 1986). This latter book contains a chapter identifying the misuse of historical analogies in making judgments, chapter 3, 34–57.

2. A Primer on the Oil Industry

1 Daniel Yergin, *The Prize* (New York: Simon & Schuster, 1991), 5–10.

2 Alanna Petroff and Tal Yellin, "What It Costs to Produce Oil," CNNMoney, November 23, 2015, https://money.cnn.com/interactive/economy/the-cost-to-produce-a-barrel-of-oil/index.html.

3 The classic study remains Yergin, *The Prize.*

4 Zainab Calcuttawala, "The $1.7 Trillion Oil Industry Isn't Going Anywhere," OilPrice.com, October 23, 2016, https://oilprice.com/Energy /Crude-Oil/The-1.7-Trillion-Oil-Industry-Isnt-Going-Anywhere.html.

5 "World Energy Investment 2017," International Energy Agency, July 2017, https://www.iea.org/reports/world-energy-investment-2017.

6 International Energy Agency, *Oil 2021: Analysis and Forecast to 2026* (Paris: International Energy Agency, 2021), 52.

7 For a summary of global annual investment in the oil and gas industry, see Barclay's annual report *Global Exploration and Production Spending*, various years.

8 "Global Fossil Infrastructure Tracker," Global Energy Monitor. https:// globalenergymonitor.org/projects/global-fossil-infrastructure-tracker/.

9 "Number of Ships in the World Merchant Fleet as of January 1, 2021, by Type," Statista, November 2021. https://www.statista.com /statistics/264024/number-of-merchant-ships-worldwide-by-type /#:~:text=The%20number%20of%20crude%20oil%20tankers%20 rounded%20up,You%20need%20a%20Single%20Account%20for%20 unlimited%20access.

10 United States, Energy Information Agency, *Short Term Energy Outlook*, December 2020, 19.

11 "Global Crude Oil and Oil Products Storage in Use and Available as of March 2020," Statista, February 2020. https://www.statista.com /statistics/509052/global-available-oil-storage-capacity-by-type/.

12 Dale D. Murphy, *The Structure of Regulatory Competition: Corporations and Public Policy in a Global Economy* (Oxford: Oxford University Press, 2006), chapter 2.

13 Dave Keating, "Germany's Merkel Defends the Internal Combustion Engine," *Forbes*, November 27, 2020, https://www.forbes.com/sites /davekeating/2020/11/27/merkel-defends-the-internal-combustion -engine/?sh=52e3775d15cd.

14 Eric Walz, "12 State Governors Support a Ban on Internal Combustion Engine Vehicles in the U.S. by 2035," FutureCar, April 21, 2021, https:// m.futurecar.com/4565/12-State-Governors-Support-A-Ban-on-Internal -Combustion-Engine-Vehicles-in-the-U-S--by-2035#:~:text=The%20 governors%20of%20California%2C%20New,gasoline%2Dpowered%20 vehicles%20by%202035.

15 International Energy Agency, *World Energy Outlook 2018*, 153.

16 Douglas Broom, "The Dirty Secret of Electric Vehicles," World Economic Forum, March 27, 2019, https://www.weforum.org/agenda/2019/03 /the-dirty-secret-of-electric-vehicles/.

17 "Tesla & Other EV Sales – Global & Country by Country," CleanTechnica, https://cleantechnica.com/tesla-sales/.

18 "Estimated Worldwide Motor Vehicle Production between 2017 and 2020, by Type," Statista, https://www.statista.com/statistics/1097293/worldwide-motor-vehicle-production-by-type/.

19 "2019 (Full Year) USA: GM General Motors Sales," – Car Sales Statistics, January 4, 2020, https://www.best-selling-cars.com/usa/2019-full-year-usa-gm-general-motors-sales/?doing_wp_cron=1643034200.39173 60305786132812500#:~:text=In%202019%2C%20General%20Motors%20delivered,size%20pickup%20trucks%20and%20SUVs.

20 Deivis Centeno, "U.S. Ford Motor Company Sales Decrease 3 Percent during 2019 Calendar Year," Ford Authority, January 13, 2020, https://fordauthority.com/2020/01/ford-motor-company-sales-numbers-figures-results-2019-calendar-year/#:~:text=U.S.%20Ford%20Motor%20Company%20Sales%20Decrease%203%20Percent%20During%202019%20Calendar%20Year&text=Ford%20Motor%20Company%20sales%20decreased,year%20in%20the%20United%20States.

21 These include the labor conditions present in the mines extracting the minerals necessary to produce the necessary batteries, as well as the need to generate the additional electricity, much of which will come from electricity plants powered by carbon-based fuels.

22 For a summary of various oil-demand scenarios, see the International Energy Agency, *World Energy Outlook 2017* (Paris: OECD Publishing 2018), chapter 4, Outlook for Oil and Gas.

23 "Products Made from Oil and Natural Gas," US Department of Energy, https://www.energy.gov/sites/prod/files/2019/11/f68/Products%20Made%20From%20Oil%20and%20Natural%20Gas%20Infographic.pdf.

24 Peter Tertzakian, *A Thousand Barrels a Second: The Coming Oil Breakpoint and the Challenges of an Energy Dependent World* (Toronto: McGraw-Hill Education, 2007), 143.

25 The reader wanting such data is encouraged to consult the above sources directly for the most current detailed breakdown of supply and demand figures.

26 International Energy Agency, *World Energy Outlook 2009*, 81.

27 Tertzakian, *A Thousand Barrels a Second*.

28 International Energy Agency, *Oil 2021: Analysis and Forecast to 2026* (Paris: International Energy Agency, 2021), 14.

29 International Energy Agency, *World Energy Outlook 2017*, 54.

30 International Energy Agency, *Oil 2021: Analysis and Forecast to 2026*, 143.

31 Ibid., 143.

32 International Energy Agency, *World Energy Outlook 2017*, 163.
33 "China Surpassed the United States as the World's Largest Crude Oil Importer in 2017," US Energy Information Administration, February 5, 2018, https://www.eia.gov/todayinenergy/detail.php?id=34812.
34 International Energy Agency, *Oil 2019*, 16.
35 International Energy Agency, *World Energy Outlook*, 2014.
36 Jim Krane, International Energy Agency, *World Energy Outlook 2016*, 115.
37 In 1973 the Texas Railroad Commission, which had up until then imposed measures of restraint on US production levels to prop up domestic price, abandoned such efforts. Price had escalated and the need to protect US producers from cheap imports no longer applied.
38 In 2010 the United States used on average 19,157 mbd of oil: of this, 9.4 mbd was imported. United States, Energy Information Agency, *Annual Energy Review 2010*, (Washington: Energy Information Agency, 2011), 134.
39 Michael T. Klare, *Blood and Oil: The Dangers and Consequences of Americas Growing Dependency on Imported Petroleum* (New York: Metropolitan Books, 2004).
40 Two examples of this are Simmons, *Twilight in the Desert*; and Jeffrey Rubin, *Why Your World Is about to Get a Whole Lot Smaller* (New York: Random House, 2009). Both of these books appeared when oil prices were particularly high and in which worries about shortages animated popular thinking. Both also are intellectual descendants of the previous warnings. See Donella H. Meadows, Dennis I. Meadows, Joregen Randers, and William W. Beherens III, *The Limits to Growth* (Washington, DC: Potomac Associates, 1972).
41 Blake Clayton, *Market Madness: A Century of Oil Panics, Crises, and Crashes* (Oxford: Oxford University Press, 2015).
42 Leonardo Maugeri, "Oil: The Next Revolution," Discussion Paper #2012-10 (Boston: Harvard Kennedy School, Belfer Center for International Affairs, 2012), 39.
43 Jason Dziuba, Randy Ollenberger, Ray Kwan, and Christian Witkopf, "The 400 Billion Barrel Opportunity for Friendly Oil, and Canada's Evolving Role," *BMO Capital Markets*, March 2020.
44 For strong critiques of the environmental and social impacts of oil sands development, see William Marsden, *Stupid to the Last Drop* (Toronto: Vintage Canada, 2008), and Andrew Nikiforuk, *Tar Sands: Dirty Oil and the Future of a Continent* (Toronto: Greystone Books, 2010). For a rejoinder on the Alberta Oil Sands, see Alastair Sweeney, *Black Bonanza: Canada's Oil Sands and the Race to Secure North America's Future* (Toronto: John Wiley & Sons, 2010).

45 Recent efforts to tap emerging fields in the Gulf of Mexico are a clear example of this: such efforts have only been slowed, not stopped, by the BP Deepwater Horizon Macondo field spill, finally capped in 2010. Abrahm Lustgarten, *Run to Failure: BP and the Making of the Deepwater Horizon Disaster* (New York: W.W. Norton & Company, 2012).

46 The Obama administration approved Royal Dutch Shell to begin Arctic drilling efforts in the summer of 2015. See "Shell Wins Approval to Seek Oil off Alaska's Arctic Coast," Bloomberg, May 11, 2015, http://www .bloomberg.com/news/articles/2015-05-11/shell-wins-u-s-approval-to -explore-for-oil-off-alaska-s-arctic.

47 International Energy Agency, *World Energy Outlook 2017*, 175.

48 The Saudi Arabian oil minister Ali Al-Naimi granted an extensive interview with CBS's *60 Minutes* and journalist Lesley Stahl in which he noted this belief. "The Oil Kingdom: Part One," YouTube, December 7, 2008, https://www.statista.com/statistics/264024/number-of-merchant -ships-worldwide-by-type/#:~:text=The%20number%20of%20crude%20 oil%20tankers%20rounded%20up,You%20need%20a%20Single%20 Account%20for%20unlimited%20access.

49 See the respective country reports on energy production issued by the International Energy Agency: "Iran," IEA, https://www.iea.org /countries/iran; and "Iraq," IEA, https://www.iea.org/countries/iraq.

50 Daniel Gilbert and Chelsey Dulaney, "Chevron Posts Lowest Quarterly Profit in Five Years," *The Wall Street Journal*, January 30, 2015, http:// www.wsj.com/articles/chevron-results-top-expectations-on-asset-sales -refining-strength-1422625804.

51 ExxonMobil, "2017 Financial Statements and Supplemental Information." https://corporate.exxonmobil.com/-/media/Global/Files/investor -relations/annual-meeting-materials/financial-statements/2017-financial -statements.pdf.

52 Indeed, one of the major symptoms of the so-called resource curse is the progressive erosion of a country's non-oil industrial competitiveness. As oil becomes increasingly profitable, it draws investment capital, human resources, and management attention toward itself, starving other industries. See Terry Lynn Karl, *The Paradox of Plenty: Oil Booms and Petro States* (Berkeley: University of California Press, 1997).

53 Marion Candau, "Russia's Economy: Still Dependent on Oil," Eurativ, March 16, 2018, https://www.euractiv.com/section/energy -environment/news/russias-economy-still-dependent-on-oil/.

54 At the height of the oil boom Canada's oil industry accounted for approximately 30 per cent of the listings on the Toronto Stock Exchange.

In the case of Norway, oil exports over the preceding decade have allowed the country to create an SWF totaling hundreds of billions of dollars. Gordon L. Clark, Adam D. Dixon, and Ashby H.B. Monk, *Sovereign Wealth Funds: Legitimacy, Governance, and Global Power* (Princeton, NJ: Princeton University Press, 2013).

55 "Petroleum and Other Liquids," US Energy Information Administration, https://www.eia.gov/outlooks/aeo/pdf/AEO2020%20Petroleum%20 and%20Other%20Liquids.pdf.

56 "Oil and Petroleum Products Explained," US Energy Information Administration, https://www.eia.gov/energyexplained/index.php?page =oil_where.

57 David Vogel, *Kindred Strangers: The Uneasy Relationship between Politics and Business in America* (Princeton, NJ: Princeton University Press, 1996).

58 Daniel Yergin, *The New Map: Energy, Climate, and the Clash of Nations* (New York: Penguin Press, 2020), 27.

59 United States Energy Information Agency, *Short Term Energy Outlook*, December 2020, 18.

60 Other fields included in the top ten include Cantarell, Mexico (discovered 1976, current production rate 1.9 mbd); Burgan in Kuwait (discovered 1938, current production 1.5 mbd); Daiqing, China (discovered 1959, production 1 mbd); Kirkuk, Iraq (discovered 1927, produces 900,000 bd); Rumailia, North Iraq (discovered 1958, produces 700,000 bd); Shegli, China (discovered 1962, produces 534,000 bd); and Marlim, Brazil (discovered 1985, production 521,000 bd).

61 Chris Isidore, "Saudi Aramco Is the World's Most Profitable Company," CNN Business, April 1, 2019, https://www.cnn.com/2019/04/01 /investing/saudi-aramco-profit/index.html.

62 Paul Stevens, "Saudi Aramco: The Jewel in the Crown," in *Oil and Governance: State-Owned Enterprises and the World Energy Supply*, ed. David G. Victor, David R. Hults, and Mark Thurber, chapter 5 (Cambridge: Cambridge University Press, 2012), 193.

63 Ibid., 174.

64 Ibid.

65 Valérie Marcel, *Oil Titans: National Oil Companies in the Middle East* (Baltimore: Brookings Institution Press, 2006), 173–4.

66 David G. Victor, David R. Hults, and Mark Thurber, eds., *Oil and Governance: State-owned Enterprises and the World Energy Supply* (Cambridge: Cambridge University Press, 2012), 192–3.

67 Marcel, *Oil Titans*, 143.

68 Stanley Reed, "Saudi Arabia Insisted Aramco Was Worth $2 Trillion. Now It Is," *The New York Times*, December 16, 2019, https://www .nytimes.com/2019/12/16/business/energy-environment/saudi -aramco.html#:~:text=Saudi%20Aramco%2C%20the%20world's%20 biggest,trillion%20on%20the%20Saudi%20exchange.

69 "The World's Largest Oil Reserves By Country," WorldAtlas, https:// www.worldatlas.com/articles/the-world-s-largest-oil-reserves-by -country.html.

70 "Russia Is World's Largest Producer of Crude Oil and Lease Condensate," US Energy Information Administration, https://www.eia .gov/todayinenergy/detail.php?id=22392.

71 Various sources ascribe this famous quote to Winston Churchill's radio address in 1939.

72 Thane Gustafson, *Wheel of Plenty: The Battel for Oil and Power in Russia* (Cambridge, MA: Belknap Press of Harvard University, 2012), 481.

73 Michael Porter, *Competitive Advantage: Creating and Sustaining Superior Performance* (New York: The Free Press, 1980).

74 This list is compiled by *Fortune* magazine and can be found at http:// fortune.com/global500/. Their market value dominance has only recently been eclipsed by the meteoric rise of technology and social media companies.

75 Steve Coll, *Private Empire: ExxonMobil and American Power* (New York: Penguin Press, 2012), chapter 1.

76 Pauline Jones Luong and Erika Weinthal, *Oil Is Not a Curse: Ownership Structure and Institutions in Soviet Successor States* (Cambridge: Cambridge University Press, 2010), 25–6.

77 Victor, Hults, and Thurber, eds., *Oil and Governance*, 11.

78 Marcel, *Oil Titans*.

79 David R. Hults, "Hybrid Governance: State Management of National Oil Companies," in *Oil and Governance*, ed. Victor, Hults, and Thurber, chapter 3 (Cambridge: Cambridge University Press, 2012). See the diagram on pf. 69 for an illustration of this diverse model.

80 Marcel, *Oil Titans*, chapter 3.

81 "Which Economies Are Most Heavily Reliant on Oil?" Compliance Alert, https://calert.info/details.php?id=970#:~:text=Countries%20 where%20fuel%20accounts%20for,%2C%20Libya%2C%20Sudan%20 and%20Venezuela.&text=For%20an%20idea%20of%20which,as%20 a%20share%20of%20GDP.

82 Energy Intelligence Research, *The Quest for Dominance*, chapter 4.

83 Elizabeth Economy and Michael Levi, *By All Means Necessary: How China's Resource Quest Is Changing the World* (Oxford: Oxford University Press, 2014), 53.
84 Alex Prud'homme, *Hydrofracking: What Everyone Needs to Know* (Oxford: Oxford University Press, 2014), 26–30.
85 Ibid., 28.
86 "Crude Oil Production in the United States Increased to 11473 BBL/D in October from 10809 BBL/D in September of 2021," Trading Economics, https://tradingeconomics.com/united-states/crude-oil-production.
87 International Energy Agency, *Oil 2019: Analysis and Forecast to 2024* (Paris: OECD Publishing, 2019), 52.
88 Ibid.
89 For a balanced account of this, see Daniel Raimi, *The Fracking Debate: The Risks, Benefits, and Uncertainties of the Shale Revolution* (New York: Columbia University Press, 2018), chapter 3.
90 "Q: Can Tap Water Be Lit on Fire because of Fracking?" Facts about Canada's Oil and Natural Gas Industry, https://oilandgasinfo.ca/know -fracking/can-tap-water-be-lit-on-fire-because-of-fracking/. See also "Is Fracking Connected to Burning Tap Water?" Coloradans for Responsible Energy Development, https://www.cred.org/is-fracking-connected-to -burning-tap-water/.
91 Raimi, *The Fracking Debate*, chapter 10.
92 Steve A. Yetiv, *Crude Awakenings: Global Oil Security and American Foreign Policy* (Ithaca, NY: Cornell University Press, 2004), 5.
93 International Energy Agency, *World Energy Outlook 2014* (Paris: OECD Publishing 2014), 96.

3. The Legacy of Oil: 1858–2000

 1 Daniel Yergin, *The Prize: The Epic Quest for Oil, Money, and Power* (New York: Simon and Schuster, 1990).
 2 This book uses West Texas Intermediate and Brent Crude as its benchmark standards for oil prices. Both are light and sweet (having low sulfur content, making them easy to refine into gasoline), and are widely traded on global oil markets. Various other sources are also prices on world markets. For a more detailed explanation of various oil prices and their meaning, see "A Detailed Guide on the Many Different Types of Crude Oil," OilPrice.com, December 2, 2009, https://oilprice.com/Energy /Crude-Oil/A-Detailed-Guide-On-The-Many-Different-Types-Of-Crude -Oil.html.

3 Yergin, *The Prize*, chapter 2.
4 Blake Clayton, *Market Madness: A Century of Oil Panics, Crises, and Crashes* (Oxford: Oxford University Press, 2015).
5 Alfred Chandler, *The Visible Hand: The Managerial Revolution in American Business* (Cambridge, MA: Harvard University Press, 1977).
6 Mark J. Rowe, *Strong Managers, Weak Owners: The Political Roots of American Corporate Finance* (Princeton, NJ: Princeton University Press, 1994).
7 Ida Tarbell, *The History of the Standard Oil Company* (New York: McClure & Philips Company, 1904).
8 Standard Oil's breakup created a number of regional companies bearing the Standard name: Standard Oil of New Jersey, which eventually became Exxon; Standard Oil of New York, which became Mobil; and Standard Oil of California, the forbearer of Chevron.
9 John Hofmeister, *Why We Hate the Oil Companies: Straight Talk from an Industry Insider* (New York: Palgrave Macmillan, 2010).
10 It was also a victory for private ownership interests: the stock price of Standard Oil's descendants jumped quickly once investors saw their books and cash flows. Rockefeller, who still held large blocks of stock in the remaining companies, became richer than ever.
11 Anthony Sampson, *The Seven Sisters: The Great Oil Companies and the World They Made* (New York: Viking Press, 1975), 32.
12 Robert McNally, *Crude Volatility: The History and the Future of Boom-Bust Oil Prices* (New York: Columbia University Press, 2017).
13 Paul Kennedy, *The Rise and Fall of British Naval Mastery* (London: Macmillan Press, 1991).
14 Yergin, *The Prize*, 164–5.
15 Kennedy, *Rise and Fall*, 254–77.
16 The British government acquired 51 per cent of its stock and two board seats in the process. Yergin, *The Prize*, 161.
17 Yergin, *The Prize*, chapters 6–8.
18 Fareed Zakaria, *From Wealth to Power: The Unusual Origins of America's World Role* (Princeton, NJ: Princeton University Press, 1998), chapter 5.
19 Randall, *United States Foreign Oil Policy Since World War I*, chapters 2–3.
20 Ibid., 25.
21 Zakaria, *From Wealth to Power*
22 Randall, *United States Foreign Oil Policy*, 14–17.
23 Ibid., 29.
24 Ibid.
25 Louis Turner, *Oil Companies in the International System* (London: George Allen & Unwin, 1978), 25.

26 Jeremy A. Yellen, *The Greater East Asia Co-Prosperity Sphere: When Total Empire Met Total War* (Ithaca, NY: Cornell University Press, 2019).

27 Yergin, *The Prize*, 339–43.

28 Rosemary A. Kelanic, *Black Gold and Blackmail: Oil and Great Power Politics* (Ithaca, NY: Cornell University Press, 2021).

29 Clayton, *Market Madness*, 62.

30 Yergin, *The Prize*, chapter 6.

31 Nominally, there were thirty-eight descendants emerging out of the Standard Oil breakup. Of these, the most significant were Standard Oil of New Jersey (which became Exxon), Standard Oil of New York (which became Mobil), Standard Oil of California (later Chevron) and Standard Oil of Indiana (which became Amoco). McNally, *Crude Volatility*, 37.

32 See Sampson, *The Seven Sisters*, 187–201.

33 G. John Ikenberry, *Reasons of State: Oil Politics and the Capacities of American Government* (Ithaca, NY: Cornell University Press, 1988), 65.

34 That would of course change after the discovery of substantial offshore oil deposits in the North Sea, but those would not be developed for another half-century.

35 Meghan L. O'Sullivan, *Windfall: How the New Energy Abundance Upends Global Politics and Strengthens America's Power* (New York: Simon and Schuster, 2017), 248.

36 Yergin, *The Prize*, 202–4.

37 John M. Blair, *The Control of Oil*, (New York: Vintage Books, 1978), chapter 3.

38 Sampson, *The Seven Sisters*, 168–9.

39 John Lewis Gaddis, *Strategies of Containment: A Critical Appraisal of American National Security Policy During the Cold War* (Oxford: Oxford University Press, 1985).

40 Richard K. Vietor, *Energy Policy in America Since 1945: A Study of Business Government Relations* (Cambridge: Cambridge University Press, 1984), 91.

41 As described by David Vietor: "Few other regulatory schemes in America's history can match the Mandatory Oil Import Program for labyrinthine complexity, or for the distortion of markets and interest-group dissension that it caused." Ibid.

42 Louis Turner, *Oil Companies in the International System*, (London: The Royal Institute of International Affairs, 3rd edition, 1978), chapter 4.

43 Srilata Zaheer, "Overcoming the Liability of Foreignness," *Academy of Management Journal* 38, no. 2 (1995): 341–63.

44 They had been able to do so largely because the US government provided their domestic companies little bargaining support in their dispute with Mexico. Yergin, *The Prize*, 271–9.

45 Edward W. Chester, *United States Oil Policy and Diplomacy: A Twentieth Century Overview* (Westport, CT: Greenwood Press, 1983), 140–57.

46 Louis Turner, *Oil Companies*, 116.

47 Niall Ferguson, *Empire: The Rise and Demise of the British World Order and the Lessons for Global Power* (London: Penguin Books, 2002), chapter 6.

48 Kenneth Pollack, *The Persian Puzzle: The Conflict Between Iran and America* (New York: Random House, 2005).

49 Blair, *The Control of Oil*, 221.

50 Blair, *The Control of Oil*, 226–7.

51 Sampson, *The Seven Sisters*, 242–5.

52 Blair, *The Control of Oil*, 262.

53 Turner, *Oil Companies*, 174.

54 McNally, *Crude Volatility*, 131.

55 "Average Annual OPEC Crude Oil Price from 1960 to 2021," Statista, January 2022, https://www.statista.com/statistics/262858/change-in -opec-crude-oil-prices-since-1960/#:~:text=The%202021%20annual%20 average%20OPEC,during%20the%202016%20oil%20crisis.

56 Rory Miller, *Desert Kingdoms to Global Powers: The Rise of the Arab Gulf* (New Haven, CT: Yale University Press, 2016), 22.

57 "OPEC Crude Oil," Statista, https://www.statista.com/statistics /262858/change-in-opec-crude-oil-prices-since-1960/#:~:text=The%20 2021%20annual%20average%20OPEC,during%20the%202016%20oil%20 crisis.

58 McNally, *Crude Volatility*, 139.

59 Mahmood El Gamal and Amy Myers Jaffe, *Oil, Dollars, Debt and Crises: The Global Curse of Black Gold* (Cambridge: Cambridge University Press, 2009).

60 Miller, *Desert Kingdoms*, 31.

61 Nimah Mazaheri, *Oil Booms and Business Busts: Why Resource Wealth Hurts Entrepreneurs in the Developing World* (Oxford: Oxford University Press, 2016).

62 Richard Auty, "Natural Resources and Civil Strife: A Two Stage Process," *Geopolitics* 9, no. 1 (2004): 29–49.

63 C.W., "What Dutch Disease Is, and Why It's Bad," *The Economist*, November 5, 2014, https://www.economist.com/the-economist -explains/2014/11/05/what-dutch-disease-is-and-why-its-bad.

64 Richard Auty, "Natural Resources and Small Island Economies: Mauritius and Trinidad and Tobago," *Journal of Development Studies* 53, no. 2 (2017): 264–77.

65 Michael L. Ross, "What Do We Know about Export Diversification of Oil Rich Countries?" *Extractive Industries and Society*, June 16, 2019.

66 Some of the more relevant literature includes Terry Lynn Karl, *The Paradox of Plenty: Oil Booms and Petro States* (Berkeley: University of California Press, 1997); Michael L. Ross, *The Oil Curse: How Petroleum Wealth Shapes the Development of Nations* (Princeton, NJ: Princeton University Press, 2012); Jeff Colgan, *Petro-Aggression: When Oil Causes War* (Cambridge: Cambridge University Press, 2013); Pauline Jones Luong and Erika Weithal, *Oil Is Not a Curse: Ownership Structure and Institutions in Soviet Successor States* (Cambridge: Cambridge University Press, 2010); and Emily Meierding, *The Oil Wars Myth: Petroleum and the Causes of International Conflict* (Ithaca, NY: Cornell University Press, 2020).

67 Vietor, *Energy Policy*, 217.

68 Kenneth M. Pollack, *The Persian Puzzle: The Conflict between Iran and America*, (New York: Random House, 2005).

69 John Lewis Gaddis, *Strategies of Containment: A Critical Appraisal of American National Security Policy during the Cold War* (Oxford: Oxford University Press, 2005).

70 Pollack, *The Persian Puzzle*, chapter 5.

71 President Jimmy Carter, State of the Union Address, January 23, 1980, quoted in Keith Crane, Andreas Goldthau, Michael Toman, Thomas Light, Stuart Johnson, Alireza Nader, Angel Rabasa, and Harun Dogo, *Imported Oil and U.S. National Security* (Infrastructure, Safety, and Environment and National Security Research Division, RAND corporation, 2009), 60.

72 A full video of that speech is available at "President Jimmy Carter – 1980 State of the Union," YouTube, September 22, 2009, https://www.youtube.com/watch?v=6_-szG7E0PU.

73 Rachel Bronson, *Thicker than Oil: America's Uneasy Partnership with Saudi Arabia* (Oxford: Oxford University Press, 2006).

74 For a critical examination of the relationship between Saudi Arabia and the United States, see Craig Unger, *House of Bush, House of Saud: The Secret Relationship between the World's Two Most Powerful Dynasties* (New York: Scribner Publishers, 2004).

75 Bronson, *Thicker than Oil*, 27.

76 Richard A. Clarke, *Against All Enemies: Inside America's War on Terror* (New York: The Free Press, 2004), chapter 3.

77 Steve Yetiv, *Crude Awakening: Global Oil Security and American Foreign Policy* (Ithaca, NY: Cornell University Press, 2004).

78 For an analysis and critique of the economic arguments behind increased merger and acquisition activity that occurred among many global corporations at the end of the 1990s, see Daniel Yergin and Joseph Stanislaw, *The Commanding Heights: The Battle for the World Economy* (New York: Simon & Schuster, 1998), 406–7; William Greider, *One World Ready or Not: The Manic Logic of Global Capitalism* (New York: Simon & Schuster, 1997), chapter 9; and John Micklethwait and Adrian Woodridge, *A Future Perfect: The Essentials of Globalization* (New York: Crown Business, 2000), 205–45.

79 Robert Corzine, "Rockefeller Revived: Robert Corzine Investigates Why the World's Biggest Oil Companies Are Eyeing Each Other's Assets," *Financial Times*, November 27, 1998, 21.

80 Llewelyn Hughes, *Globalizing Oil: Firms and Oil Market Governance in France, Japan, and the United States* (Cambridge: Cambridge University Press, 2014), chapter 4.

81 There were some economic concerns raised about the proposed mergers, primarily about undue concentration in the industry. The BP–Amoco merger would end up controlling almost all output of the Prudhoe field in Alaska, one of the major continental US producing fields, while the ExxonMobil merger would place 14 per cent of all domestic gas stations under the control of one company. This forced the US government to make an awkward determination of what did or did not constitute "undue concentration" in the industry. The proposed benefits of combined with the careful limitation ownership over gas stations to below the rough guideline of 15 per cent, reassured public concerns against the creeping spectre of industry concentration.

82 Daniel Yergin, *The Quest: Energy, Security, and the Remaking of the Modern World* (New York: Penguin Press, 2011), chapter 4.

83 Ralph Atkins, "Growth Seeker in the Land of Giants: The Heat Is on for the Oil Subsidiary of the Veba Conglomerate. Its Chairman Tells Ralph Atkins about the Directions in Which It Could Move," *Financial Times*, January 12, 1999, 15.

84 Daniel Yergin, "Bigger Oil: Merger Mania Will Not Stop With Exxon-Mobil," *Financial Times*, December 1998, 21.

4. The Oil Market, 2000–2014: Rising Prices and the Perils of Profit

1 Brooke Clayton, *Market Madness: A Century of Oil Panics, Crises, and Crashes* (Oxford: Oxford University Press, 2015).

2 In the United States, economic growth rates measures measured 1.1 per cent and 1.8 per cent in 2001 and 2002, respectively. International

Monetary Fund, World Economic Database 2013, http://www.imf.org /external/pubs/ft/weo/2013/01/weodata/index.aspx.

3 Ian Seymour, "Oil in the 1990s," *Energy Policy*, October 1992, 909–12.

4 This was the period in which financial and strategic control of Russian oil production shifted to a group of oligarchs, each of whom profited immensely. See Yuri Felshtinsky and Vladimir Pribylovsky, *The Corporation: Russia and the KGB in the Age of President Putin* (New York: Encounter Books, 2008). See also Marshal I. Goldman, *Petrostate: Putin, Power, and the New Russia* (Oxford: Oxford University Press, 2008).

5 Martin Wolf, *The Shifts and the Shocks: What We Learned, and Have Still to Learn, about the Global Financial Crises* (New York: Penguin Press, 2014).

6 Statistics for this paragraph are taken from the publicly available data section of the United States Energy Information Administration (EIA) website: http://www.eia.gov/dnav/pet/PET_PRI_SPT_S1_D.htm.

7 Joseph Stiglitz, *The Roaring Nineties: A New History of the World's Most Prosperous Decade* (New York: W.W. Norton & Company, 2003).

8 For an overview of the various economic afflictions that had caused global economic growth to abruptly slow down at the end of the decade, see Stiglitz, *The Roaring Nineties*. Stiglitz was also critical of the US and international response to the international economic shocks afflicting the global economy at the end of the 1990s, such as the eruption of the Asian financial crisis as well as the ongoing economic turbulence in Russia that culminated in the formation of the Russian oligarchs. See Joseph E. Stiglitz, *Globalization and Its Discontents* (New York: W.W. Norton & Company, 2002).

9 The strategy and conduct of the war on terror has in the years since become subject to immense critical scrutiny: many have taken issue with the strategies chosen to combat terror and the suitability of the current US force structure to wage it. A sampling of some of these works includes Clarke, *Against All Enemies*, as well as Thomas P.M. Barnett, *The Pentagon's New Map: War and Peace in the Twenty-First Century* (New York: Penguin Group, 2004), as well as *The Pentagon's New Map: Blueprint for Action* (New York: Penguin Group, 2004).

10 Alan Greenspan, *The Age of Turbulence: Adventures in a New World* (New York: Penguin Press, 2007), 228.

11 For an analysis and critique of the economic arguments behind increased merger and acquisition activity that occurred among many global corporations at the end of the 1990s, see Yergin and Stanislaw, *The Commanding Heights*, 406–7; William Greider, *One World Ready or Not: The Manic Logic of Global Capitalism* (New York: Simon & Schuster,

199), chapter 9; and John Micklethwait and Adrian Woodridge, *A Future Perfect: The Essentials of Globalization* (New York: Crown Business, 2000), 205–45.

12 Yergin, "Bigger Oil," 21.

13 During the period 2000–7 US growth rates averaged roughly between 1 and 4 per cent per year. China's ranged from 8 per cent to an upper bound of 14 per cent per year. Almost all countries experienced positive growth rates, putting increased pressure on the global economic system. See International Monetary Fund, Data and Statistics, http://www.imf .org/external/data.htm.

14 The US trade deficit with the rest of the world ballooned during this period, measuring over $411 billion dollars in 2000 and measuring over $800 billion dollars in both 2006 and 2007. However, these figures are misleading: much of the trade deficit represented the final assembly of premade products in low-wage countries. These dynamics led to the lion's share of financial return to be retained by the countries doing product design and development. For trade statistics, see US Census Bureau, "U.S. Trade in Goods with World, Seasonally Adjusted," http://www.census.gov/foreign-trade/balance/c0004.html#2000. For a description of the structure of integrated modern trade, see Fareed Zakaria, *The Post-American World* (New York: W.W. Norton Publishers, 2008), 186. See also Stephen S. Poloz, "Financial Intermediation under the New Trade Paradigm: EDC and Integrative Trade," Ottawa, Export Development Canada, January 25, 2007, https://docplayer.net/19372330 -Financial-intermediation-under-the-new-trade-paradigm-edc-and -integrative-trade.html..

15 International Monetary Fund, *World Economic Outlook 2007: Globalization and Inequality*, October 2007, chapter 1, p. 6.

16 Jim O'Neil, chief economist of the investment bank Goldman Sachs, is credited with the popularization of the term BRIC. He expounds those views in Jim O'Neil, *The Growth Map*, (New York: Penguin Group, 2011).

17 Growth rates cited from the International Monetary Fund, "World Economic Outlook Databases," https://www.imf.org/external/pubs/ft /weo/2019/01/weodata/weorept.aspx?sy=2001&ey=2002&scsm=1&ssd =1&sort=country&ds=.&br=1&c=223%2C924%2C922%2C534%2C111&s =NGDPD&grp=0&a=&pr.x=48&pr.y=6.

18 Ibid., https://www.imf.org/external/pubs/ft/weo/2019/01/weodata /weorept.aspx?sy=2001&ey=2002&scsm=1&ssd=1&sort=country&ds=.& br=1&c=223%2C924%2C922%2C534%2C111&s=NGDPD&grp=0&a=&pr .x=48&pr.y=6.

19 Martin Jacques, *When China Rules the World* (London: Penguin Books, 2009), chapter 11.
20 On the public-sector side, see International Energy Agency, *World Energy Outlook 2007: China and India Insights* (Paris: OECD/IEA Publishing, 2008), 73. On the private-sector side, see ExxonMobil, *Outlook for Energy*, various years. See also BP, *Statistical Review of Energy*, various years.
21 International Energy Agency, *World Energy Outlook 2019*, 132-4.
22 International Energy Agency, *World Energy Outlook 2007*, 79.
23 International Energy Agency, *World Energy Outlook 2008*, 42.
24 *World Energy Outlook 2007: China and India Insights* (Paris: International Energy Administration, 2007), 118–26.
25 ExxonMobil and British Petroleum also continued very public forecasts on the global oil market, which gained strong credibility within oil market watchers generally. See British Petroleum and Exxon Mobil, *Energy Outlooks*, various years.
26 International Energy Agency, *World Energy Investment Outlook 2003* (Paris: OECD Publishing, 2003), 131.
27 Robert McNally, *Crude Volatility: The History and the Future of Boom-Bust Oil Prices* (New York: Columbia University Press, 2017), 196.
28 Kenneth S. Deffeyes, *When Oil Peaked* (New York: Hill and Want, 2010).
29 Roger D. Blanchard, *The Future of Global Oil Production* (Jefferson, NC: McFarland & Company Publishers, 2005).
30 Many countries chose to report the same levels of official reserves year after year, without changing them to take into account ongoing production efforts. For example, Kuwait's reported proven reserve levels stood unchanged at 94 billion barrels each year between 1991 and 2002, despite having produced over 8 billion barrels of oil in that time, and the country did not add any new discoveries. Ibid., 93.
31 Matt Simmons, *Twilight in the Desert: The Coming Saudi Oil Shock and the World Economy* (New York: Wiley Books, 3006).
32 Ibid., 98.
33 Ibid.
34 Jeff Rubin, *Why Your World Is about to Get a Whole Lot Smaller* (Toronto: Vintage Canada, 2010).
35 Michael T. Klare, *Resource Wars: The New Landscape of Global Conflict* (New York: Henry Holt & Company, 2001).
36 Rubin, *Why Your World*.
37 John S. Duffield, *Over a Barrel: The Costs of U.S. Foreign Oil Dependence* (Princeton, NJ: Princeton University Press, 2008).

38 George Akerlof, *Animal Spirits: How Human Pychology Drives the Economy, and Why It Matters for Global Capitalism* (Princeton, NJ: Princeton University Press, 2010).

39 Charles Kindleberger and Robert Z. Aliber, *Manias, Panics, and Crashes: A History of Financial Crises* (Hoboeken: John Wiley and Sons, 5th edition, 2005).

40 Mahmoud A. El-Gamal and Amy Myers Jaffe, *Oil, Dollars, Debt, and Crises: The Global Curse of Black Gold* (Cambridge: Cambridge University Press, 2010), 81–4.Ironically, it was the US financial system's reputation for transparency, stability, and strong regulation which motivated the influx of foreign dollars that eventually contributed to the growing instability of that system.

41 Ibid.

42 Christopher Balding, *Sovereign Wealth Funds: The New Intersection of Money & Politics* (Oxford: Oxford University Press, 2012), chapter 6. See also Edwin M. Truman, *Sovereign Wealth Funds: Threat or Salvation* (Washington, DC: Peterson Centre for International Economics, 2010).

43 Ragurham Rajan, *Fault Lines: How Hidden Fractures Still Threaten the World Economy* (Princeton, NJ: Princeton University Press, 2013), chapter 1.

44 During the presidency of George Bush, this fiscal flexibility allowed a large tax cut to be enacted at the same time that the country was conducting the war on terror, rapidly raising deficit spending. How sustainable this is, and projections for the long-term fiscal position of the United States, can be found in *The Long Term Fiscal Position of the United States*. At this writing the accumulated US fiscal deficit is overhang that tops US$18 trillion.

45 Useful sources for looking at the 2008 financial crisis include Martin Wolf, *The Shifts and the Shocks: What We Learned – And Have Still to Learn – From the Financial Crisis* (London, Penguin Publishers, 2015), as well as Ben S. Bernanke, *The Courage to Act: A Memoir of a Crisis and Its Aftermath* (New York: W.W. Norton and Company, 2015).

46 Clayton, *Market Madness*, 159–60.

47 McNally, *Crude Volatility*, 193–5.

48 Data for this paragraph drawn from the United States Energy Information Agency, http://www.eia.gov/dnav/pet/pet_pri_spt_s1_d.htm.

49 Statistics for this paragraph are taken from the publicly available data section of the United States Energy Information Administration, http://www.eia.gov/dnav/pet/PET_PRI_SPT_S1_D.htm.

50 McNally, *Crude Volatility*, 194.

51 The US SPR was capable of providing a drawdown rate of 4.4 mbd within thirteen days of a presidential decision. McNally, *Crude Volatility*, 200.
52 Ibid., 200.
53 Ibid.
54 International Energy Agency, *World Energy Outlook 2008*, 104.
55 Ibid., 323.
56 Yetiv, *Crude Awakenings*, chapter 7.
57 Ibid., 94.
58 Giuliano Garavani, *The Rise and Fall of OPEC in the Twentieth Century* (Oxford: Oxford University Press, 2019), chapter 7.
59 IEA, *World Energy Outlook 2008*, 328.
60 McNally, *Crude Volatility*, 174.
61 "Oil Production in Saudi Arabia from 1998 to 2020," Statista, July 2021, https://www.statista.com/statistics/265190/oil-production-in-saudi-arabia-in-barrels-per-day/.
62 Ibid.
63 Blake Clayton and Michael A. Levi, "Fiscal Breakeven Oil Prices: Uses, Abuses, and Opportunities for Improvement," *Council of Foreign Relations*, Discussion Paper, 2015.
64 International Energy Report, *Monthly Oil Market Report* (Paris: International Energy Agency, June 11, 2009), 16.
65 International Energy Agency, *Monthly Oil Market Report* (Paris: International Energy Agency, January 1, 2009), 20.
66 Barclay's Capital, *The Original E & P Spending Survey: Analysis of Worldwide E & P Expenditures* (December 16, 2009), 9.
67 Ibid., 9.
68 Statista, various country reports.
69 Jeff Colgan, "The Emperor Has No Clothes: The Limits of OPEC in the Oil Market," *International Security* 68, no. 3 (2014): 600–3.
70 Dow Jones Industrial Average, Company Reports, various years.
71 Steve Hargreaves, "Exxon 2008 Profit: A Record $45 Billion," CNN Money, January 30, 2009, http://money.cnn.com/2009/01/30/news/companies/exxon_earnings/.
72 Ronald D. White., "Exxon Mobil Shatters U.S. Record for Annual Profit," *Los Angeles Times*, January 21, 2009, https://www.latimes.com/archives/la-xpm-2009-jan-31-fi-oilearns31-story.html.
73 Barclay's Capital, Equity Research (Analysts James D. Crandell and James C. West, Barclay's Capital), "Outlook 2009 E & P Spending," 1.
74 Ibid.
75 Barclay's Capital, *Global Exploration Expenditure and Update*, May 18, 2012, 7–9.

76 International Energy Agency, *World Energy Outlook*, 307.

77 ExxonMobil also added capacity by purchasing other domestic companies. In June 2010 it purchased XTO energy for $41 billion, adding significant capacity to domestic US natural gas production capacity.

78 Exxon Mobil Corporation, *10-K Annual Report to Shareholders* (New York: Securities and Exchange Commission, 2011), 16.

79 Exxon Mobil Corporation, *Annual 10-K Shareholders Report* (New York: Securities and Exchange Commission, 2012), 5.

80 Chevron Corporation, *2011 Annual Report to Shareholders*, 13.

81 ConocoPhillips, *Summary Annual Report to Shareholders*, Spring 2012.

82 Company Annual Reports, various years.

83 Energy Intelligence Research, *The Quest for Dominance: NOC-IOC Rivalries, Alliances, and the Shape of the New Global Oil Industry* (New York: Energy Intelligence Research, 2008), 86.

84 Lyudmyla Hvozdyk and Valerie Mercer-Blackman, "What Determines Investment in the Oil Sector? A New Era for National and International Oil Companies," *Inter-American Development Bank Working Paper Series*, No. IDB- WP-209, August 2010, 35.

85 El-Gamal and Jaffe, *Oil, Dollars, Debt, and Crises*, 148.

86 James Henderson and Ekaterina Grushevanko, "The Future of Russian Oil Production in the Short, Medium, and Long Term," *The Oxford Institute for Energy Studies: Energy Insight #57*, September 2019, 7.

87 "Oil Production in Russia from 2000 to 2020," Statista, July 2021, https://www.statista.com/statistics/265187/oil-production-in-russia-in-barrels-per-day/#:~:text=In%202020%2C%20Russia%20produced%20approximately,world's%20third%2Dlargest%20oil%20producer.

88 "Oil Production in Brazil from 2008 to 2020," Statista, July 2021, https://www.statista.com/statistics/265184/oil-production-in-brazil-in-barrels-per-day/.

89 Energy Intelligence Research, *The Quest for Dominance: NOC-IOC Rivalries, Alliances, and the Shape of the New Global Oil Industry* (New York: Energy Intelligence Group, 2008), 121. Statoil, for example, has invested in Algeria, Libya, Egypt, Angola, Nigeria, Azerbaijan, Venezuela, Iran, and Russia.

90 "Oil Production in Norway from 2000 to 2020," Statista, July 2021, https://www.statista.com/statistics/265186/oil-production-in-norway-in-barrels-per-day/.

91 Statista, *The Oil Industry in Canada*, 17.

92 United States Energy Information Administration, *Annual Energy Outlook 2013 With Projections to 2020* (Washington, DC: US Department of Energy, 2013), 83.

93 Ibid., 32–7.

94 Revenues from current and projected oil sales have now become deeply embedded in the global financial system: raising concerns that the leveraged financial value of these assets far exceed the oil's actual value. Kent Moors, *The Vega Factor: Oil Volatility and the Next Global Crises* (New York: John Wiley & Sons, 2011).

95 El-Gamal and Jaffe, *Oil, Dollars, Debt, and Crises*, 148.

96 Kindleberger and Aliber, *Manias, Panics, and Crashes: A History of Financial Crises* (New York: John Wiley & Sons, 5th edition, 2005).

97 Steven Mufson, "This Week's OPEC Meeting Is the Most Important in Years," *The Washington Post*, November 25, 2014, https://www .washingtonpost.com/news/wonk/wp/2014/11/25/this-weeks-opec -meeting-is-the-most-important-in-years/?utm_term=.e3bba6338ffa.

5. The Politics, Geopolitics, and Global Governance of Oil: 2000–2014

1 Thomas Friedman, "First Law of Petropolitics, *Foreign Policy*, May–June 2006, 31.

2 Some books chronicling the debilitating effect of oil production on domestic institutions include Leif Weimar, *Blood Oil: Tyrants, Violence, and the Rules That Run the World* (Oxford: Oxford University Press, 2016); and Nicholas Shaxson, *Poisoned Wells: The Dirty Politics of African Oil* (New York: Palgrave Macmillan, 2016).

3 The six factors this survey measures are labeled voice and accountability, political stability and absence of violence, government effectiveness, regulatory quality, rule of law, and control of corruption. It presents time-series data that shows how countries evolve along these facets over time. "Worldwide Governance Indicators," World Bank, http://info .worldbank.org/governance/wgi/index.aspx#home.

4 "Freedom in the World 2019: Democracy in Retreat," Freedom House, https://freedomhouse.org/report/freedom-world/freedom -world-2019.

5 *Foreign Policy* magazine, in collaboration with the nonprofit group Fund for Peace, developed a Fragile States Index that measured how resilient domestic governments were to external, and often unpredictable, shocks: http://foreignpolicy.com/2015/06/17/fragile-states-2015-islamic-state -ebola-ukraine-russia-ferguson/.

6 Condolezza Rice, "Testimony before the Senate Foreign Relations Committee," April 6, 2006. Quoted in Gal Luft, "United States: A Shackled Superpower," in *Energy Security Challenges for the 21st Century:*

  A Reference Handbook, ed. Gal Luft and Anne Korin (Santa Barbara: Praeger Security International, 2009), 144.

7 Rachel Bronson, *Thicker than Oil: America's Uneasy Partnership with Saudi Arabia* (Oxford: Oxford University Press, 2006).

8 Steve A. Yetiv, *The Petroleum Triangle: Oil, Globalization, and Terror* (Ithaca, NY: Cornell University Press, 2011).

9 Richard A. Clarke, *Against All Enemies: Inside America's War on Terror* (New York: The Free Press, 2004).

10 Doug Stokes and Sam Raphael, *Global Energy Security and American Hegemony* (Baltimore: The Johns Hopkins University Press, 2010), chapter 3.

11 John Esterbrook, "Rumsfeld: It Would Be a Short War," CBS News, November 15, 2002, http://www.cbsnews.com/news/rumsfeld-it-would-be-a-short-war/.

12 Yetiv, *The Petroleum Triangle.*

13 Jessica Stern, *Terror in the Name of God: Why Religious Militants Kill* (New York: HarperCollins 2003), 120–1.

14 Keith Crane, Andreas Goldthau, Michael Toman, Thomas Light, Stuart Johnson, Alireza Nader, Angel Rabesa, Harun Dogo, *Imported Oil and U.S. National Security* (Santa Monica: RAND Corporation, 2009), 73–4. To quote directly, this source argues that "future oil-related military operations are likely to be highly intermittent and characterized more by crises response, counterterrorism, training of local security forces, and localized stability operations. An operation of this type is much less costly that the invasion and occupation of Iraq has turned out to be."

15 Thomas Barnet, *The Pentagon's New Map: War and Peace in the 21st Century* (New York: G.P. Putnam and Sons, 2004).

16 Elisabeth Bumiller and Adam Nagourney, "Bush: 'America Is Addicted to Oil,'" *The New York Times,* February 1, 2006, https://www.nytimes.com/2006/02/01/world/americas/01iht-state.html.

17 John Hofmeister, *Why We Hate the Oil Companies: Straight Talk from an Energy Insider* (New York: St. Martin's Press, 2010).

18 Antonia Juhasz, *The Tyranny of Oil: The World's Most Powerful Industry, and What We Must Do to Stop It* (New York: Harper Publishers, 2008).

19 "Obama Says He Would Impose Windfall Profits Tax," Reuters, June 9, 2008, https://www.reuters.com/article/us-usa-politics-obama/obama-says-he-would-impose-oil-windfall-profits-tax-idUSWAT00963020080609.

20 Barack Obama, Remarks after winning the Iowa caucuses, Des Moines, Iowa, January 3, 2008.

21 Barack Obama, Democratic Presidential Nomination Address, Denver Colorado, August 28, 2008.

22 Barack Obama, Inauguration Speech, January 20, 2009.

23 Thomas Friedman, *Hot, Flat, and Crowded* (New York: Farrar, Straus and Giroux, 2008).

24 Senator Richard Lugar, United States Senate, "A Bill to Establish a Western Hemisphere Energy Cooperation Forum," March 12, 2009.

25 One sample of such literature that garnered significant attention is Martin Jacques, *When China Rules the World: The End of the Western World and the Birth of a New Global Order* (New York: Penguin Books, 2009).

26 David Baldwin, *Economic Statecraft* (Princeton, NJ: Princeton University Press, 1985).

27 Joshua Kurlantzick, *State Capitalism: How the Return of Statism Is Transforming the World* (Oxford: Oxford University Press, 2016), chapter 2.

28 Elizabeth C. Economy and David Levy, *By All Means Necessary: How China's Resource Quest Is Changing the World* (Oxford: Oxford University Press, 2014), chapter 4.

29 Bo Kong, *China's International Petroleum Policy* (Santa Barbara: Praeger Security International, 2010), chapter 1.

30 Bo Kong, *China's International Petroleum Policy*, 119–21.

31 William J. Norris, *China's Economic Statecraft: Commercial Actors, Grand Strategy, and State Control* (Ithaca, NY: Cornell University Press, 2017), chapter 3.

32 Flynt Leverett and Jeffrey Bader, "Managing China–U.S. Energy Competition in the Middle East," *The Washington Quarterly* 29, no. 1 (2005–6): 187–201.

33 Janeer Elass and Amy Myers Jaffe, *Iraqi Oil Potential and Implications for Global Oil Markets and OPEC Politics* (Houston: James A. Baker III Institute for Public Policy, July 2011), 11–12.

34 Amy Myers Jaffe and Kenneth B. Medlock, "China and Northeast Asia," in *Energy & Security: Toward a New Foreign Policy Strategy*, ed. Jan H. Kalicki and David L. Goldwyn (Washington, DC: Woodrow Wilson Center Press, 2005), 274–8.

35 Theodore H. Moran, *China's Strategy to Secure Natural Resources: Risks, Dangers, and Opportunities* (Washington, DC: Peterson Institute for International Economics, 2010), 14–17.

36 David Zweig and Bi Jinhai, "China's Global Hunt for Energy," *Foreign Affairs* (September–October 2005), 27–8.

37 Andrew B. Kennedy, "China's Search for Oil: A Critique," in *The New Politics of Strategic Resources: Energy and Food Security Challenges in the 21st Century*, ed. David Steven, Emily O'Brien, and Bruce Jones (Washington, DC: Brookings Institution Press, 2015), 25.

38 CNOOC, *Annual Report 2010*, 3.
39 PetroChina, *United States Securities and Exchange Commission Form 20-F*, 2012, 18.
40 Barclay's Capital, *Global E & P Capital Spending Update*, May 2012, 9.
41 Michael T. Klare, "China's Global Shopping Spree: Is the World's Future Resource Map Tilting East?" HuffPost, June 1, 2020, http://www.huffingtonpost.com/michael-t-klare/chinas-global-shopping-sp_b_522081.html.
42 Robert B. Zoellick, "Whither China: From Membership to Responsibility?" Remarks to National Committee on US–China Relations, New York City, September 21, 2005.
43 Leif Wenar, *Blood Oil: Thieves, Tyrants, and the Rules That Run the World* (Oxford: Oxford University Press, 2015).
44 The standard reference of these efforts remains Louis Turner, *Oil Companies in the International System* (London: Royal Institute of International Affairs, 1978). See chapter 5 for a documentation of the relationship between home and host governments.
45 Amy Myers Jaffe and Stephen W. Lewis, "Beijing's Oil Diplomacy," in *Survival*, 44, no. 1 (2002): 127.
46 Moran, *China's Strategy to Secure Oil Resources*, 47.
47 Joshua Kurtlantzick, *State Capitalism: How the Return of Statism Is Transforming the World* (Oxford: Oxford University Press, 2016), 3995 (Kindle edition).
48 David M. Lampton, *The Three Faces of Chinese Power: Might, Money, and Minds* (Berkeley: University of California Press, 2008), 105.
49 "Saudi Arabia Facts and Figures," Organization of the Petroleum Exporting Countries, https://www.opec.org/opec_web/en/about_us/169.htm.
50 Jim Krane, *Energy Kingdom: Oil and Political Survival in the Persian Gulf* (New York: Columbia University Press, 2019), chapter 4.
51 Alexandra Gillies, *Crude Intentions: How Oil Corruption Contaminates the World* (Oxford: Oxford University Press, 2020).
52 Andrei Schleifer and Robert W. Vishny, *The Grabbing Hand: Government Pathologies and Their Cures* (Boston: Harvard University Press, 2002).
53 Gordon L. Clark, Adam D. Dixon, and Ashby H.B. Monk, *Sovereign Wealth Funds: Legitimacy, Governance, and Global Power*, (Princeton, NJ: Princeton University Press, 2013), 30–3.
54 Clark, Dixon, and Monk, *Sovereign Wealth Funds*, chapter 2.
55 Christopher Balding, *Sovereign Wealth Funds: The New Intersection of Money and Politics* (Oxford: Oxford University Press, 2012), chapter 4.

56 Ibid., 21.

57 Ibid., 121.

58 Edwin M. Truman, *Sovereign Wealth Funds: Threat or Salvation?* (Washington, DC: Peterson Institute for International Economics, 2010).

59 Kindleberger and Aliber, *Manias, Panics, and Crashes: A History of Financial Crises* (New York: Wiley, 1978).

60 Jonathan Kirshner, *American Power after the Financial Crisis* (Ithaca, NY: Cornell University Press, 2014).

61 A standard reference on the brutal emergence of the Russian oligarchs is well told in Thane Gustafson, *Wheel of Fortune: The Battle for Oil and Power in Russia* (Cambridge, MA: The Belknap Press of Harvard University, 2012).

62 Marshall I. Goldman, *PetroState: Putin, Power and the New Russia* (Oxford: Oxford University Press, 2008), chapter 3.

63 Gustafsson, *Wheel of Fortune*, chapter 3.

64 United States Energy Information Administration, https://www.eia.gov /beta/international/analysis.php?iso=RUS.

65 Gustafsson, *Wheel of Fortune*, 186.

66 Putin's alternating of roles between president and prime minister has allowed him to skirt the term-limit rules that limit time in office.

67 Putin jailed Mikhail Khordokovsy, chairman of the Russian company Yukos, after he had become too outspoken a critic of the Kremlin.

68 Gustafsson, *Wheel of Fortune*, 360.

69 Steven Levitsky and Lucan A. Way, *Competitive Authoritarianism: Hybrid Regimes after the Cold War* (Cambridge: Cambridge University Press, 2010), 189–91. On the process of consolidating Russia into a petrostate, see Marshall I. Goldman, *Petrostate: Putin, Power, and the New Russia* (Oxford: Oxford University Press, 2008).

70 Gustafsson, *Wheel of Fortune*, 7304 (ebook edition).

71 Goldman, *PetroState*.

72 "SIPRI Military Expenditures," Stockholm International Peace Research Institute, https://www.sipri.org/databases/milex.

73 Ibid.

74 Richard K. Vietor and Hilary White, "Saudi Arabia: Finding Stability after the Arab Spring," HBS Case #9714053 (Boston: Harvard Business School Publishing), 1.

75 Sheyla Urdaneta, Anatoly Kurmanaev, and Isayen Herrera, "Venezuela, Once an Oil Giant, Reaches the End of an Era," *The New York Times*, October 8, 2020, https://www.nytimes.com/2020/10/07/world /americas/venezuela-oil-economy-maduro.html.

76 Ibid.

77 Alexei Barrionuevo, "Brazil Takes More Control of Oil Fields, with Long-Term Risks." *The New York Times*, August 17, 2009, https://www.nytimes.com/2009/08/18/world/americas/18brazil.html#:~:text=Brazil%20Takes%20More%20Control%20of%20Oil%20Fields%2C%20With,Seeks%20More%20Control%20of%20Oil%20Beneath%20Its%20Seas.

78 In this case it may be more profitable to pursue regulatory coordination among large energy consumers: "the codified adjustment of standards in order to recognize or accommodate regulatory framework from other countries." Likely easier said than done in an arena as highly security conscious as oil supply. See Daniel W. Drezner, *All Politics Is Global: Explaining International Regulatory Regimes* (Princeton, NJ: Princeton University Press, 2007), 11.

79 Ann Florini and Benjamin K. Sovacool, "Who Governs Energy? The Challenges Facing Global Energy Governance," *Energy Policy* 37 (2009): 5240. See also Amitav Acharya, *Why Govern? Rethinking Demand and Progress in Global Governance* (Cambridge: Cambridge University Press, 2016).

80 Jeff D. Colgan, Robert O. Keohane, and Thijs Van De Graaf, "Punctuated Equilibrium in the Energy Regime Complex, *Review of International Organizations* 7, no. 2 (2012): 117–43.

81 "Membership," IEA, July 16, 2021, https://www.iea.org/about/membership.

82 David K. Victor and Linda Yueh, "The New Energy Order: Managing Insecurities in the Twenty-First Century," *Foreign Affairs* 89 (2010): 66.

83 "China," IEA, https://www.iea.org/countries/China/.

84 "The Government's Revenue," Norwegian Petroleum, https://www.norskpetroleum.no/en/economy/governments-revenues/.

85 Angelique Chrisafis, "Son of Equatorial Guinea's President Is Convicted of Corruption in France," *The Guardian*, October 27, 2017, https://www.theguardian.com/world/2017/oct/27/son-of-equatorial-guineas-president-convicted-of-corruption-in-france.

86 Gilles, *Crude Intentions*, various chapters.

87 John Gerard Ruggie, *Just Business: Multinational Corporation and Human Rights* (New York: Norton Press, 2015).

88 https://www.pwyp.org/.

89 https://eiti.org/.

90 For a statistical overview of the increase in global oil production, see the International Energy Agency, *World Energy Outlook* (Paris: OECD Publishing, 2016), 121–35.

6. The Politics and Markets of a Price Fall: 2014–2019

1 Simeon Kerr, "Saudi Purge Hopes to Raise $13 Billion by Year End from Graft Purge," *Financial Times*, February 11, 2018, https://www.ft.com /content/1beb9206-0da5-11e8-8eb7-42f857ea9f09.

2 "Crude Oil Prices Down Sharply in Fourth Quarter of 2014," US Energy Information Administration, https://www.eia.gov/todayinenergy /detail.php?id=19451.

3 Energy prices drawn from http://www.bloomberg.com/energy.

4 In 2014 the investment bank Goldman Sachs issued a warning that commodity prices would likely remain low for an extended period of time. Glenys Sim, "Goldman Forecasts Lower Commodity Prices as Cycle Ends," Bloomberg, July 16, 2014, https://www.bloomberg.com /news/articles/2014-07-16/goldman-sees-lower-commodity-prices -over-five-years-on-supplies.

5 Investment in non-OPEC production sites in Brazil, the United States, and oil sands development in Canada all contributed to this surge in production, which was projected to reach and all-time high of 56 mbd by 2040. International Energy Agency, *World Energy Outlook 2014* (Paris: OECD Publishing, 2014). 114.

6 Robert McNally, *Crude Volatility: The History and The Future of Boom-Bust Oil Prices* (New York: Columbia University Press, 2017).

7 At its November 2014 meeting OPEC ministers argued that "stable oil prices – at a level which did not affect global economic growth but which, at the same time, allowed producers to receive a decent income and to invest to meet future demand – were vital for world economic wellbeing. Accordingly, in the interest of restoring market equilibrium, the Conference decided to maintain the production level of 30.0 mb/d." This presumably meant a concerted effort to drive out higher-priced suppliers in an effort to reduce the overall glut. "OPEC 166th Meeting Concludes," Organization of the Petroleum Exporting Countries, http:// www.opec.org/opec_web/en/press_room/2938.htm.

8 Speech by Ali al-Naimi, Minister of Oil, Saudi Arabia, delivered February 23, 2016, at the annual CERA oil convention in Houston, Texas.

9 This claim follows reports of Saudi Arabia's strategy to float a portion of Saudi Aramco's value on public stock exchanges as part of its "Saudi 2030" economic strategy. "Saudi Aramco Flotation 'Coming Soon,'" BBC News, October 30, 2019, https://www.bbc.com/news /business-50232253

10 McNally, *Crude Volatility*, 215–16.

11 They certainly seem capable of doing this in financial markets. See
    Kenneth Rogoff and Carmen Reinhardt, *This Time Is Different: Eight
    Centuries of Financial Folly* (Princeton, NJ: Princeton University Press, 2011).
12 Daniel Kahneman, *Thinking Fast and Slow* (New York: DoubleDay, 2010).
    Here Kahneman describes the halo effect and the tendency to follow
    leaders who are overoptimistic and confident.
13 For thorough overviews of common fallacies in prediction and
    expectation, see Nassim Nicholas Taleb, *The Black Swan: The Impact of
    the Highly Improbable* (New York: Random House, 2010): see also Daniel
    Kahneman, *Thinking Fast and Slow.*
14 International Energy Agency, *World Energy Outlook 2015,* 108.
15 Haynes and Boone LLP, *Oil Patch Bankruptcy Monitor,* November 30, 2020.
16 Clifford Krauss, "U.S. Oil Companies Find Energy Independence Isn't so
    Profitable," *The New York Times,* June 30, 2019, https://www.nytimes
    .com/2019/06/30/business/energy-environment/oil-companies-profit
    .html.
17 Statistics Canada. Table 25-10-0054-01. Capital expenditures, oil and gas
    extraction industries, Canada (x 1,000,000).
18 David Wethe, "Tens of Thousands Are Getting Laid Off in U.S. Shale
    Patch," Bloomberg, March 21, 2020, https://www.bloomberg.com/news
    /articles/2020-03-20/tens-of-thousands-are-getting-laid-off-in-the-u-s
    -shale-patch.
19 Company Annual Report: Operating Years 2016.
20 Royal Dutch Shell, Annual Report, 2016. http://reports.shell.com/annual
    -report/2016/strategic-report/segments/upstream/investments-and
    -portfolio.php.
21 This includes deepwater drilling, in which technological improvements
    might hold the key to significantly lowering costs. Lynn Cook, Sarah Kent,
    and Paul Kiernan, "Shell's Titanic Bet: Can Deep-Water Drilling Be Done
    on the Cheap?" *The Wall Street Journal,* March 20, 2017, https://www.wsj
    .com/articles/shell-goes-on-a-deep-water-drilling-diet-1490024220.
22 "Chevron, Exxon Mobil Tighten Their Grip on Fracking," LFS
    Technologies, March 19, 2020, http://www.lfstechnologies.com/chevron
    -exxon-mobil-tighten-their-grip-on-fracking..
23 "Oil Production in the United States from 1998 to 2020*," Statista, July
    2021, https://www.statista.com/statistics/265181/us-oil-production-in
    -barrels-per-day-since-1998/.
24 Sarah Ladislaw, "Dissecting the Idea of U.S. Energy Dominance," *The
    Oxford Institute for Energy Studies: Oxford Energy Forum* 111 (November
    2017): 5–8.

25 Meghan L. O'Sullivan, *Windfall: How the New Energy Abundance Upends Global Politics and Strengthens American Power* (New York: Simon and Schuster, 2017).
26 That spill, which ended up dumping millions of gallons of crude oil into the Gulf of Mexico, is well chronicled in Abrahm Lustgarten, *Run to Failure: BP and the Making of the Deepwater Horizon Disaster* (New York: W.W. Norton & Company, 2012).
27 United Nations, "The Paris Agreement," https://unfccc.int/process-and -meetings/the-paris-agreement/the-paris-agreement.
28 Megan L. O'Sullivan, "U.S. Energy in an Age of Energy Abundance," *The Oxford Institute for Energy Studies: Oxford Energy Forum* 111 (November 2017): 8–11.
29 O'Sullivan, *Windfall*.
30 Laidislaw, "Dissecting the Idea of Energy Dominance," 6–7.
31 Richard Nephew, *The Art of Sanctions: A View From the Field* (Columbia: Columbia University Press, 2918), 7–15.
32 Meghan L. O'Sullivan, *Shrewd Sanctions: Statecraft and State Sponsors of Terrorism* (Washington, DC: The Brookings Institution, 2003).
33 Stuart Anderson, "Trump's Trade War Cost U.S. Company Stock Prices $1.7 Trillion," *Forbes*, June 1, 2020, https://www.forbes.com/sites/ stuartanderson/2020/06/01/trumps-trade-war-cost-us-company-stock -prices-17-trillion/?sh=64752a4f5279.
34 https://www.washingtonpost.com/business/energy/all-about-the-us -sanctions-aimed-at-putins-russia/2020/12/18/db9633d2-414a-11eb-b.
35 Dan De Luce and Robert Windrem, "Trump Faces Bipartisan Pushback over Arms Sales to Saudie Arabia, UAE," NBC News, June 5, 2019, https://www.nbcnews.com/politics/congress/trump-faces-bipartisan -pushback-over-arms-sales-saudi-arabia-uae-n1014191.
36 The multilateral deal signed by Iran, the United States, China, Russia, France, Britain, and the European Union that set limits on Iranian nuclear production.
37 Steve Lohr, "U.S. Moves to Ban Huawei from Government Contracts," *The New York Times*, August 7, 2019, https://www.nytimes.com/2019/08 /07/business/huawei-us-ban.html.
38 For a fuller elaboration of these realities, see Erica S. Downs, "Who's Afraid of China's Oil Companies?" as well as Erica Downs, *China's Quest for Energy Security* (Santa Monica: RAND, 2000). See also Theodore H. Moran, *China's Strategy to Secure National Resources: Risks, Dangers, Opportunities* (Washington, DC: Peterson Institute for International Economics, 2010).

39 "Crude Oil Production in China Decreased to 3962 BBL/D/1K in October from 4042 BBL/D/1K in September of 2021," Trading Economics, https://tradingeconomics.com/china/crude-oil-production.

40 "China's Crude Oil Imports Surpassed 10 Million Barrels per Day in 2019," US Energy Information Administration, March 23, 2020, https://www.eia.gov/todayinenergy/detail.php?id=43216.

41 Tsvetana Paraskova, "China's [sic] Becomes World's Next Top Oil Importer," OilPrice.com, February 6, 2018, https://oilprice.com/Energy/Crude-Oil/Chinas-Becomes-Worlds-Next-Top-Oil-Importer.html.

42 Ibid.

43 Valerie Marcel, "The Cost of an Emerging National Oil Company," Research paper (London: Chatham House, Royal Institute of International Affairs), March 2016.

44 Nick Cunningham, "China's Oil Industry Is Faltering, Production Falls 5%," OilPrice.com, May 16, 2016, https://oilprice.com/Energy/Crude-Oil/Chinas-Oil-Industry-Is-Faltering-Production-Falls-5.html..

45 David Steven, Emily O'Brien, and Bruce Jones, eds., *The New Politics of Strategic Resources: Energy and Food Security Challenges in the 21st Century*, (Washington, DC: Brookings Institution Press, 2016), 24–5.

46 Bo Kong, *China's International Petroleum Policy* (Santa Barbara: Praeger Series International Security, 2010).

47 Chih-shian Liou, "Bureaucratic Politics and Overseas Investment by Chinese State-Owned Companies: Illusory Champions," *Asian Survey* 49, no. 4 (2009): 677.

48 William Norris, *Chinese Economic Statecraft*, 1777–80 (Kindle edition).

49 For an overview and summary of these developments, see Andrew B. Kennedy, "China's Search for Oil Security: A Critique," in *The New Politics of Strategic Resources: Energy and Food Challenges in the 21st Century*, ed. David Steven, Emily O'Brien, and Bruce Jones, chapter 2 (Washington, DC: Brookings Institution Press, 2015), 23–39.

50 An analysis of China's Five-Year Economic Plan for 2016–20 can be found at https://www.uscc.gov/sites/default/files/Research/The%2013th%20Five-Year%20Plan_Final_2.14.17_Updated%20%28002%29.pdf.

51 David Steven, Emily O'Brien, and Bruce Jones, eds., *The New Politics of Strategic Resources: Energy and Food Security Challenges in the 21st Century* (Washington, DC: Brookings Institution Press, 2016), 24–5. See also Erica Downs, "Who's Afraid of China's Oil Companies?" in *Energy Security: Economics, Politics, Strategies, and Implications*, ed. Carlos Pascual and Jonathan Elkind (Washington, DC: Brookings Institution Press, 2010), chapter 4.

52 "Does China Dominate Global Investment?" ChinaPower, https://chinapower.csis.org/china-foreign-direct-investment/#:~:text=As%20of%202019%2C%20just%20over,top%20destinations%20for%20Chinese%20FDI.&text=The%20US%20Bureau%20of%20Economic,percent%20of%20US%20investment%20inflows.

53 Ibid.

54 "Factbox: China's Oil Majors Tap New Discoveries as They Step Up Drilling," Reuters, February 1, 2019, https://www.reuters.com/article/us-china-oil-exploration-factbox/factbox-chinas-oil-majors-tap-new-discoveries-as-they-step-up-drilling-idUSKCN1PQ3Q2.

55 Oil & Gas 360, "China Opens Up to Foreign Investment in Oil Sector," OilPrice.com, May 24, 2017, https://oilprice.com/Energy/Natural-Gas/China-Opens-Up-To-Foreign-Investment-In-Oil-Sector.html.

56 Julianne Geiger, "China's Mad Scramble to Boost Domestic Oil Production," OilPrice.com, March 26, 2019, https://oilprice.com/Energy/Crude-Oil/Chinas-Mad-Scramble-To-Boost-Domestic-Oil-Production.html.

57 The increase in US domestic oil production caused by fracking motivated the Republican-dominated US Congress to press for and eventually pass a bill repealing a ban on the export of domestically produced crude oil. The bill passed in December 2015, allowing US oil production to add additional volume to the export market.

58 Steve A. Yetiv, *Myths of the Oil Boom: American National Security in a Global Oil Market* (Oxford: Oxford University Press, 2015), 37.

59 A description and overview of the Saudi Arabian economic plan can be found at http://english.alarabiya.net/special-reports/saudi-vision-2030.html.

60 Anjli Rival and Simeon Kerr, "Saudi Arabia Expected to Sign Off on Long-Awaited IPO This Week," *Financial Times*, October 14, 2019, https://www.ft.com/content/ff0da45c-ee86-11e9-ad1e-4367d8281195.

61 Quote of $60/barrel taken from Sam Wilkin, "IMF Sees Saudi Break-Even Oil Price Drops Less than Forecasted," Bloomberg, October 19, 2016. https://www.bloomberg.com/news/articles/2016-10-19/imf-sees-saudi-break-even-oil-price-falling-less-than-expected.

62 Report for Selected Countries and Subjects (imf.org). Country report on Russia, International Monetary Fund World Economic Outlook database. Report generated December 20, 2020. "World Economic Outlook Database," International Monetary Fund, https://www.imf.org/en/Publications/WEO/weo-database/2021/October.

63 Daniel Cloud, "Revenge of the Ruble: What the Crisis Means for Putin," *Foreign Affairs*, December 18, 2014, https://www.foreignaffairs.com /articles/russia-fsu/2014-12-18/revenge-ruble.

64 James Henderson and Ekaterina Grushevenko, "The Future of Russian Oil Production in the Short, Medium, and Long-Term," *The Oxford Institute for Energy Studies*, Energy Insight #57, September 2019, 9.

65 Goldman Sachs Report cited by Irina Slav, "Russia Continues to Raise Its Oil Production," OilPrice.com, November 2, 2016, http://oilprice.com /Energy/Crude-Oil/Russia-Continues-To-Raise-Its-Oil-Production.html.

66 Nayla Razzouk, Angelina Rascouet, and Golnar Motevalli, "OPEC Confounds Skeptics, Agrees to First Oil Cuts in 8 Years," Bloomberg, November 30, 2016, https://www.bloomberg.com/news/articles/2016-11-30/opec-said-to -agree-oil-production-cuts-as-saudis-soften-on-iran.

67 Grant Smith, "OPEC–Russia Deal Could Drain Almost Half the Oil Surplus," Bloomberg, December 12, 2016, https://www.bloomberg.com /news/articles/2016-12-12/opec-russia-deal-could-drain-almost-half -the-global-oil-surplus.

68 David Sheppard, "Russia Ready to Discuss Oil Output Cut with OPEC," *Financial Times*, January 28, 2016, https://www.ft.com/content/efed8686 -c5d1-11e5-b3b1-7b2481276e45.

69 Ibid., 3.

70 According to the *Wall Street Journal*, many OPEC oil producers require prices to remain at $100 or more to meet stated expenditure requirements; Elliot Bentley, Pat Minczeski, and Jovi Juan, "Which Oil Producers Are Breaking Even?" *The Wall Street Journal*, July 26, 2017, http://graphics.wsj.com/oil-producers-break-even-prices/.

71 International Energy Agency, *Oil Market Report 2019*, 67.

72 Data sourced from "GDP Growth (Annual %) – Russian Federation," World Bank national accounts data, http://data.worldbank.org /indicator/NY.GDP.MKTP.KD.ZG?locations=RU&name_desc=false.

73 International Monetary Fund, World Economic Outlook Databases, https://www.imf.org/external/pubs/ft/weo/2019/01/weodata/weorept .aspx?sy=2014&ey=2019&scsm=1&ssd=1&sort=country&ds=.&br=1&c=2 23%2C922&s=NGDP_RPCH%2CNGDPD&grp=0&a=&pr1.x=61&pr1.y=10.

74 David Segal, "Petrobras Scandal Leaves Brazilians Lamenting a Lost Dream," *The New York Times*, August 7, 2015, https://www.nytimes .com/2015/08/09/business/international/effects-of-petrobras-scandal -leave-brazilians-lamenting-a-lost-dream.html.

75 Daniel Silva and Bard Wilkinson, "Judge Orders Arrest of Ex-Brazil President Lula da Silva," CNN, April 5, 2018, https://www.cnn.com/2018/04/05 /americas/brazil-lula-ruling-corruption-election-intl/index.html.

76 Jeff Colgan, *Petro Aggression*, 4027 and 4782 (Kindle edition).

77 Freedom House, Country Report, Venezuela, https://freedomhouse.org /report/freedom-world/2019/venezuela.

78 Tsvetana Paraskova, "U.S. Sanctions Severely Cripple Venezuela's Oil Production," OilPrice.com, September 18, 2019, https://oilprice.com /Latest-Energy-News/World-News/US-Sanctions-Severely-Cripple -Venezuelas-Oil-Production.html.

79 Shawn Donnan, "Falling Oil Price Raises Prospect of Bailouts for Crude Producers," *Financial Times*, January 28, 2016, https://www.ft.com /content/c942a4c2-c5df-11e5-b3b1-7b2481276e45.

80 International Energy Agency, Oil 2019: Analysis and Forecast to 2024 (Paris: OECD Publishing, 2018), 73–4.

81 Leif Wenar, *Blood Oil: Tyrants, Violence, and the Rules That Run the World* (Oxford: Oxford University Press, 2016).

82 United States Energy Information Administration, "What Countries Are the Top Producers and Consumers of Oil?" https://www.eia.gov/tools /faqs/faq.php?id=709&t=6.

83 Michelle Bellefontaine, "Alberta Premier Announces 8.7% Oil Production Cut to Increase Prices," CBC, December 2, 2018, https:// www.cbc.ca/news/canada/edmonton/alberta-premier-oil-differential -announcement-1.4929610.

84 Robson Fletcher, "Eye-roll Nation: Why Our Sympathy for Economic Pain Often Stops at Provincial Borders," CBC, November 29, 2018, https://www.cbc.ca/news/canada/calgary/alberta-oshawa-jobs-gm -general-motors-layoffs-1.4923771.

85 For a sampling of books churned out detailing the pros and cons of additional pipeline construction in Canada, see Denis McConaghy, *Breakdown: The Pipeline Debate and the Threat to Canada's Future* (Toronto: Dundurn Press, 2019); Jim Prentice (with Jean-Sébastien Rioux), *Triple Crown: Winning Canada's Energy Future* (Toronto: HarperCollins, 2017).

86 Dan Healing, "Foreign Share of Oilsands Production Fell over Past 4 Years, Analysis Shows," CBC, September 3, 2019, https://www .cbc.ca/news/canada/calgary/oilsands-alberta-production-foreign -investment-1.5268376.

87 Colgan, *Petro Aggression*, chapters 7 and 9.

88 International Energy Agency, *World Energy Outlook 2018*, 64.

89 Ibid., 67.

90 International Energy Agency, *Oil 2019: Analysis and Forecast to 2024* (Paris: OECD Publishing, 2019), 49.

91 "Iran Crude Oil: Production," CEIC, https://www.ceicdata.com/en /indicator/iran/crude-oil-production.

92 Ibid.

93 Jim Krane, *Energy Kingdoms: Oil and Political Survival in the Persian Gulf* (New York: Columbia University Press, 2019).

94 Ibid., 67.

95 Polling data done by Gallup: Art Swift, "Opposition to Fracking Mounts in the U.S.," Gallup, March 30, 2016, https://news.gallup.com /poll/190355/opposition-fracking-mounts.aspx.

96 Steve Coll, *Private Empire: Exxon Mobil and American Power* (New York: The Penguin Press, 2012).

97 To see a video copy of the speech, visit the Bank of England's website: http://www.bankofengland.co.uk/publications/Pages/speeches /2015/844.aspx.

98 International Energy Agency, *The Oil and Gas Industry In Transition* (Paris: OECD Publishing, January 2020), 33.

99 "Net Zero: A Fiduciary Approach," BlackRock, https://www.blackrock .com/corporate/investor-relations/blackrock-client-letter.

100 Ed Crooks and Lilita Clark, "Rockefellers Join Anti-fossil Fuel Drive," *Financial Times*, September 22 2014, https://www.ft.com/content /c201f2e8-4279-11e4-847d-00144feabdc0.

101 Clifford Kraus, "U.S. Oil Companies Find Energy Independence Isn't so Profitable," *The New York Times*, June 30, 2019, https://www.nytimes .com/2019/06/30/business/energy-environment/oil-companies-profit .html.

102 James Murray, "How the Six Major Oil Companies Have Invested in Renewable Energy Projects," NS Energy, January 16, 2020, https://www .nsenergybusiness.com/features/oil-companies-renewable-energy/.

103 International Energy Agency, *World Energy Outlook 2016* (Chapter 3, Executive Summary).

7. 2020 and Beyond: Oil in the Post-pandemic World

1 *The Economist*, May 15, 2021.

2 "WHO Coronavirus (COVID-19) Dashboard," World Health Organization, https://covid19.who.int/.

3 Louis Turner, *Oil Companies in the International System* (London: Royal Institute of International Affairs, 1978), 23.

4 Valérie Marcel and John V. Mitchell (contributor), *Oil Titans: National Oil Companies in the Middle East* (Baltimore: Brookings Institution Press, 2006), 57.

5 "Message in a Bottleneck: Don't Give up on Globalisation," *The Economist*, March 31, 2021, https://www.economist.com/weeklyedition/2021-04-03.

6 Jeff Colgan, "The Emperor Has No Clothes: The Limits of OPEC in the Global Oil Market," *International Organization* 68, no. 3 (2014): 599–632.

7 Denis McConaghy, *Breakdown: The Pipeline Debate and the Threat to Canada's Future* (Toronto: Dundurn Press, 2019).

8 International Energy Agency, *World Energy Outlook*, various years.

9 Lisa Friedman and Coral Davenport, "On Day 2 of the Climate Summit, Biden Revives a Venture to Increase Investment in Renewable Energy," *The New York Times*, April 23, 2021, https://www.nytimes.com /live/2021/04/23/us/earth-day-climate-summit-biden#on-day-2-of -the-climate-summit-biden-revives-a-venture-to-increase-investment-in -renewable-energy.

10 "President Biden Invites 40 World Leaders to Leaders Summit on Climate," The White House, March 26, 2021, https://www.whitehouse .gov/briefing-room/statements-releases/2021/03/26/president-biden -invites-40-world-leaders-to-leaders-summit-on-climate/.

11 Climate Champions, "GFANZ: Net Zero Financial Alliance Launches," Race to Zero, April 21, 2021, https://racetozero.unfccc.int/net-zero -financial-alliance-launches/.

12 Franklin Tugwell, *The Energy Crisis and the American Political Economy* (Stanford, CA: Stanford University Press, 1988), 127.

13 Malcolm Gladwell, *The Tipping Point: How Little Things Can Make a Big Difference* (New York: Little Brown and Company, 2006).

14 Roberto Baldwin, "GM Announces Goal to Eliminate Gas and Diesel Vehicles by 2035," Car and Driver, January 28, 2021, https://www .caranddriver.com/news/a35352321/gm-eliminate-gas-vehicles-2035/.

15 Jerry Hirsch, "GM Plans to Phase Out Gas and Diesel Cars by 2035," *Forbes*, January 28, 2021, https://www.forbes.com/wheels/news/gm -phase-out-gas-diesel-cars-2035/.

16 Reuters, "Internal-combustion Vehicle Bans across the World," Autoblog, November 18, 2020, https://www.autoblog.com/2020/11/18/internal -combustion-engine-bans-around-the-world/.

17 "Oil Giants, under Fire from Climate Activists and Investors, Mount a Defense," *The New York Times*, September 23, 2019, https://www.nytimes .com/2019/09/23/climate/oil-industry-climate-investment.html.

18 Daniel Drezner, *All Politics Is Global: Explaining International Regulatory Regimes* (Princeton, NJ: Princeton University Press, 2007).

19 Charles L. Glaser and Rosemary A. Kelanic, eds., *Crude Strategy: Rethinking the US Military Commitment to Defend Persian Gulf Oil* (Washington, DC: Georgetown University Press, 2016).

20 Jeff Colgan, *Petro Aggression: When Oil Causes War* (Cambridge: Cambridge University Press, 2013), chapters 7 and 9.

21 To review Saudi Arabia's plan for its own future, see http://vision2030 .gov.sa/en.

22 "Saudi Arabia: Individual – Taxes on Personal Income," PWC, January 2, 2022, http://taxsummaries.pwc.com/ID/Saudi-Arabia-Individual -Taxes-on-personal-income.

23 Benjamin Smith, *Hard Times in the Lands of Plenty: Oil Politics in Iran and Indonesia* (Ithaca, NY: Cornell University Press, 2007), 97.

24 Robert D. Blackwill and Jennifer M. Harris, *War by Other Means: Geoeconomics and Statecraft* (Cambridge, MA: Harvard University Press, 2016), 209.

25 Sarah M. Brooks and Marcus J. Kurtz, "Oil and Democracy: Endogenous Natural Resources and the Political "Resource Curse," *International Organization* 70 (Spring 2016): 279–311.

26 Thad Dunning, *Crude Democracy: Natural Resource Wealth and Political Regimes* (Cambridge: Cambridge University Press, 2008), 35.

27 Colgan, *Petro Aggression*, 1308 (Kindle edition).

28 Daniel Yergin, *The New Map* (New York: Penguin Press, 2020).

29 Karen Dawisha, *Putine's Kleptocracy: Who Owns Russia?* (New York: Simon and Schuster, 2014).

30 Measures of governance quality emanated from the World Bank's annual survey of governance indicators, which indicate that Russia's overall governance quality has declined over the past five years. See http://info .worldbank.org/governance/wgi/#reports.

31 One popular measure of country competitiveness has been developed by the IMD's world competitiveness rankings, which placed Russia as the forty-fourth most competitive economy in the world: http://www.imd .org/wcc/news-wcy-ranking/.

32 James Henderson and Ekaterina Grushevenko, "The Future of Russian Oil Production in the Short, Medium, and Long Term," *The Oxford Institute for Energy Studies: Energy Insight #57*, September 2019.

33 Steve Yetiv, *Myths of the Oil Boom* (Oxford: Oxford University Press, 2015), 121.

34 Heather A Conley, James Mina, Ruslan Stefanov, and Martin Vladiminov, "The Kremlin Playbook: Understanding Russian Influence in Central and

Eastern Europe," Center for Strategic and International Studies (New York: Rowman & Littlefield, 2016).

35 See evidence provided by James Comey, director of the Federal Bureau of Investigation, in testimony before Congress given March 20, 2017. See http://www.cnn.com/. Of course, one key observer questioning that allegation remains Donald Trump himself.

36 Some have tried. For arguments that directly link US military doctrine and strategy to the desire to exert global energy hegemony, see Doug Stokes and Sam Raphael, *Global Energy Security and American Hegemony* (Baltimore: Johns Hopkins University Press, 2010).

37 Joseph Stiglitz and Linda J. Bilmes, *The Three Trillion Dollar War: The True Cost of the Iraq Conflict* (New York: Norton Press, 2008).

38 Keith Crane, Andreas Goldthau, Michael Toman, Thomas Light, Stuart Johnson, Alireza Nader, Angel Rabasa, and Harun Dogo, *Imported Oil and U.S. National Security* (Santa Monica: RAND Corporation, 2009), 74.

39 Other countries are also looking to develop their shale oil resources. Their potential is at present hard to gauge, but they may eventually prove the productive bonanza that the US has recently experienced. Ajay Makan, "Russia and LatAm to Be Next Shale Oil Stars," *Financial Times*, January 15, 2014.

40 Alan Greenspan, *The Age of Turbulence: Adventures in a New World* (New York: Penguin Books, 2008).

41 Bo Kong, *China's International Petroleum Policy* (Santa Clara: Praeger Security Publishers, 2010), 90–3.

42 Recent works that outline the varieties of state capitalism present, as well as their various approaches to economic statecraft, include Joshua Kurlantzick, *State Capitalism: How the Return of Statism Is Transforming the World* (Oxford: Oxford University Press, 2016), as well as Robert D. Blackwill and Jennifer M. Harris, *War by Other Means: Geoeconomics and Statecraft* (Cambridge: Belknap/Harvard University Press, 2016).

43 William J. Norris, *China's Economic Statecraft: Commercial Actors, Grand Strategy, and State Control* (Ithaca, NY: Cornell University Press, 2017).

44 Andrew Chatzky and James McBride, "China's Massive Belt and Road Initiative," Council on Foreign Relations, January 28, 2020, https://www.cfr.org/backgrounder/chinas-massive-belt-and-road-initiative.

45 For a summary of these arguments, see Roland Danneruther, "China and Global Oil: Vulnerability and Opportunity," *International Affairs* 87, no. 6 (2011): 1345–50.

46 That quote is usually attributed to economist Paul Samuelson.

47 "The IEA Has Delivered an Overdue Message," *Financial Times*, May 18, 2021, https://www.ft.com/content/4b524b96-7311-4fd7-9b2e-ff989dfb2b84.

48 David Sheppard, "Brent Crude Hits $70 as Traders Bet on Sustained Revival in Oil Demand," *Financial Times*, May 18, 2021, https://www.ft.com/content/83b10e14-d143-4951-a315-cd4170320ac3.

49 "The Death of the Internal Combustion Engine," *The Economist*, August 12, 2017,https://www.economist.com/leaders/2017/08/12/the-death-of-the-internal-combustion-engine..

50 Emily Meierding, *The Oil Wars Myth: Petroleum and the Causes of International Conflict* (Ithaca, NY: Cornell University Press, 2020).

51 Michael Ross, *The Oil Curse: How Petroleum Wealth Shapes the Development of Nations* (Princeton, NJ: Princeton University Press, 2012); Colgan, *Petro Aggression*.

52 Kyle Bakx, "Old, Unproductive Oil and Gas Wells Could Cost up to $70B to Clean Up, Says New Report," CBC News, April 8, 2019, https://www.cbc.ca/news/business/orphan-wells-alberta-aldp-aer-1.5089254#:~:text=Business-,Old%2C%20unproductive%20oil%20and%20gas%20wells%20could%20cost%20up%20to,%2440%20billion%20and%20%2470%20billion.

53 Steven Pinker, *Enlightenment Now: The Case for Reason, Science, Humanism, and Progress* (New York: Penguin Books, 2018).

Index

 **UTP** insights

Books in the Series

- John Joe Schlichtman, Jason Patch, and Marc Lamont Hill, *Gentrifier*
- Robert Chernomas and Ian Hudson, *Economics in the Twenty-First Century: A Critical Perspective*
- Stephen M. Saideman, *Adapting in the Dust: Lessons Learned from Canada's War in Afghanistan*
- Michael R. Marrus, *Lessons of the Holocaust*
- Roland Paris and Taylor Owen (eds.), *The World Won't Wait: Why Canada Needs to Rethink Its International Policies*
- Bessma Momani, *Arab Dawn: Arab Youth and the Demographic Dividend They Will Bring*
- William Watson, *The Inequality Trap: Fighting Capitalism Instead of Poverty*
- Phil Ryan, *After the New Atheist Debate*
- Paul Evans, *Engaging China: Myth, Aspiration, and Strategy in Canadian Policy from Trudeau to Harper*